Fallacies in Education

Fallacies in Education

Why Schools Are Mired in Mediocrity

Randy K. Trani and Robert K. Irvine

ROWMAN & LITTLEFIELD EDUCATION

A division of

ROWMAN & LITTLEFIELD PUBLISHERS, INC.
Lanham • New York • Toronto • Plymouth, UK

Published by Rowman & Littlefield Education
A division of Rowman & Littlefield Publishers, Inc.
A wholly owned subsidary of The Rowman & Littlefield Publishing Group, Inc.
4501 Forbes Boulevard, Suite 200, Lanham, Maryland 20706
http://www.rowmaneducation.com

Estover Road
Plymouth PL6 7PY
United Kingdom

British Library Cataloguing in Publication Information Available

Library of Congress Cataloging-in-Publication Data

Trani, Randy K. (Randy Keith), 1967–
    Fallacies in education : why schools are mired in mediocrity / Randy K. Trani and
    Robert K. Irvine.
        p. cm.
    Includes bibliographical references.
    ISBN 978-1-60709-467-8 (cloth : alk. paper) — ISBN 978-1-60709-468-5 (pbk. : alk.
paper — 978-1-60709-469-2 (electronic)
    1. Educational change—United States.   2. Public schools—United States.   I. Irvine,
Robert K., 1968–   II. Title.
    LA217.2.T727 2010
    370.973—dc22   2009032106

Printed in the United States of America

∞ ™ The paper used in this publication meets the minimum requirements of American
National Standard for Information Sciences—Permanence of Paper for Printed Library
Materials, ANSI/NISO Z39.48-1992.

To the teachers.

Contents

Acknowledgments

Acknowledgments have to start with all of the wonderful teachers we both had when we were young and knew everything. Professional influences are too many to mention but they have all been profound. The staff at Corbett School has been particularly influential and inspiring. We want to personally thank Lori and Carrie for their help editing the manuscript. Bob Dunton has been a mentor and leader without whose example and guidance this book would never have even been conceived.

We would be remise if we did not thank the coffee houses and brew pubs of the greater Portland Metro area for their culinary delights, free electricity, and WIFI that kept the word processor and idea generators operating.

Of course we would be in big trouble if we did not acknowledge the debt we owe our parents, step parents, and in-laws. Thankfully, as we have aged we are constantly amazed at how much wiser they get every year.

Thanks go out to Stan whose loaned raft found us drifting down the Grande Ronde River where we conceived this book two years ago.

Finally, and by far most importantly, we want to thank our families. Emma, Zack, Tessa, Aurora, and Finn, we are so proud of you and thank you for giving us the time to write. And, of course we need to thank our whole reasons for being, the epicenters of our universe. (We know there can't be more than one epicenter . . . . but there just is.) We thank you for your forbearance, tolerance, and for that one time when you laughed at our jokes. Thank you Diane and Elisa, or should we say Elisa and Diane, either way one will be mad that she was not first . . . . so thanks girls . . . no, that will really piss them off. . . . to our ladies . . . no, they won't like it if we say "our." . . . . how about to the women we were lucky enough to find and who were dumb enough to marry us . . . thank you! Will you please let us do this again? Please?!

Perhaps the most valuable result of all education is the ability to make yourself do the thing you have to do, when it ought to be done, whether you like it or not.

—Thomas H. Huxley, English biologist, 1825–1895

Chapter 1

Introduction

"Much of what you know or were taught about education is wrong, and it gets in the way of creating excellent schools."

This statement is the starting point of this book, and while it may not surprise you, we hope that some of the specifics will. We hope that you will find the point well argued and cogent, but most importantly, we hope that you will find it useful as a voter, educator, student, parent, or concerned citizen.

To be sure, the current configuration of schools and the education system is the result of good intentions and thought, but we believe that there is as much myth, obfuscation, and wrong thinking as there is good design and planning. In the following pages, we examine what we think are the key variables that can help or inhibit the creation of an excellent learning environment, and more importantly, what to do instead.

Howsoever a person might measure the excellence of a school, we believe that the proof of a school's effectiveness lies in the students it graduates. Moreover, we believe that any reasonable person can look at a school, its students and teachers, and the overall environment, and come to an accurate assessment of its worth. Regardless of complex funding formulas, testing methods, and reports, most people can recognize a good school when they see it.

While a thoughtful person can indeed recognize a good school, the simple fact is that there is no short cut, no easy answer, no silver bullet, or legislative mandate that can, a priori, create a superior school. In fact, we believe that any such effort to use legislation to improve schools is nothing more than a legislative attempt to bandage self-inflicted wounds, and more often than not, results in schools becoming less effective rather than more effective.

Fundamentally, it is the local conditions and the staff of a local district, along with their relative investment or apathy, and their initiative or resistance to solutions that sets the expectations and determines the results. Willingness to take calculated risks and tailor solutions to local conditions is critical and far more important than conforming to a national benchmark that is inherently arbitrary and designed for the "average school." We think it is instructive to remember that laws designed for the "average school," probably work as well as the automobile designed to hold the "average" family of 2.3 people.

Education is necessarily an intimate and personal process, and everything that the authors have experienced supports the notion that it is impossible to mass produce or industrialize education. We believe that it is very rare to find someone who liked being treated as a faceless number. What matters in education are individuals and relationships, and the school system must recognize this fact. Moreover, it is crucial that the school design an environment to create such relationships; this means that as a rule, our target is one teacher to twenty-four kids for as many consecutive years as possible.

Classes larger than 1:24 are simply too big to be effective, and no manner of jiggering the numbers by adding aides and parents can make up the difference in the long term. Good and bad schools are the result of deliberate decisions, but too often, the decisions and their consequences are divorced. We hope that this book will help people recognize those connections and see how some of our most cherished assumptions about economy, school organization, curriculum, teacher education, and traditions work against the goal of building excellent schools.

As argued, many of the strongest beliefs that Americans hold on the topic of education are wrong, and they get in the way of creating excellent schools. The following chapters explore what we regard as some of the most important "un-truths" associated with education. We begin with an introductory chapter dedicated to unlearning common knowledge about education.

In chapter one, we tackle what we consider to be the biggest obstacle to creating excellent schools, namely all of the ideas and beliefs about school size and the efficacy of the "comprehensive high school." Fundamentally, we believe that big schools and big districts are a problem. Big schools, big bureaucracies—big things have a great deal of momentum and inertia, they are not flexible, they are difficult to steer, resist change, and have a tendency to become detached from their constituencies. Big invariably becomes unwieldy and resistant to improvements, innovation, and solutions.

From the basic problem of becoming too big, schools and districts develop myriad problems, from an inability to respond to threats and opportunities to a lack of accountability for academic achievement. Big schools breed additional layers of administration, stricter rules, stiffer processes, and most problematic of all—anonymity. Studies by the dozen, as we discuss in the following chapters, continue to affirm that for students, relationships matter. However, this is true for all people, and the more divorced people become from their institutions, the less those institutions matter. We believe that any school that is large enough to allow a student to become anonymous is too big.

Unfortunately, it is common knowledge that bigger high schools are better. Consequently, this is where we begin; from here, the book moves to a discussion of goals, purposes, and roles aimed at unlearning common knowledge about education, and radically reforming the educational process to create excellent schools.

Before we move on, we believe that it is appropriate for us to introduce ourselves and briefly explain how this book came to be. Between them, the authors have taught at the elementary, middle, and high school levels, as well as at the collegiate level including junior colleges and universities.

One author, Randy Trani, is currently the principal of the Corbett K–12 school. Randy is also a past Oregon High School Principal of the year, as well as a past Oregon Middle Level Association middle school principal of the year. As a teacher in small rural schools in Alaska, Randy taught as an elementary, middle, and high school teacher. Randy also taught in Oregon as a middle and high school biology teacher.

As of this writing, the Corbett Middle School is Oregon's only "School to Watch," a prestigious designation awarded by the National Forum. Additionally, the Corbett High School has been recognized by Newsweek Magazine as a top ten high school in the nation on the basis of participation by students in Advanced Placement program.

The other author, Robert Irvine, has taught at the community college and university level, and continues to teach through a distance education program at the University of Eastern Oregon as well as at Blue Mountain Community College. Bob also works with non-profit organizations, local governments, schools, community colleges, businesses, and Indian tribes as a development consultant.

We hope, and indeed we are pretty sure, that our combination of teaching and administrative experience enables us to highlight the different models and assumptions at work within the field of "education." In particular, it has become apparent to us that there are inherent contradictions within the accepted standard practices. For example, it is generally accepted that elementary schools should be small, and elite private colleges likewise tout their smallness as possessing intrinsic advantages, but we are told that high schools are more efficient when larger and that the largeness allows more opportunities for students.

We ask why small was good at the beginning and end, but not in the middle? We also came to ask why in the state of Oregon, where we live, are large schools funded at a higher level per student than small schools. Why, too, is the drop-out rate for large schools higher than for small schools, and why do they have more administrators per student?

Seeking the answers to these questions brought us to this book and to our undiminished belief that "much of what we all know or were taught about education is wrong and it gets in the way of creating excellent schools."

However extensive we might want to believe our own experience, we recognize the inherent limitations, and for that reason we have tried to punctuate points with case studies and evidence from multiple districts or jurisdictions. Likewise, if you as a reader know of strong supporting or contradictory evidence we would very much like to know of it and can be contacted via the publisher. We are adamant that the conversation about the future of education must be one that is as comprehensive as possible, and we welcome new data.

Chapter 2

Common Knowledge That Gets in the Way of Education

The United States has a unique and progressive history in the effort to provide universal education for its citizens. Beginning in Massachusetts and moving throughout the nation, the idea of universal, compulsory education for all of its citizens has produced a body of received wisdom or "common" knowledge about the education process. One of the temptations that this book works to combat is the desire to regard the "common knowledge" as accurately reflecting the lessons of decades of careful analysis and research.

If the common knowledge were accurate, it would be much easier to create excellent schools. Unfortunately, common knowledge is getting in the way. The lessons that people take for granted embrace everything from the proper size of a school to the way schools should be organized. Consequently, anyone truly working to make an excellent school faces not only the inherent problems of cultivating excellence, but also must fight these misconceptions and well-meaning but wrong assumptions.

Consider the analogy of wiring a building. Running wire in new construction allows almost infinite possibilities. All walls, floors, and ceilings are open and available to serve as a raceway to wire. Wiring an existing building by contrast demands working around what already exists, cleaning and removing what no longer suits the purpose, and it also puts up barriers to change.

Continuing the analogy, a person seeking to make an excellent school does not have the liberty of working in the proverbial new construction. Instead, this person must work around the accumulated debris, existing walls, insulation, dust, and the decades of repairs and add-ons, which constitute a monumental obstacle.

Unfortunately, making an excellent school requires leaders to not only put systems, policies and protocols in place, but also to identify and respond to obstacles and barriers. A portion of this book, and this chapter in particular, are therefore dedicated to identifying some of the most problematic issues that anyone who seeks to make an excellent school will face. Moreover, it is not enough to identify the problem. Because a school is a social institution, making an excellent one requires working within the community to help others recognize the flaws in the common knowledge.

CONTEXT FOR COMMON KNOWLEDGE ABOUT EDUCATION

Given that within the field of "Education" and especially universal education, the United States has been something of a leader, it often seems that its methods are not only ancient and wise, but also well tested and documented. However, truly universal education for everyone is only a few generations old. Indeed, professional associations and states only began to standardize the credentials for teachers during the Progressive Era in the early 20th century.

Just because the nation's rhetoric championed universal access to education does not mean it was a fact. Consider, for example, the pernicious effects of racial segregation which ensured that many citizens received sub-par educations well into the 1960s. Today, many education commentators argue that economic segregation produces the same results.

The point of these observations is that although the United States has a long history as a comprehensive education provider, there is much variation and many contradictions within that history. If anything, the record demonstrates that no "one" way of educating young people has proven to be the best and only way to do it. In short, there is no ancient, received wisdom about how to conduct public education.

There is no one method or approach to which one can point as absolutely correct. In the absence of such documented wisdom, the United States has crafted education laws that allow for considerable variation, individual and local initiative, and experimentation. Furthermore, the nation's institutions of higher education have hardly established an optimal method, curriculum, or approach. Truly, many have tried. Even a casual look at the educational research over the past decade or two quickly produces a sense of overwhelming contradictions, as well as the far too common use of acronyms.

Indeed, the best way to train teachers is in itself a much smaller undertaking than creating excellent schools or ensuring an excellent education for students, and that topic too remains a vexing and unsolved challenge. As a nation, we have not been able to master this smaller task, and it leaves the larger problem of creating an excellent school even more daunting.

DIVINING MEANING AND METHOD

The upshot of these observations is that common knowledge is a poor, contradictory, and confusing guide. The authors have attempted to sift through the common knowledge and identify a core set of beliefs. The balance of this chapter is a rough and ultimately idiosyncratic, if not unscientific, review of the major categories of common knowledge about education.

The authors believe that somehow there is an underlying hope, faith, or fervent optimism that educators can find the perfect formula for educating America's youth. The hope seems to be that however difficult to find, the formula will yield a simple and beautiful truth: something on the line of $E = MC^2$ if not $A^2 + B^2 = C^2$.

Fundamentally, the authors believe that researchers, legislators, and advocates will not find this Holy Grail. Instead, the authors believe that great schools require hard work, good people, and thoughtful examination of needs, opportunities, and resources as well as an ability to make intelligent compromises. Unfortunately, common knowledge tends to get in the way. However, any meaningful attempt to create a great school and to replicate the process requires an understanding of the forces that impede its implementation.

While the authors are reluctant to characterize common knowledge as the "enemy," this knowledge is a force that gets in the way of meaningful and effective change. Given the obstacles posed by common knowledge when trying to create or build a great school, it makes sense to examine them a little more closely. The result of that examination should be an understanding of the challenges that common knowledge pose and a strategy to overcome that faulty logic. The categories of common knowledge include the following.

- School Size
- Grade Level
- Elementary School Configuration
- Subject Area Specialists in Middle School
- Ninth Grade Division
- High School Configuration
- Schools as Universal Incubators and Parents
- Schools as Social or Legal Police Force
- Roles of People and Groups in a School

SCHOOL SIZE

The topic of school size merits a chapter all its own, but it also deserves discussion here. Assumptions about school size constitute one of the most insidious pieces of common knowledge. Consider the following common beliefs and the inherent inconsistencies:

- Small elementary schools are good.
- Slightly larger middle schools are desirable.
- Big high-schools are best.
- Small colleges are desirable and price themselves accordingly.

Looking at these assumptions and most people's experience, it should be clear that big schools are favored over small schools. Obviously, bigness and smallness are relative, but for ease of categorization, it is easy to use athletic divisions as shorthand for classification by size.

The assumptions above also give rise to some reasonable questions. These questions include: what fundamental change or changes take place between elementary school, high school, and college? Do the advantages of a small elementary school disappear because the students age? Why suddenly at age twelve is it appropriate to go from one teacher to six or more? Why suddenly at age fourteen is it better to be thrown into a huge school and have all of one's relationships fractured?

Consider these questions in light of the preponderance of evidence that demonstrates that relationships are the most important factor for success in school. Across the nation, the standard pattern is for multiple elementary schools to funnel students into a single middle school, and for multiple middle schools to funnel students to a single high school.

The community of Walla Walla in Washington State is a good example. The school district lists fourteen schools, and seven are elementary schools, including Homelink, a home-schooled resource for grades K–8. Of the remaining seven, four are middle schools, but Homelink is double counted. The remaining four schools consist of the main high school, and three alternative programs. Essentially, seven elementary schools funnel into one high school.

Traditional logic, championed by Harvard President James Bryant Conant in the 1950s and 60s, argued for large "comprehensive" schools that could offer the fullest possible curriculum. Small schools, he argued, cannot offer multiple foreign languages or multiple arts offerings, for example.

As desirable as multiple foreign languages might be, the total available time to take classes is the same for all students, and the value of being able to choose between Mandarin and Spanish may be less important than the opportunity to take any foreign languages and develop language skills from a good teacher. Indeed, proponents of learning foreign language do not usually distinguish between languages, and for good reason.

Significantly, not only is the preference for large schools not universal, it is under criticism. For example on April 11, 2007, National Public Radio ran a story about the break-up of Northwestern High School in Baltimore. The story characterized the large comprehensive Northwestern as a "dinosaur," and one of only three remaining in the city.[1] Northwestern is but one example of many, and it is a hopeful sign.

As hopeful as Northwestern might be, the predominant pattern is to continue to funnel many elementary school students into a single middle or high school. Consider one of the fastest growing communities in Oregon, the city of Bend. In 2003, the City of Bend opened a new high school: Summit High School. Summit describes itself as a comprehensive high school; opened in 2003, it is one of three Bend high schools, and receives students from more than ten elementary schools. Clearly, the news that comprehensive high schools are dinosaurs has not filtered down to every community.

Fundamentally, large high schools have several problems that attend their size. Look at other examples that fit the preference: large institutions, organizations, organisms, vehicles, or endeavors. In these and in all examples, bigness demands more layers, more bureaucracy and more administration.

Big vehicles take longer to turn, slow down, or speed up. Big organizations become faceless, people and tasks become disconnected, and communication takes longer. These are profound problems in education. Big high schools have vice principals, security guards, attendance secretaries, school resource officers, and so forth. In short, big schools have layers that do not exist in smaller schools.

Consider the challenge of access. In a big school, access to decision makers is inherently harder to gain for teachers, students, and parents. How could that possibly be a good thing? Similarly, it is more difficult to communicate good ideas and solutions. Likewise, problems are untended or unheeded longer. Again, how in the world can this be something desired? These problems are inevitable outcomes of big schools and they work against the foundation of a good education.

A fair question is: would you or anyone opt to live in a system where you have a difficult time getting information or communicating with your peers and superiors? Would anyone opt to exist in a system where they become anonymous, faceless, and increasingly powerless? Why then do communities and American society in general continue to deliberately create education systems to do precisely this?

Critics of modern society invariably seize on alienation as a byproduct of an industrialized, computerized world. Big schools feed students into a system that inevitably creates alienation and disconnection. Students are shunted from class to class, each full of new faces, each taught by a different teacher who is told to form meaningful relationships with 150 new students every term. One of the predominant reasons for this situation, if not "the" reason, is that common knowledge that asserts that big high schools are better.

GRADE LEVEL

Ultimately, grade level is one of the most pernicious fundaments of common knowledge influencing education today. The absurdity of grade level expectations can be illustrated by the following example. Johnny was born on August 31st of 1998; by virtue of his birthday he is a fifth grade student in Oregon. His friend Frank was born on September 1st of 1998 and is in the fourth grade. Their next door neighbor, Zack was born on September 1st 1999 and is in the third grade.

Three hundred and sixty six days separate these three boys; however, they are separated by three complete grade levels. For the sake of argument, these boys are equally academically gifted and they have had the same advantages bestowed upon them by their families; in essence, they are identical save for their birthdates.

In October, they each take the state of Oregon's standardized tests in reading. Johnny scores a 212 in reading, a score that places him in the 25th percentile amongst all of his fifth grade peers, almost all of whom are much older than he is. Frank scores a 212 as well; however, he is a fourth grader, and compared to the other fourth grade students, most of whom are much younger than he is, he is in the 75th percentile. Meanwhile Zack, scores a 207 and, like poor Johnny, Zack is ranked in the 25th percentile compared to most of the much older third-grade students.

If only Zack and Johnny were born one day later, they too would be labeled as bright students rather than as students in need of serious reading intervention.

Clearly, this is absurd. Yet the common knowledge known as grade level holds three widely different sets of expectations for three students who are nearly all the same age. As they grow older, the 366 days separating their birthdates will become a statistically smaller percentage of their lives; however, the grade-level expectations and their inherent differences will follow them until they are in college.

If you are an educator and you are reading this, you will have noticed one more absurdity in our argument. It is absurd to think that these three boys are virtually identical learners save for 366 days of longevity.

Johnny is from a rich family and his parents have given him every educational advantage. Frank is from a moderately wealthy family; his parents have given him some educational advantages, but to put it bluntly, Frank is just not nearly as smart as his friend Johnny. His luck in the gene lottery was just off. Zack is in even worse shape; he has poor parents who don't speak English, he is malnourished, and his brain never developed correctly.

Even if they were all born on the same day, say September 1, 1998, and were thereby all in fourth grade, their individual differences are so vast that it would be absurd to expect them to perform equally well on a standardized test.

The common knowledge known as grade level is so pervasive and unquestioned that it has permeated every facet of our educational jargon. Take, for example, special education, the most widely scrutinized and evaluated of all educational enterprises. Students who are referred for special education testing, or special education students who are being re-evaluated, are often tested as to their present level of education performance (PLEP) in reading, writing, and mathematics.

These PLEP scores are widely reported in meetings between parents, administrators, educational psychologists, special education teachers, and regular education teachers—all of whom do not bat an eye when a child's reading scores are reported at the 1.3 grade level for comprehension, or at the 1.7 grade level for fluency.

Are we really sure that we can place a student's ability to read, write, or do math along a static continuum accurate to the tenth's place of a given grade level? Could differences in birthdates account for some portion of the differences we see in present levels of education performance? We most steadfastly say YES!

As you read this next paragraph, please add John Lennon's *Imagine* to the background music playing in your head. Imagine there is no grade level; it is easy if you try. No SPED kids below us above us, just another guy. Imagine all of the children learning at their own raaaate!

OK, turn the station, or flip your Ipod to another song as that rendition of *Imagine* may bring poor John back from the dead. We hope our point is worth replaying even if our lyrics are not.

If you imagined there was no grade level, and forgot the common knowledge we all accept regarding grade level, suddenly all students would be just where they are. There would be no one who was behind grade level; there would be no one who was ahead of grade level. The words TAG and

SPED would disappear from our education vocabulary. Words like differentiated instruction and individual education plan associated with SPED
and TAG programs would apply equally to all students. In short, we believe
that there is nothing in the SPED planning and approach that is not good
for everybody. Given that fact, for it is a fact, why only use this tool on a
limited basis?

Are we proposing an educational nirvana equivalent to the cultural one
John sang about? Yes! However, our nirvana is far easier to attain than John's
vision. A bold statement on our part to be sure, but we have seen schools
that have traveled far down the path towards educational nirvana by utilizing the best practices of multi-age instruction, coupled with a commitment
to a continuous-progress model rather than a grade-level, curriculum-based
model. These examples will be detailed in later chapters.

ELEMENTARY SCHOOL CONFIGURATION

Elementary school configurations nationwide generally fit into one of these
categories, all of which are held to be the best possible arrangement due
to a preponderance of common knowledge. A good elementary school is
either a K–5, K–6, or, if you are wild, a K–8 building. No matter how big
your elementary school is, it is certainly the smallest school in your district.
(Unless, of course, you have a very small district with only one elementary
school, one middle school, and one high school; a combination that we, as it
turns out, really love!)

Occasionally school districts have buildings that are K–3 and/or 3–5, or
K–1 and/or 2–6; however, these arrangements are usually a construct of over-
crowding in play with the physical infrastructure of the district, and responses
to that crowding and infrastructure, rather than a calculated decision aimed at
fostering intellectual growth.

Without regard to which of the three optimal building configurations a
district chooses, the vast majority of students are funneled into grade-level
classrooms where one teacher will guide them throughout their day, save for
"specials" such as P.E., music, counseling, and art. The art, music, counseling, and P.E. teachers are usually incorporated into the school's environment
to provide prep time for classroom teachers.

There are three issues that we have with current configurations of elementary schools. First, we fully embrace the idea that elementary schools should
be small. However, we take issue with the common knowledge that they
should be the smallest in the district. This criticism is not specifically aimed
at elementary schools; rather it is aimed at district configurations.

Along the lines of "what is good for the goose is good for the gander," we question the common knowledge that elementary schools should be smaller than middle schools, and even smaller than high schools. In fact, we think they all should be small and strategically located so that a student's transition from elementary school to middle, and then high school is the least disruptive as possible. Ideally, the three schools will be on the same campus and a student's identity as a student of _____ school will not be fractured two times in their K–12 career. We will espouse on this idea at length in later chapters.

Second, we do not embrace the idea of students spending only one year with a classroom, grade-level teacher. We want to be clear that a student in elementary school is much better off spending an entire year with one teacher, rather than a year with six or seven teachers, as many students do when they hit middle school. In fact, we think that spending an entire year with one highly trained, competent adult is such a boon that it would be absurd to throw away the advantages inherent to that situation after only one year.

Taking this assertion a step further we think a far better educational environment can be achieved by ditching the common knowledge about grade-level classrooms and embracing multi-age classrooms, where teachers spend multiple years with students, and adopt a continuous-progress model in place of the predominant curriculum-centered approach to education. Once again, we will argue these points ad nauseam in subsequent chapters.

Third, the use of specialists in elementary schools is the harbinger of heinous practices looming in a child's near middle level future. We fully understand the practicalities of negotiated agreements, and the need for administrators to provide prep time for teachers within the school day. We recognize the utilitarian benefits produced by sending a group of elementary students to visit P.E., music, art, and counseling specialists.

Obviously local limitations imposed upon districts through negotiated agreements may make it necessary to move kids out of their self-contained classroom and into specialist's classrooms throughout the day. However, to the maximum extent possible, we think that every effort should be made to keep students in contact with their classroom generalist rather than subject area specialists. In our experience, the very best elementary specialists would make, and have made, some of the very best classroom generalists.

MIDDLE SCHOOL CLASSES AND THEIR TEACHERS

From grades K–6, most American children experience one teacher a year. Other schools allow a teacher to stay with a cohort from Kindergarten through first grade, for example. Some schools have adopted multi-age looping classrooms where a single teacher may teach third and fourth grades, and they stay with students for two years.

These last two approaches allow students to develop a relationship with their teacher, create a sense of community, and build relationships with other students. Specifically, they form secure relationships that allow them to focus on academics and the skills that are the foundation for academic success, as opposed to having to spend energy and attention elsewhere. These approaches make sense and work better than the single grade alternative.

Why then, at grade six or seven—age twelve for most students—are they suddenly forced to have six teachers, six classrooms, and a cavalcade of continually changing classmates? What possible benefit can this change provide to students who have developed learning and coping styles based on a single classroom? Surely, the course materials do not suddenly become so advanced that no single teacher could provide instruction.

Of course we recognize that licensure restrictions might lead you to think that seventh grade science is so complex that a person with a degree in math or English could never fully comprehend it. However, our experience demonstrates that this is not true. Any competent teacher able to teach sixth grade materials could just as well teach seventh grade materials. The proof is in any interview with a competent teacher or review of the curriculum materials by any thinking individual.

> *Aside: We debated back and forth about including extensive research citations and references from scholarly journals. As a compromise with ourselves and for the sake of readability, we have tried to lean away from adding them. You will find Chapter Four chock full of them, however, as we thought the topic controversial enough to warrant citations. The line between controversial and settled is hardly obvious, but we hope that you will allow us a bit of leeway.*
>
> *We hope, for example, to spare you the reader from reading an extensive section trying to prove that relationships do actually matter. We promise we reviewed the literature and have the citations in our notes. We also figured that since we are sure many people will want to read this book out loud to their peers, spouses, and at parties that we would make the narrative flow as smoothly as possible.*

Again, the preponderance of the available research asserts that relationships matter, and never is this truer than in adolescence. The logic of taking a vulnerable population, especially youth on the cusp of puberty and the tremendous changes it entails, and further fracturing their world with multiple teachers and classrooms is confusing at best. Nonetheless, the vast majority of middle schools do exactly that, separating students from familiar patterns and disrupting the learning environment. An impartial observer, especially one who had not gone through that trauma, might well ask: why?

Even though the authors do not claim to be impartial, and did indeed go through the experience, we still ask why. The authors asked teachers, administrators, parents, and strangers; the answers, such as they are, break down as follows:

- The subject material becomes specialized and requires specific endorsements.
- The legislature or law requires that subjects be taught by people with specific endorsements.
- The students need to be prepared for the high school experience.
- Students need to be prepared for the cold, harsh reality of life that relationships are transitory and unstable (admittedly, that came from just one person, but we liked it and we are the authors).
- That is the way it has always been done.
- There is no other way to do it.
- Students get to learn from teachers specializing in the subject, and therefore have much greater enthusiasm for the subject and learning.

Granted, it is hard to argue against the notion that many strange things are done in the name of legal compliance. At the same time, it is easy to argue with the list of reasons above.

Again, the authors challenge anyone to look at the middle school curriculums and conclude that a good teacher could not teach it all. The materials are simply not that advanced. Likewise, the logic of preparing students for high school by wrecking the learning environment and making it harder to learn and continue to build an educational foundation is very difficult to follow. Furthermore, an adolescent is better served when allowed to prepare for high school in a thorough, comfortable, and effective environment.

Randy recently presented at a state middle level conference in Oregon. The theme of the conference was "navigating the turbulent middle level waters." The then current teacher of the year for the state of Oregon as well as the national teacher of the year used this analogy quite eloquently in his opening address.

His power point included a picture of nine people in a river raft in heavy white water with a guide positioned near the stern of the vessel. He compared the guide to the teacher, directing and caring for the other eight students in his raft, amidst the turbulent and sometimes dangerous waters of middle school life.

His analogy was a good one, and he pointed out that the students in the raft were the ones actually doing the work to propel the raft safely through the dangerous currents, sweepers, and boils found in those waters. He pointed out, very astutely, that it matters a great deal that the guide on the raft have a good working relationship with every student on the raft. If the students did not trust their guide, they might not paddle when he told them to paddle, and this could result in disaster for the entire raft. We could not agree more.

However, he neglected a huge part of the river rafting experience that most middle school students endure, an experience that often results in drowning. His metaphor would have been far more accurate if he had portrayed his turbulent river with forty or fifty guides on the river, each transporting a crew of middle level paddlers through the angry waters.

Each of the guides would be teaching different techniques for managing the raft, some would say you pull like this, others would say you paddle like that. Some would insist on lots of chatter in the raft while others would insist on dead silence. Some would expect all paddlers to paddle at the same rate while others would differentiate the paddling for each paddler.

The list of differences between the guides would be immense, which in itself would not be a problem, save for the fact that every 45 minutes or so, in the midst of the maelstrom called the middle school river, every single kid would have to jump out of their raft and into another raft!

Imagine the confusion that would result from hundreds of kids trying to change places in rafts every period or so as the rafts tumbled down the grade established by the whitewater. Students, excuse us we mean paddlers, would have to learn to paddle differently for every guide and how to interact with different peer paddlers six or seven times in a single day!!! With all this hopping from boat to boat, it is entirely likely that a number of students would miss the transfer and end up being swept away.

Often times no one would even miss them as no single guide, or for that matter student, ever really knew them. Their parents, if they had any, might have noticed from their perch on the shore that their kid had been swept over-board. However, who would they scream at to rescue their kid? They might try screaming at all of the guides who had ever seen their kid. Assuming the guides really knew their kid at all, what would they do about it? After all, they only had that kid for 1/6th of the day; why was it their problem? They had tons of kids to keep track of throughout their work day!

We believe that the number of drowned students resulting from this model is evidenced in test scores around the country. However, discussing school and student scores on standardized measures is out of place in this chapter, but it is instructive to note score patterns. In the state of Oregon, for example, the percentage of students passing achievement tests drop from the third to the tenth grade.

The faults of the tests aside, and there are many, we think that perhaps the premature destruction of the learning environment might play a role in the failure of students to meet achievement standards. Perhaps the disruption in educational patterns and relationship development creates challenges that impede continued academic achievement.

Finally, before leaving this piece of common knowledge, it is important to note that there are examples of effective alternatives. Some schools keep students with a single teacher through middle school. What is more, there are examples of this approach working very well. These examples will be discussed at greater length in subsequent chapters, but the fact that some schools do this successfully gives lie to the argument that legislative or licensing mandates require the common strategy of using multiple subject-area teachers for each student.

NINTH GRADE AND THE START OF HIGH SCHOOL

Some middle schools include ninth grade in their offerings, and its placement in a building or district is relatively unimportant. What is important to note is that all of the arguments about multiple teachers and classrooms for seventh and eighth grade students hold true for the freshman year as well. These arguments and the common knowledge approach to ninth grade do not need to be reiterated here. What does deserve note is that there are other ways to organize the ninth grade.

Some schools, again to be discussed at greater length in subsequent chapters, keep ninth grade classes together under a single teacher. The single-teacher approach allows students to be paired with the best likely fit in terms of the available teachers, and allows a stronger relationship to develop between students as well as between the students and the teacher. Nationwide, the freshman year produces the lowest GPA in high school.

We think this is a direct result of the many superficial relationships that students are forced to foster in the predominant configuration used for ninth grade students. Again, the very existence of schools using a single teacher for ninth grade demonstrates that it can be done. Moreover, given the unconventional nature of the classes, the schools that use it are under much greater scrutiny than others, and they continue to bear up nicely under that observation.

HIGH SCHOOL CONFIGURATION

Eventually, a break from classroom generalists is required. However, harkening back to our middle level river rafting analogy, we will never advocate for a high school configuration where a student is forced to have dozens and dozens of guides on the high school river. If you create small schools, students may have seven guides during their tenth grade year, but they will at least have those same seven guides during the subsequent two years of their high school experience.

You may have noticed that we have challenged an established bit of common knowledge regarding high schools. High schools are supposed to be comprehensive in nature, and comprehensive denotes big. Big high schools have departments! Departments are composed of a hierarchy of teachers, the most junior of which teach the least desirable classes. (Least desirable classes is read "classes with the financially poor, unmotivated, and least academically talented kids.") The most senior teachers teach the most desirable classes.

Given the way teaching assignments are organized, a student can expect to experience a new science teacher every year, at the least, and perhaps a new teacher every term at the worst. No student can expect to have a serious relationship with all of their teachers; in fact, they will be lucky if they form a substantive relationship with just one teacher! Furthermore, comprehensive high schools are prone to produce fractures and divisions within the multitudes of departments that fill their often overcrowded halls.

The creation of these divisions means that students can't create meaningful relationships with their teachers, and teachers cannot create meaningful relationship between members of different departments. A comprehensive high school of 2000 can boast a teaching staff of 70 teachers, 4 counselors, 5 administrators, and 100 classified employees. How can teachers be expected to commiserate and plan with their peers if their peers do not even share the same student population?

In essence, our number one issue with the common knowledge associated with high schools is the insistence that they must be big and comprehensive. We will, in the following chapters, demonstrate that big high schools are more expensive to operate while at the same time less efficient at producing student achievement compared to their smaller counterparts.

Comprehensive high schools may be comprehensive only in their ability to foster high student drop out rate, increased spending, and reduced learning on a per pupil basis. Perhaps they need to be comprehensive in order to serve as the universal incubator for public politically correct curricula. This will be examined in the next section.

SCHOOLS AS UNIVERSAL INCUBATORS AND PARENTS

Aside: There is no good category in which to put this discussion. The authors considered "Schools as a Catch-All," or "Schools—All Things to All People," or even "Let the Schools Do it." Any of these would work, but this title allowed for bigger words, and people talking about education should try to throw in a few big words.

At some point in the past, nostalgia has us believe that schools were, or "schoolin" was, about the "3-Rs" of Reading, Writing, and Arithmetic. That historically the nation has called these subjects the "3-Rs" is perhaps proof that more education or "schoolin" was needed. From this humble and basic beginning, the curriculum has grown and continues to grow.

As puzzling as the notation "the 3 R's" may be, what is even more puzzling is the ever-expanding list of things schools are expected to do and to teach to their students. At one point in time, reading, writing, and arithmetic were a complete curriculum, with the inclusion of science and social studies. Today, schools are expected to teach and do the following:

- Deportment
- Physical education
- Fine arts
- Foreign languages
- Home Economics
- Volunteerism and Community Activism
- Internships
- Vocational Education
- Typing
- Computer Sciences
- Testing Preparation
- Emergency Preparedness
- Provide Social Services Referrals
- Intervene in Apparent Social Crises in Families
- Provide Mental Health Services
- Provide Health Services
- Support Military Recruitment
- Support College Recruitment
- Support other Recruiters
- Provide Club Activities
- Provide After School Care
- Provide Before School Care
- Provide Meals
- Provide Nutritional Education

The 2007 news that the state of Mississippi was designated as the "most overweight," is symptomatic of the growing demands and curriculums.

The news coverage invariably pointed to the schools, as this quote from an Associated Press report notes:

> A new state law enacted this year requires schools to provide at least 150 minutes of physical activity instruction, and 45 minutes of health education instruction each week for students in kindergarten through eighth grade. Until now, gym class had been optional. The state Department of Education also is phasing in restrictions on soft drinks and snacks. All public schools are currently banned from selling full-calorie soft drinks to students.
>
> Next academic year, elementary and middle schools will allow only water, juice, and milk, while high schools will allow only water, juice, sports drinks, and diet soft drinks.
>
> The state Department of Education publishes lists of snacks that are approved or banned for sale in school vending machines. Last school year, at least 50 percent of the vending offerings had to be from the approved list. That jumped to 75 percent this year and will reach 100 percent next year.
>
> Among the approved snacks are yogurt, sliced fruit, and granola bars, while fried pork rinds and marshmallow treats are banned. One middle school favorite — Flamin' Hot Cheetos — are on the approved list if they're baked but banned if they're not.
>
> State Superintendent of Education Hank Bounds said he hopes students will take home the healthful habits they learn at school. "We only have students 180 days out of the year for seven hours in a school day. The important thing is that we model what good behavior looks like," Bounds said Monday after finishing a lunch of baked chicken.[2]

While obesity is not something to ignore, we think that the state's appallingly low literacy rates also deserve some attention.[3] While there is much that schools can do, there are also practical limitations, and these facts deserve careful consideration.

Every year, state legislatures take up a new addition to the requirements. The result is that it is increasingly impossible for a student to take what should amount to the core requirements. Consider a common graduation requirement. The specifics will vary a little by state, but the principle remains the same.

A student, in four years of high school, can take six classes a year for twenty-four potential classes. Graduation, in turn, requires twenty-two credits. To take four years of math, four years of science, four years of English, and four years of social studies requires sixteen of the total twenty-two needed, leaving six classes.

Typically, districts have a physical education requirement—let us assume a two-year requirement—which leaves four classes. A foreign language would be a good idea, perhaps two years—which leaves two classes required and four available if the student elects to take all twenty-four. Add wood shop, home economics, an arts class or two, and the slate is full.

Every time the legislature or a department of education mandates teaching another topic or class, they fail at the most basic budgeting function. If they are going to require an additional class, they should specify what they are replacing. There is no school in America where students and teachers are standing around wondering what to do with their time.

Nobody in any school in the nation is waiting and hoping that the legislature will step in to tell them what class they should take. Schools are busy places and people have full schedules, so each new item comes at the expense of another, and this fundamental condition is apparently a complete unknown to many of the state and federal lawmakers.

Similarly, every new test day required, every new attempt at accountability, takes a day away from an existing lesson. The irony, which appears lost on the federal government, is that the tests take time away from teaching the material about which they wish to test.

(One author has a non-profit client who spent more than a year trying to get paid for a mental health service the non-profit delivered. The problem was that although the organization was licensed to deliver the service, and the money was dedicated to paying for the specific service, there was no governmental code that fit the service. The suggestion that the bureaucrat make a new code was not taken seriously until lawyers and their fees became involved. Then and only then, did a bureaucrat get the inspiration to create a new code. The irony was lost on them in this instance too.)

The unfortunate reality is that schools only have so much time to teach and only so many resources. There is nothing wrong with making social decisions about how to use those resources and on what to focus. However, the discussion does need to be rooted in reality and with the understanding that a school cannot do everything and be everything without significantly increased resources.

The common knowledge that schools are the panacea to all social problems must be challenged. Obviously, schools are important, but their first duty must be to provide a solid education for students, not an easy way to shuttle off fundamental social problems. Providing an effective learning environment and teaching academics should be more than enough of a job for a school; adding the job of parent, moral guide, and censor is too much.

SCHOOLS AS SOCIAL OR LEGAL POLICE FORCE

Unfortunately for someone advocating almost any social agenda, be it abstinence or physical education, schools are one of the first places that they turn to in order to advance their program. This has become increasingly true in the murky area of behavior and relationships between the sexes, races, sexual orientations, religions, and cultures.

In this litigious and sensitive time, it is worth noting here that most people learn, at least in part, by making mistakes. Schools provide a laboratory for young people to learn academics and social skills. It is difficult to imagine how this could be otherwise, given the fact that schools group dozens of young people together and expect them to get along.

Obviously, the state has an interest in preventing harm and there is no good argument for tolerating bullying, but there is a danger in over-legislating conduct. Indeed, creating an environment of fear does not do anyone any good. Furthermore, if young people cannot make mistakes and learn from them, then everyone will pay the costs.

Again, nobody advocates tolerating poor behavior but cases of six and eight-year-olds charged with harassment for slapping or teasing is inherently unproductive. Even more to the point, such prosecutions are disruptive to entire school districts and take resources away from education. Such events undermine the efforts to create an excellent school by creating uncertainty, tension, and distrust. If anything, this discussion is a call for common sense. Most teachers and administrators recognize what is and is not allowable and they are well positioned to stop such behavior.

MISCONSTRUED ROLES OF PEOPLE OR GROUPS IN SCHOOLS

First and foremost, a school must have students and teachers. Additional roles are secondary and could well be eliminated. However, some other roles are essential and deserve to be considered. Other role players include the principal, parents, support personnel, and the school board. Each deserves some discussion in light of the effort to identify where common knowledge breaks down and is downright wrong.

Worth noting from the beginning is that any critic will likely be able to find examples where excellent schools have been forged by exceptional individuals who have overcome apathy or opposition from one or more of the groups occupying a role denoted below.

Remarkable administrators and teachers have worked together to create an excellent school regardless of disinterested parents. Likewise, teachers and parents have managed to overcome incompetent administrators to create excellent schools. However, doing this is inherently more difficult and presents a pathway that is much less likely to lead to success.

Given the important tasks and roles that different groups play, the argument in this book is that it is much easier to create an excellent school if everyone is working toward a common goal. Moreover, it is easier if everyone recognizes the pitfalls and errors common to the efforts of creating excellent schools.

STUDENTS

Common knowledge tends to assert that students are empty vessels awaiting facts and skills from a school to fill them and make them "educated." This perception denies an active role to students and it relegates them to that of an observer in the process. The truth is that almost any student in any school can tell you which teachers are good at their jobs, what administrators are good at their jobs, in what classes they learn, and in which classes they do not. This font of wisdom is almost universally disregarded.

When high school students move on to college or trade school, their opinions often do matter, and many schools routinely survey students. Some schools use such information in decisions about hiring, tenure, and advancement. A legitimate question is why this is not the case a year or two earlier. Are abuses possible? Surely, the answer is yes, but the wholesale disregard for the opinion of students seems poorly considered.

Again, any student can tell you what teachers are good at their jobs, but an excellent school is one in which the students are allowed to participate in a meaningful fashion. Even more importantly, students cannot be allowed to be anonymous. Anonymous student are, by definition, those who are not connected to their schools, classmates, teachers, and administrators. When schools allow students to be anonymous, they give tacit approval to mediocrity and allow students to "slide by," with a minimal effort, contribution, and ultimately a poor education.

The opposite of anonymous students are children and youth who are known to one another, to their teachers, and to the administration. Obviously, a large school has inherent disadvantages in this effort. Similarly, administrators have a difficult task when confronting an entire school, which is yet another reason to keep schools relatively small.

Students who are not anonymous are also students whose stories, conditions, abilities, challenges, and circumstances are known. This demands more of everyone and it can only be done with a consistent, committed effort, but it is something that is much easier to do in a small school.

Young people are nothing if not good judges of genuine concern. An effort to engage and connect with students must be consistent and it must be something valued. A sporadic effort with much rhetoric but no substance may be worse than nothing at all.

Furthermore, in many conceivable situations, it may be easier for students to be anonymous, especially when facing difficulties at home or with fitting in. Again, perfection in terms of engaging students may be impossible to attain, but the effort will produce dividends for everyone and will lead directly to creating an excellent school.

LABOR VERSUS MANAGEMENT

Obviously, teachers are critical for any school and all the more so for an excellent one. However, far too often teachers are regarded as a replaceable part, and the market generally has plenty. Fundamentally, this is a situation that gets in the way of creating excellent schools, and many things feed into this perception.

One of the primary forces encouraging the view of teachers as interchangeable parts is the historic animosity between labor and management. Teachers are typically represented by the largest labor union in the United States and the thousands of reactionary school boards are not typically a bastion of progressive and innovative thinking. American labor law assumes an adversarial relationship between labor and management. Not surprisingly, this is a self-fulfilling prophecy. Even more problematic is the fact that principals often wind up arrayed against teachers, as representatives of "management."

Perhaps worst of all is that parents typically make up school boards, and this can put teachers and parents as antagonists, labor versus management. The result is that people who should be working together become the "other," and the effectiveness of schools is severely undercut. Simply put, this adversarial relationship gets in the way of creating excellent schools.

The purpose of this discussion is not to denigrate labor unions, or to suggest that teachers do not deserve their compensation, but rather to identify a very significant impediment to creating an excellent school. Fundamentally, the way that schools are operated and run creates a built-in impediment to effective operation. School officials pay a great deal of lip service to building a team environment, but arraying principals against teachers does not seem to be a thoughtful arrangement.

TEACHERS

Looking at teachers and the way they are regarded by "common knowledge" reveals that there is a great deal of disagreement. Anyone who has experienced school know there is tremendous variation between teachers, and that same experience demonstrates that good teachers make all the difference.

The above noted truism dictates that teachers should be the focus of an excellent school, its budget, its recruitment, retention efforts, and its operation.

Unfortunately, this is rarely the case. What is more, it is difficult to recognize and reward excellent teachers. Worse, the job environment for too many teachers is marked by a lack of resources and indifference. In any job, a lack of resources is demoralizing, and it is a rare individual who can overcome a lack of support.

Considering the market conditions, one might conclude that teachers are a proverbial dime-a-dozen. Indeed, Economics 101 invites the question: "how important can they be when viewed in light of a seemingly unending supply?" The truth is that while schools may have no trouble finding a teacher, they face a profound challenge in finding excellent teachers. Precisely because excellent schools require excellent teachers, or teachers who can be excellent, the goal must be to hire the best.

As a rule, it is easier to hire or find the "one best" of anything than to find the twenty best or hundred best. This is another advantage that small schools have when compared to larger schools. The turnover is less at a small school, and the board or administration is faced with having to hire the one best biology teacher rather than five new science teachers. The difference is hardly academic and it allows smaller schools to be much more selective.

A critic may ask how every school can even hope to hire the best, when by definition half of all teachers are below average. The only answer can be that a person or group working to create an excellent school does not have to worry about all schools, only their school. Furthermore, raising expectations and standards should lead to better products, which is a basic tenet of market philosophy. When consumers demanded safer cars, airbags became standard. There is still disparity between the safest and less safe cars, but they are all are safer than the cars manufactured forty years ago.

Common knowledge asserts that quantified measures are the only way to assess a teacher's effectiveness. This assertion flies in the face of what everybody knows from experience. Which teachers are good and effective is self-evident. Students, parents, administrators, and other teachers know which teachers are the best. If there are any doubts, one need look no further than other teachers who work to get their own kids into specific classrooms.

Another common belief is that a teacher is either a good teacher or a bad teacher, either effective or ineffective, across kids, subjects, and ability to motivate. This too makes no sense in light of basic experiences that every person has. Some people work better with one type of personality than another. This is not a problem, unless it is ignored. Consider for a moment that everyone accepts the notion that a business or corporation will work hard to create project teams made of individuals who work well together.

Further, everyone accepts the notion that a talented person may fit one team or office or organization but not another. Likewise, every coach and sports journalist notes the importance of "team chemistry" and how some people fit together better than others. Can it be any surprise that this is true for teachers and students too? Why then do so many schools avoid making the same effort? Simply put, why is it that schools do not work to make deliberate and consistent good fits between teachers and the students they teach? The answer is that excellent schools and excellent staffs do this.

Carrying the team analogy further, many observers believe that as teams work together over multiple seasons they become better, more efficient, and more "team-like." If this is true, why are classes mixed and matched from year to year, tossing different kids together without regard to continuity of classmates? Once again, schools are treated as unique; people seem to assume that there is little value in creating a "learning team" within the student body.

Clearly, students help other students learn, and the students in a classroom work together (or not) to create an environment that makes learning easier or more difficult. Just think of a classroom that you have known, one in which students did not trust each other, one in which everything was in flux. Then consider how much more difficult it is to learn in such an environment than one in which students know each other, are familiar with each other's strengths and weaknesses, and where mutual trust has been built. Education can take place in each, but in which would you rather put your kids?

We think the answer is self evident and that excellent schools do all they can to keep kids and teachers together for as long as possible to create the best possible environment.

In truth, many schools do work to put kids with compatible teachers, but the process is inconsistent, imprecise, and poorly understood. For all the ink spilled to identify styles of learning, precious little has gone into identifying ways to put kids with the teachers that can reach them.

Of course, a cynic might argue that this is too "soft" or imprecise an endeavor to get right every time. The cogent response to this criticism is that it is indeed difficult to be perfect at anything, but that does not obviate the value of trying to do so. Moreover, if a school deliberately works to match kids and teachers, needs and styles, the process will get better as everyone comes to recognize the value of the attempt.

TEACHERS' WORK YEAR

One of the most pervasive pieces of common knowledge is that teachers have it good, with a long summer vacation, lots of holidays, and time off. In truth, teaching is exhausting. Ask any parent at the end of a long school break if they look forward to a little peace and quiet when their children return to school. Teaching and managing the high-energy environment of a classroom is a demanding task that requires skill and ability. Obviously, there are important changes that could be made to the school calendar, and these are discussed later.

The point to these observations is that what teachers do is not easy and it is a difficult job by any measure. When society devalues these abilities, it is not only disheartening, it sets an example for students and young people to likewise disregard the value of the education they are privileged to receive. Ultimately, creating an excellent school demands that society, or at least the local community, place a value on teachers and their contributions.

PARENTS

A good way to start a three or four-way argument is to ask any two people about the proper role of parents in education. Even a casual look at parental involvement suggests a general trajectory that moves parents farther and farther away as their children get older and, hopefully, abler. In early elementary school, it is common for parents to volunteer in classrooms, while most universities set aside a single weekend for the parents to venture into the same town as their children. The trend suggests an easy regression analysis showing a fairly even line of disengagement.

For many teachers, the less parental involvement the better, especially when it appears that many parents only get involved when something is wrong. At other times critics insist that schools cannot be parents and that parents need to quit abdicating their responsibilities to educate their own children. Somewhere there must be a middle ground where parents can be involved before there is a crisis, and a way for parents to be contributors to an excellent school.

Perhaps the most obvious way is for parents to value education and support teachers and schools in their efforts to raise the proverbial bar. Excellent schools do not become excellent by expecting or tolerating mediocrity. Excellent schools have excellent expectations and do not teach to minimum standards.

Since the passage of "No Child Left Behind," there has been an ongoing debate about the appropriateness of teaching to a test. Advocates of such a program say that if the test is the benchmark, then it makes sense to aim at that mark. Others decry the approach as somehow disingenuous and akin to cheating.

Unfortunately, the debate about teaching to a test misses the point, in much the same way the tests themselves do. We believe that teaching to a test is essentially aiming low. In almost no other task do people set a goal at the lowest acceptable achievement. On the other hand, if a person does aim low, they rarely admit it. Why in the world would a government create a system that encourages institutions to be minimally acceptable? At least part of the answer must involve the expectations and demands of parents for their children.

Any effort to create an excellent school must invariably face the truth that not all parents care about education. Many parents care but do not themselves have the skills or abilities to help their children, or to discern good practices from bad. Indeed, some parents are well meaning, but are hampered by their uncritical acceptance of the common knowledge discussed throughout this chapter.

Unanimity is rare at best, and often unknown when it comes to public education. Nonetheless, a respectful attempt to involve and educate parents cannot harm an effort. At the same time some parents will remain steadfastly uninvolved, but it is in society's interest to ensure an excellent education for everyone. To quote John Dewey rather loosely, it is imperative that parents working for an excellent education must want for all children what they want for their own.

Cynically, many administrators and teachers must prefer to be left alone to do their best work, rather than be badgered and "advised" by parents. If the alternatives are indifference or opposition, indifference must be preferred. At the same time, parents must have appropriate avenues available to them to make constructive contributions to the effort to create an excellent school.

SUPPORT PERSONNEL

Support personnel, secretaries, janitorial staff, coaches, cooks, and aides form part of the context for any school. These necessary functions bring unique perspectives to the effort and the exact nature of the relationship between a secretary or janitor, and the possibility of creating an excellent school is muddled at best. The real truth is that without direct and purposeful involvement, these staff members are likely to be detrimental to the effort.

Common knowledge suggests that the support personnel are almost invisible and have nothing to do with the education of children. However, these people have everything to do with creating the educational environment. If their contribution is not recognized and actively managed, then it will always be a potential problem because the support staff often knows more about the entire institution than many teachers or parents.

When it comes to the role of support staff, it is important to recognize a truism about schools. Schools and education invariably suffer from the perception that everyone is an expert, by virtue of their own "schoolin." This belief in their own expertise is no less true for support personnel. Like most parents, most secretaries and janitors know that they are education experts. Simply put, to ignore these staff members in the project of creating an excellent school is to invite criticism from within, which is one of the most destructive forms of criticism, as it carries the veneer of inside knowledge.

Generally, the fewer the support personnel the better, for it likely means that the funding is going to teachers and classrooms. Recognizing the important role that support staff play is the starting point for any school and it is important that teachers, administrators, and students have consistent modeling of respectful behavior. Moreover, involving the support staff in discussions about the philosophy of the school and explaining why the school does what it does can go a long way to keeping support staff truly supportive.

CONCLUSIONS

In this chapter, we have surveyed the most important or impactful assumptions underlying what is embraced as "common knowledge" that gets in the way of creating excellent schools. In Chapter Three, we take a more positive approach and identify what we think are the six secrets to creating an excellent school. These six secrets deliberately counter many of the problematic common knowledge issues discussed here, and that we hope flow logically from this discussion.

To be sure, we will revisit some of the topics later, especially the myth about the benefits of large schools, which is probably the piece of wrongheaded common knowledge that is the most difficult to dispel.

NOTES

1. National Public Radio, "Troubled Schools Turn Around by Shrinking," by Larry Abrahamson, April 11, 2007.

2. Emily Wagster Pettus, "Mississippi Ranked Fattest State in Nation," Associated Press, August 28, 2007.

3. See, for example, the National Adult Literacy Survey data on Mississippi State. A state spotlight is available at: http://www.nasaa-arts.org/spotlight/stspot_1104.shtml

Chapter 3

Six Secrets for Creating Excellent Schools

There are at least six secrets to creating excellent schools. We hesitate to call them "secrets" as most of them are far from controversial or unknown. With that said, it is amazing how many districts seem to forget the secrets of creating an excellent school, and implement programs that violate these tenants.

There are actually only five secrets, as the sixth secret is basically a reminder not to do anything that violates the previous five rules of thumb. However, we feel it is necessary to include the sixth reminder, because too often the erosion of the primary five occurs by adopting programs that are only meant to improve education but actually hurt the process.

SECRET NUMBER ONE: 1 EXCELLENT TEACHER AND 24 STUDENTS

The first secret to creating excellent schools will not shake the foundations of education. If you want to create excellent schools, you need to fashion a system where one excellent teacher is paired up with around twenty-four students. Read this secret carefully and you will note that it has two important parts. The first half is by far the more critical portion of the secret, that being the word "excellent," as in "excellent teacher."

With this secret, as in this chapter and indeed throughout this book, we will draw on observations from our personal experiences in education in the hopes that they may lend some credence to our assertions. Throughout our careers in education, we have noted the difference that excellent teachers can and do make with regard to student achievement.

Randy's experiences as principal of The Corbett School highlights the importance of excellent teachers as it relates to student achievement. Specifically, it is this experience that solidified our belief in the importance of pairing one excellent teacher with approximately 24 students.

As this discussion moves forward, we want to emphasize this particular point; namely, we are not advocating anything that we have not seen work. Moreover, we have seen these secrets, rules, or principles work to excellent results. Therefore, we want to highlight the experiences and results of the Corbett School District in Corbett, Oregon.

Corbett is a small district with around 800 students in grades K–12. The high school at Corbett is one of the most prolific in the state and the nation in terms of the percentage of students who participate in Advanced Placement (AP) course work.

In 2004 and 2005, the high school at Corbett was one of the top five AP schools in Oregon. In 2006 it achieved the rank of the highest rated Oregon school ever which placed it in the top 1 percent in the nation, the 2007 test results vaulted them into the top 100 in the nation, and their AP participation rate during the 2008 school year placed them eighth in the United States. Results from the 2009 tests should move Corbett near if not into the top five in the United States.

This is a remarkable accomplishment when you consider that Corbett is the only truly neighborhood school among the top 10 in the country. The other schools are magnet schools and charter schools, many of which screen students at the door with regard to admittance.

Not surprisingly, the school has garnered considerable attention for its achievements, and it is worth figuring out how this happened. Was Corbett's success with regard to AP participation a result of exceptional leadership or was some other factor to credit?

To be sure, the superintendent of Corbett schools, Bob Dunton, set the stage for Corbett's impressive academic achievement. His leadership and vision were critical to Corbett success. Additionally, Randy hopes that his efforts in the district further added to the successes of the school and district. However, both Bob Dunton and Randy are quick to point out that the astounding successes of Corbett would not have been possible without a cadre of exceptional teachers.

A short list of some of the attributes of the teachers at Corbett may help to illustrate what an exceptional group of educators they are and what exceptional teachers look like as well. One attribute exceptional teachers seem to share is a remarkable propensity to continue their formal education long after they are more than qualified for their current position. For instance, 20 percent of all teachers at Corbett have their administrative licenses, 15 percent of classroom teachers are also certified SPED instructors, and the average high school instructor is highly qualified in more than two areas.

The importance of continuing education should not be glossed over and there is growing evidence and belief nationally that this matters. For example, the Bill and Melinda Gates Foundation recently emphasized funding for this very purpose. Not surprisingly, excellent schools already do this, but unfortunately, it is far from common.

In Corbett, the annual staff budget for professional development for thirty-three teachers is approximately $250,000 or 6 percent of the total operating budget. This is a significant investment and a major expense that was difficult to develop. However, the investment has paid marvelous dividends and is cost effective.

The following rhetorical list of questions may be informative as to the qualifications held by Corbett teachers.

• How many art teachers do you know who are also Advanced Placement United States History and Psychology teachers?
• What other school do you know where five out of twelve high school teachers are highly qualified mathematics instructors, while only one of them teaches advanced mathematics?
• What AP Calculus and AP Statistic teacher have you ever met that spent the first eighteen years of his career teaching grade school?
• How many teachers do you know who are highly qualified to teach every core subject? (At Corbett, two out of twelve high school teachers hold those endorsements.)
• How rare is it to find a teacher who can teach AP World History, AP Government and Economics, all subjects in grades 6–8, and maintain the entire district's computer network?
• How many award winning filmmakers do you know who are also passionate Spanish instructors?
• How many middle schools have teachers who are highly qualified to teach every subject to middle-level students while also being qualified to teach courses such as Spanish, Economics, English, and French at the secondary level?
• How many elementary schools have teachers who, in addition to being experts on multi-age education, are also reading specialists or bilingual in Italian, French, or Spanish, and are also SPED certified or non-practicing administrators?
• Finally, what school would be complete without a band instructor who earned his master's degree in music in one of the most rigorous programs in the country and who can literally play every instrument in the band

at a concert level, while at the same time being recognized as a master
instructor in the vocational arts of mechanics and woodworking?

You, dear reader, may be tiring of Corbett at this point and rightfully ask "so
what?"

It is all very fine and good to have a group of teachers collected together
who have a paper pedigree that makes them highly qualified to teach everything. We know that many of the most well educated people in our society,
college professors, are among some of the worst classroom practitioners.
Suffice it to say that in addition to being well educated, lifelong learners, the
teachers at Corbett are equally adept at delivering instruction in such a manner
as to create an environment where students learn at an alarming rate.

Our point with the investment in the professional development of staff is
that it is a wise investment and we have evidence that supports this. In truth,
we don't think that anything we have said so far will garner any visceral
objections from our readers. Isn't it obvious that student achievement will
increase if students are surrounded by excellent teachers like those at Corbett?
Perhaps, and we hope this is the case, a reader may be wondering how Corbett
got lucky enough to assemble such an assortment of excellent educators. The
answer is hard work and a commitment to supporting excellent teachers.

Excellent teachers are both found and made. The finding of excellent
teachers happens through carefully screening applicants at job fairs and in the
casual interactions administrators have with teachers during the normal work
year. An administrator's influence on the direction that their district is headed
is no greater than during the hiring process. If you hire the best, the chances
of becoming a great school increase dramatically.

However, the academic pedigrees possessed by the teachers at Corbett
were not fully in place when the teachers were hired. No, the Corbett School
actively supported the creation of their extremely over-qualified teachers by
instituting one of the most aggressive professional growth programs in the
state of Oregon.

Teachers at Corbett found themselves in the strange situation of not being
able to take college course work faster than the district would pay for it.
More masters degrees, reading endorsements, administrative licensures, and
courses needed to become highly qualified teachers were paid for by the
Corbett School District than the teachers brought through the door at their
initial hire date.

As we mentioned earlier, as much as 6 percent of the district's entire operating budget was routinely spent on professional development. Exceptional
teachers were not only found but also made at the Corbett School, and it seems
a logical extension that the same thing can be done elsewhere as well.

Significantly, not only does professional development build a cadre of excellent teachers, but the environment keeps them in Corbett. The school district has created an environment where they are encouraged to learn, valued for it, and they stay. Retention eliminates hiring costs, which can be significant. Moreover, the supportive environment leads to a lower use of substitutes, sick days, and other expenses that are essentially discretionary for the teachers. Excellent teachers also reduce discipline problems and their spiraling expenses.

SECRET NUMBER TWO: EXCELLENT TEACHERS STAY WITH THEIR STUDENTS

The next secret actually will ruffle a few feathers. Once you have that excellent teacher working closely with twenty-four students, you need to try and keep them together for as long as possible. By creating multi-age looping classrooms where a continuous-progress model represents the backbone of all instruction, you can create a situation in which excellent teachers are kept in close contact with their students for an extended period of time.

Once again, we will point to practices at Corbett to illustrate how the second secret to creating excellent schools looks in the real world. At Corbett, multi-age looping classrooms are used through grade eight. Initially classrooms were crafted with two-year increments in grades 1–8. Furthermore, most high school classes are multi-age with students ranging from 9th to 12th grade participating in courses such as Spanish, pre-calculus, and many more.

What did all of this looping and multi-age instruction lead to? For three years prior to the switch to multi-age instruction, Corbett posted consecutive years of some of the lowest math and reading achievement in the state of Oregon on the State's tenth grade achievement test. Corbett now routinely produces some of the top scores in the state of Oregon. Corbett middle and high school are recognized nationally as some of the best schools in the country.

Administration in Corbett believes that the remarkable success of students in the older grades is a direct result of a commitment to multi-age looping classrooms in the younger grades. Success of multi-age instruction prompted the administration to examine extending the two-year looping to a three or four year pattern through grade eight.

Starting in 2009, the plan is to combine students in grade K–2, 3–5, and 6–8 into multi-age looping classrooms. The rationale for moving to such a model is founded on the same reasons as the initial switch to two-year blended classrooms that created the marked school improvement mentioned briefly in the previous paragraph. There are many resources you can consult for a description of the varied benefits of multi-age instruction. A brief FAQ about multi-age education and a bibliography of multi-age resources is located at the end of the book.

Multi-age instruction mandates that teachers teach each student rather than teach the class. In a typical single-level, grade-level classroom, instruction is aimed at the middle of the class. There is an assumption, called "Grade Level," which permeates single-grade classrooms with regard to every subject. A third grade classroom has a third grade reader, and they do third grade math, and they do third grade social studies, and third grade science.

The notion of grade level is entrenched in most schools. Those of you who have been in, and around schools have surely heard the fervor in a teacher's voice when some new person inadvertently teaches something in one grade level that is reserved for a higher grade level. You might hear teachers in single-grade-level schools say things like, "You can't teach Oregon Trail in second grade; we do that in third grade!" Or, "We don't teach multiplication until third grade."

Also, how often do we hear specialists explain to parents of talented or gifted students, as well as special education students, that their student has a reading level of 3.4 or 11.8. We are so in love with the idea of grade level that we kid ourselves into believing that we can not only pigeon hole a student into a single grade level, but that we can specify with certainty to the tenths place their position along the grade-level continuum. Indeed teachers identify themselves as grade-level teachers as in, "I am a third grade teacher, I have been for 20 years and I can not imagine teaching second or fourth grade."

Given that the idea of grade level is ingrained in many teachers' minds, it is no wonder that they accept without questioning the idea that every fourth grade student should work out of the same reader, do the same social studies and science lessons, as well as work on the same math. They accept it and do it, even though if you ask them about the variation amongst their students, they are the first to tell you that their students are as varied and mixed in ability as adults are.

By teaching to a grade level through the use of grade-level materials such as readers and math texts, you effectively teach the class and neglect the students. A typical class reader is probably perfect for the middle third of a given class, much too easy for the top third and simply too hard for the bottom third.

Multi-age classrooms eliminate, by necessity, the use of grade-level texts and curriculum. When teachers are faced with a multi-age classroom, they have two choices.

First they can chose to split the class in half, or in thirds if it is a three grade mix, and teach the second grade students one lesson, while the third grade students are silent, only to reverse the process after they are done with their second grade students. However, teachers who try this will quickly realize that they have essentially doubled their workload while cutting their time to work with students in half. This first solution is a poor one and does not result in effective multi-age class instruction. Indeed, most teachers realize this within a few months of trying to operate their multi-age classroom in this fashion.

The second solution, and the one we are hoping we can convince our readers to adopt, is to treat each student as an individual. With this approach, the teacher must design instruction that can be easily differentiated across a wide range of student achievement levels. We will give a brief introduction of what this type of instruction should look like here; however, a much more thorough explanation will be provided in chapters five, six, and seven.

The first step in our preferred approach is to establish a two- or three-year curriculum to fit a multi-age configuration. For example, if the classroom in question is a two-year, multi-age classroom, then the place to start is by creating a two-year curriculum, if it is a three-year classroom, then design a three-year curriculum.

Imagine you are teaching a seventh- and eighth-grade multi-age classroom and your social studies curriculum consists of European history and early American history. During one year, you teach European history and the next you teach early American; some students learn European as seventh graders and American as eighth graders, for others it is reversed.

Now, within each year's worth of curriculum this approach does not teach the same thing to all kids. To refine the example further, let's focus in on European history and in particular a unit on the Middle Ages. The teacher will not design a unit where everyone reads the same thing, completes the same work sheet, does the same simulation, and creates the same 3-D model of a siege engine.

Instead, the teacher or teachers will design units that provide for the diversity of their multi-age classroom. This approach may force a teacher to collect 100 different texts, both fiction and non-fiction, about the Middle Ages. The texts will range in reading levels from "second grade" to "twelfth grade." However, because the teachers have spent so much time with those specific students (they have them all day for two years) they will be able to quickly connect texts about the Middle Ages with their students at *their* particular reading level.

Assignments are open-ended thematic based assignments. Perhaps each student will create a museum piece from the Middle Ages based upon what he or she has read in texts that were at his/her reading level. Obviously, each student will have read different materials and have become "expert" at varying levels upon their varied topics. The museum pieces the students create will represent the diversity of the classroom. The teacher's charge will be to insure that each student makes continuous progress.

Pay close attention to the words "continuous progress." A focus on continuous progress is what differentiates a good multi-age classroom from a typical graded classroom. A typical graded classroom, and a school structure designed to support graded classrooms, will pay more attention to aligning the curriculum so that each grade-level interchange is characterized by a smooth hand off of curriculum rather than a smooth hand-off of students.

Recall earlier when we mentioned that you do not have to hang out long in a grade-level school before you hear someone say something along the lines of "You can not teach that! We teach that in _____ grade." This represents a commitment to ensuring that curriculum is smoothly handed off from one grade level to the next.

In a multi-age school, students could learn about the Middle Ages in every grade first through sixth and no one would be concerned that someone was stealing their curriculum. Instead, the concern would transfer to each individual student. When this happens, teachers would have conversations like the following.

> "You know Johnny did a whole bunch with stained glass windows in fourth grade; now that he is in a fifth/sixth grade classroom he needs to do something else."

This stands in direct opposition to the "grade-level school," where the fifth-grade teacher might very well say;

> "I always teach about stained glass windows; I am not sure what I will do now that Johnny (and his peers) learned about them in fourth grade when you taught the curriculum out of order!"

The focus shifts from children and their needs to curriculum and the articulation of that curriculum the moment the school changes the model from multi-age to single-grade classrooms.

To this point we have only spoken of multi-age classrooms with regard to grades K–8. We do not want to give the false impression that multi-age instruction is only practical or wanted in those earlier grades. In fact, in small high schools multi-age instruction is often the norm rather than the exception.

For example, the authors both have experience where chemistry and physics were taught every other year. Thus, each class was a mix of juniors and seniors every year. Significantly, this approach worked very well, but hinged on the presence of an excellent teacher able to teach both physics and chemistry. Before we explain our concept of multi-age instruction in grades 9–12 we want to take this time to explicitly point out that through grade eight we ardently believe that instruction of students should be carried out by generalists and not specialists.

We do not anticipate this last statement will raise any eyebrows amongst our readers who focus on grades K–5. However, we do anticipate that some people who work with grades 6–8 may take issue with our appeal to generalists in those grades. Legislation regarding teacher licensure at the middle level is increasingly aimed at producing middle-level teachers who are specialists in science, math, social studies, or English. This trend, in our opinion, is absolutely contrary to best practice, particularly best practices with regard to middle-level education.

The standard rallying cry around middle-level education is to form meaningful relationships between teachers and students. If this really is a key component of effective middle-level education, then it is simply not possible to design a worse system to instruct middle-level students than to have them see seven or eight different subject area specialists in the course of their educational week.

Conversely, you could not design a better situation for forming those lasting relationships than to implement a schedule in which middle-level students spend one, two, or three years with a highly trained generalist.

Any argument that asserts that it is impossible to find teachers who are expert enough to teach all of the breadth of content at the middle grades rings false to our ears and runs contrary to our experience. First, we have seen it done at an astoundingly high level. Second, we do not want adults teaching our children who are not at least competent enough to lead middle-level students through the "rigors" of the middle-level curriculum.

Our greatest fear is that our daughters will some day run into a middle-level English teacher who looks at them blankly when they are asking for help on a pre-algebra or algebra problem. The second you separate your instruction into subject area specialists, you send the message to the students that some people are good at math; others are good at science, while some are good at English. We do not want students to experience this type of pigeon holing until their high school years at the earliest.

We do recognize that in high school there comes a point where students are ready for instruction by subject area specialists. That point happens when you are unable, due to licensure requirements, and graduation requirements, to find people who are able to teach all content areas at an extremely high level. It is difficult to find a subject area specialist who is simultaneously highly qualified to teach AP Calculus, Art, Music, AP World History, AP English, and Spanish 3. Eventually the content does outstrip the abilities of most generalists, and specialists are not only required but warranted.

However, when we talk of utilizing subject area specialists in high school, we always want to maintain a focus on multi-age instruction whereby we keep an excellent teacher in contact with students for as many years as possible. One way this can be accomplished is to avoid the sudden switch to subject area specialists the second a kid becomes a ninth grader! Our experience tells us this is possible.

For example, at Corbett, ninth grade students still receive instruction in AP Human Geography, Physics/Chemistry, Algebra 1/Algebra 2, Health, and English from one core teacher; however, their remaining two periods are spent with subject area specialists in Spanish, Band, or P.E. In the Corbett model, ninth grade students still spend a majority of their day with one teacher. Students still have an opportunity to form a long-lasting, meaningful relationships with an adult while at the same time transitioning to the intricacies of juggling the multiple expectations of their three other teachers.

In whatever manner a school designs the transition from full day generalists in grades K–8 to full day specialists in grades 9–12, we recommend the following approach. Avoid creating classes that are only for seniors, or juniors, and so forth. Course work in your high school should be achievement based. If you have a freshman or sophomore who is ready for AP Calculus or AP Physics, make sure your schedule allows her to attend those classes! If you have junior or senior who is ready for freshman English, make sure your schedule allows him to attend that class.

The next imperative is that the school hire specialists who are broadly qualified in their discipline. Do not hire a physics teacher, a biology teacher, and a chemistry teacher; rather hire a science teacher who can teach all three subjects and perhaps even more!

By employing broadly qualified subject area specialists such as the one previously described, a student can spend three or four years with the same science teacher, same math teacher, same social studies teacher, and so forth. Once again, you will have created a situation in which a highly expert teacher will get to form a relationship with a student and maintain that relationship over a long period of time. They may only see that student for one period a day in grades 10–12, but a more typical scenario would be for them to see three or four different teachers in that discipline over the same time period.

A reader may well wonder where to find someone who is broadly qualified enough to teach all types of science or all levels of mathematics; we believe we have the answer in secret number four. To foreshadow a bit, we recommend that you hire the people who know they can teach it all, and then pay for their professional development so they earn the paper that proclaims they can do it all. In short, send them back to school on your dime!

Enough of the argument for multi-age classrooms for now. We will explain our rationale further in subsequent chapters. So, for now we have identified two secrets to creating excellent schools: first you need to hire excellent teachers, and next you must keep them in contact with 24 students for as long as possible. (Multi-age classrooms accomplish this task nicely.) Once those two secrets are satisfied, it is critical that an excellent school feed its teachers.

SECRET NUMBER THREE: FEED THE TEACHERS—GIVE THEM EVERYTHING THEY NEED

It will not do any good to have an excellent teacher working with 24 students for years if the teacher is starving. Excellent schools must feed the teachers and give them everything they need; this is the third secret of creating excellent schools.

Our experiences have shown that the morale of even the most gifted teacher can be broken down. If the teachers are starving for resources, those teachers' effectiveness in the classroom is greatly diminished. Furthermore, what good teacher would want to teach in situations where the basic accruements of their profession are rationed? Such a situation will invariably create a situation where the teachers who are able to leave and get other jobs, typically the best teachers, will leave, and those who remain will be the least able.

We will start with an example around something as simple as the copy machine. How many schools and districts ration copy paper? How many teachers are given a code that counts the number of pages they are allowed to copy in a given month? How many teachers have been forced to ask their administrator if they can borrow some of the administrator's copy rations for the month, as they so unwisely mismanaged the 200 pages they were rationed for their 30 students that month? We believe the answer is far too many.

Imagine you are a teacher, an excellent teacher, a highly educated professional, who dedicates far more of your time than called for in any negotiated agreement to your profession. Imagine that a school entrusts you with the education of our children, you are entrusted with keeping them safe, and yet we do not trust you to make the decision as to whether you should make a copy of something for your class!

What message do we send to the most essential part of the educational process, our teachers, when we ration copy machine use? What does it mean when long distance telephone access, text books, pens, paper, pencil sharpeners, clocks that work, laboratory equipment, or desks are rationed? This is not an exhaustive list, but we have probably made our point. Namely, we believe that when you ration the basic necessities of a teacher's day to day world, you do not send the message that they are the most essential part of the educational process.

In fact, when it comes to this third secret we recommend that you think of teachers like this. "Teachers Must be the Priority!" All other parts of the educational process are less important. Before any of the priorities suffer one moment of need, a school should cut some non-instructional position to ensure that it can meet these priorities.

We anticipate that many of you are thinking about your current situation in which the budget just does not allow for the kind of unfettered spending that we are advocating with regard to teacher needs. Without knowing the specifics of your individual situation we of course can not speak directly to the room in your budget to follow our advice. However, before you throw up your hands and ignore our advice consider for a moment just a few of the items in your budget that we would cut before you failed to meet the needs of your teachers.

Our supposition is that every other part of the education process is subservient to the needs of the teachers. We have witnessed schools and districts that make the decision to starve their teachers while they maintain staffing in other areas like administration, counseling, teachers on special assignment, reading specialists, classroom aides, and many other positions that funnel dollars out of the classroom and away from the teachers.

The next example is not meant to pick on counselors, it is meant to illustrate a common staffing decision that we believe leads down a path of mediocrity rather than exceptionality. It is not uncommon for a school of 700 K–6 grade students to have a full time counselor. The counselor may represent 1 out of 31 certificated teachers in a typical grade-level school with 24 students per classroom. A mid-career counselor's salary and benefit package could easily cost a district from $50-$90 thousand per year depending upon the district in which they are employed.

The counselor can expect to spend about 1 hour and 15 minutes per student in a year, if the time is divided equally amongst all students and he/she spends five hours per day in a 160 day year counseling. Meanwhile the school is in a fiscal predicament and each teacher is rationed 200 pages per month of copy machine use, or 8 pages per month per student. If the counselor's salary and benefit package were translated into copy paper, each teacher could have between $1600 and $3000 dollars worth of copy paper use per year!

Eliminate one position, eliminate one hour and 15 minutes worth of counseling per student per year, and you have fed the most important part of the educational process. The position you eliminate may not be that of counselor, it may be an administrator, a teacher on special assignment, or any of the other non-instructional positions you currently support at your school. Also, you may need to eliminate more than one position to meet your teachers' needs.

Our point is not to pick on counselors any more than it is to pick on administrators, teachers on special assignments, reading specialists, classroom aides, or other non-instructional personnel. However, consider that in a multi-age classroom the teachers become far more familiar with the students than a counselor could ever become. Further, consider how few minutes per year a counselor is able to spend with each student. Lastly, note that for serious mental health issues most school counselors are not qualified to counsel students, and instead recommend that the students seek more qualified advice from a mental health practitioner.

To put it simply, we hesitate to place counseling high up on our list of non-instructional staffing priorities. Having these types of positions on staff is not a bad idea. Indeed, we think if you can afford to feed your teachers' needs and hire counselors, administrators, teachers on special assignments, and classroom aides, then you should. However, we think that too often the classroom climate is negatively impacted by the inability of administrators to say "no" to good ideas like counselors.

Each situation in each school is different; there may be situations in which in order to create an excellent school you do need to hire a counselor or other non-instructional personnel. However, we think that in the vast majority of cases the creation of exceptional schools will be fostered by hiring excellent teachers, keeping them in contact with around 24 kids for as long as possible, and providing them with the all of the equipment and supports they need to teach effectively.

If we were in charge of operating a school and we suddenly had a $100,000 annual windfall, we would add another classroom teacher long before we would add many other kinds of support personnel such as administrators or counselors. Excellent schools are created on the backs of teachers, not on the support personnel that tend to take a disproportionate share of school budgets across the country.

SECRET NUMBER FOUR: INVEST LAVISHLY IN TEACHERS' PROFESSIONAL DEVELOPMENT

Along the lines of providing for the teachers' needs you should make an incredible investment in the professional development of your staff. An expansive investment in the professional development of your teachers is the fourth secret of creating excellent schools.

Business has long recognized that it is far cheaper to retain employees and retrain them than it is to hire replacement employees. Companies recognize that one of their largest investments is in their personnel. Companies recognize this despite the fact that many companies have substantial physical holdings that often represent an even greater investment than their employee pool.

For instance stores and hospitals have a considerable amount of their net worth wrapped up in equipment, stock, and overhead, yet what makes companies such as Nordstrom, Starbucks, or Methodist Hospital System among the 100 Best Companies to work for according to *Fortune Magazine* is the great length to which they go to retain employees.

Schools have no assets like equipment, inventory, or investments; 85 percent of schools' investments are its personnel! To the authors, this makes it obvious that a school should make an even greater effort to retain their personnel than a for-profit company does. One way for a school to retain its personnel is to invest heavily in professional development.

Our opinion of professional development is also the one that we have regarding student instruction. We have mentioned earlier that we champion the idea of a continuous-progress model for student education, a model where the curriculum is routinely differentiated for each learner in every subject. This model should not stop at age 18. Our ideas about professional development lean heavily on a continuous-growth model where professional development is differentiated for each staff member.

Just as we think the "one size fits all" instruction method is not the best way to teach kids, we think that there are relatively few professional development programs that are appropriate for all of your staff members. We do not think that the common practice of hiring an outsider to come to a staff development training at the start of the school year is necessarily the best way to develop an effective professional development program in your district.

Obviously, there are situations in which it is desirable to have a whole group professional development opportunity where an expensive, outside-the-district agent is brought in to deliver a staff development in-service. *This is especially true, if you want to hire us!* With our presentations aside, we think most of the time group professional development activities should be directed at small group situations, rather than whole school affairs. In other words, differentiate for the audience.

The best way to differentiate professional development opportunities for your staff is to allow the staff members to develop their own individual professional development plans. Next, you need to support those plans monetarily. Recall earlier we described the extent that the Corbett School District supported professional development opportunities for its staff members by making it impossible for them to take course work faster then the district could pay for it.

We believe that education is important, and that creating life long learners is one of the goals of public education. With those two beliefs in mind, it would be hypocritical for a school not to support its teachers' efforts at continuing their professional development through advanced course work in fields and areas that most benefit them as professionals.

Further, we know from experience that when you support teachers' efforts at continuing professional development, you engender a commitment to the district on the part of the teacher. Turnover drops when you supply your teachers with everything they need, and one mainstay of an excellent teacher's life is continued access to personally meaningful professional development opportunities.

You may be thinking to yourself, "How in the world am I going to afford to pay for every college course a teacher wants to take?" We feel even more strongly about meeting this need of your teachers then we do about making sure you support their more mundane needs such as copy paper. We recommended you eliminate non-instructional positions from your district to make sure teachers had classroom supplies; we are even more adamant that you support the professional growth needs of your teachers!

If you need to eliminate two or three positions to support the professional growth needs of your staff, then you should do so! Unlike buying paper for your teachers, buying professional development opportunities pays dividends in the form of better informed teachers who are energized and thus are more effective teachers. Teachers who are energized and better informed produce higher student academic achievement, and this is the main point of education.

Our list of secrets is growing. We imagine that most readers agreed with us that it is important to hire excellent teachers. We hope we have challenged some of your beliefs with regard to keeping teachers with the same 24 students for years at a time through multi-age classrooms. We also hope that we have challenged your thinking with regard to supplying them with all of their needs both in the classroom and from a professional development standpoint, even if to meet those needs requires you to eliminate non-instructional positions. We hope secret number five challenges your assumptions and preconceived ideas as well.

SECRET NUMBER FIVE: FOCUS LIKE A LASER ON ONE THING

The fifth secret takes some planning, forethought, and commitment to first implement, and then sustain. You need to decide what your school is going to be the best at and focus on that goal like a laser.

First of all, we assert that creating large schools, particularly large high schools, constitutes a devastating blow to effective education. We have dedicated parts of previous and subsequent chapters to convince the reader that if you have a small school, you are in luck, and if you have a large school, you will need to work hard to overcome your bad luck. In fact, we will encourage you to tear it down, or somehow change your big school into a small school.

So, although we have not tried to convince you of our assertion that big schools are bad, we ask you to assume for now that they are indeed bad, and recognize that all of the intricacies of this fifth secret are aimed at smaller schools.

One of the many problems with large schools, and the only one we will address here, is that large high schools attempt to be comprehensive. They offer an array of courses that may include jazz band, AP Calculus, 4-H, automotives, child care, economics, and many more options. Large high schools try to be comprehensive, and they may actually have the resources to attempt this feat. However, their attempts are doomed from the outset due to problems intrinsic within their very largeness. (Please trust us for a few more chapters, and allow us the freedom to state without evidence that big schools are bad!)

Furthermore, because large high schools are called comprehensive, most of them do not attempt to be the best at one thing and focus on it like a laser. Rather they attempt to be comprehensive, and we believe that this eventually means that in the end they wind up doing all things poorly. The large schools opt for an approach that can be likened to being a mile wide and an inch deep rather than an inch wide and a mile deep!

Perhaps it is possible to operate a large high school and minimize some of the problems associated with largeness by abandoning the comprehensive approach and focusing on one thing. However, we can not imagine one high school that focuses in on only one thing, say agriculture education that was a good fit for 2,500 students.

Secondly, we assume, and we hope you will too, that education is at least a K–12 process and that all grade schools should have one thing that they want to focus on like a laser, that is to get their students ready for middle school. All middle schools should focus on getting their students ready for high school.

With those two assumptions in mind, that large high schools are bad and that grade schools and middle schools should focus on getting students ready for high school, we can move onto the fifth secret; deciding what your small high school will be the very best at and focusing in on it like a laser.

The hard part about deciding what you want to be the best at is deciding what you do not want to do. An all too common mistake of small high schools is to try to mimic the comprehensive nature of large high schools. It is odd that small schools mimic large, comprehensive high schools given that large high schools are not nearly as effective at delivering instruction as their smaller counterparts. The simple fact of the matter is that small schools do not have the resources to be all things to all people and therefore their attempts at being a comprehensive high school are even more tenuous than are those of their larger counterparts.

If a small school is in an agricultural community, then perhaps it makes sense to make the focus of the entire school to be the very best agriculture high school in the state. However, if a school has an agriculture program, and 90 percent of its students never ever will set foot on a farm, then maybe the focus of that school needs to be elsewhere!

Our general thoughts about what a school's laser-like goal should be tend toward an academic focus. Our rational for this is simple. Schools are primarily entrusted with, and assessed on, their instruction of students in English, math, science, and social studies, and so their focus should probably be on these areas. However, the needs of every school and community are different and we cannot speak to every situation. Certainly this is a good argument for local control of schools as opposed to a state system, but we digress.

The upshot of these observations is the injunction that once you pick a focus area in which you want your school to excel you will have to constantly fight off well-meaning individuals and organizations who will take energy away from that focus.

Imagine you have a small high school and you have determined that your focus, the thing you will be the best at, is academics. Given this scenario, it makes sense to design a program in which students earn four credits of math, science, English, social studies, as well as three credits of second language and two of fine arts. The focus of this hypothetical school is academics, and after factoring in the requirements of health and P.E., a high school student has five credits of electives to be rationed over a four-year high school career. Forces will conspire against your focus.

Soon your state legislature decides that every student in grades 9–12 should have one hour of P.E. per day to fight childhood obesity. Then they add a requirement for community service, while a local auto-shop owner insists that students need to know how to work on their cars and petitions the board to add a vocational-education department.

Following on the heels of this addition, the local chamber of commerce believes a business class should be taught, and who could argue that a performing arts focus is not a good thing for some students? At the same time, one teacher is particularly interested in teaching DECA and is trying to flex her schedule away from US history in order to teach DECA. Of course, the local head start people want to start a class in which high school students learn childcare.

These ideas are great, and while things are changing, why not add robotics, which would be fun, and so is 4-H. On top of that, it would be great if students could have a school newspaper or make a yearbook. What if a partnership could be formed between a local graphic artist and the art students in your school? The newspaper would be a great place for students to create their own advertisements for cookies that the students make in their home-economics class that desperately needs to be added so kids can learn to cook healthy meals; the list goes on and on!

Individually, each of these things is good. Not only are they good, but each idea will be put forth under the auspices of, "I have an idea that will be good for kids." However, if a school's focus is on academics, it is imperative that each suggestion be considered within the context of the focus. For example, how will adding a 4-H program, or forming a partnership with a local graphic artist help the school become the highest performing academic school in the state?

We believe that an excellent school must filter all ideas through the filter or sieve of the objective: "If it is not directed at our focus, then do not do it." No matter how good the idea is, adding non-complimentary or distracting programs, classes, or foci is inherently disruptive, destructive, and works against creating an excellent school.

School boards, administrators, parents, and everyone concerned about creating an excellent school will have to learn to say "no" to good ideas like the ones we have just listed. Saying "no" is an essential skill the community will need to develop in order to create an exceptional school. Our sixth and last secret is a huge reminder as to the power of the word "no."

SECRET NUMBER SIX: DON'T DO ANYTHING TO VIOLATE THE FIRST FIVE SECRETS

Finally, do not do anything that violates those first five secrets. The list of things that schools often do to violate the first five rules is exhaustive. We think that it might be informative to list a few of the common pitfalls that you may encounter when trying to implement the first five secrets.

For secret number one, the biggest pitfall includes good teachers, ok teachers, and increased class size. Good teachers and ok teachers are the biggest challenge and potential trap.

Consider the case of the administrator at a large school who must hire 20 new staff members each year. Unfortunately, the fact of the marketplace is that the chance of finding 20 exceptional teachers is low. It is not low because those 20 teachers do not exist; it is low because schools and individuals do not have the time to properly interview the hundreds of teachers required to consider all of the candidates in order to find 20 exceptional teachers. Therefore, instead our administrator must settle for good teachers and ok teachers. The direct result of these circumstances is that the school will not be exceptional.

In small schools personnel decisions become much more personal.

In a school where every teacher knows every teacher, and friendships can run deep across many levels of the curriculum, there can be incredible pressure to keep a good teacher or an ok teacher. A small school administrator must recognize that by retaining good and ok teachers they are dooming their school to be good or ok. We are willing, however, to note that raising expectations, professional development, and administrative help can help make excellent teachers, or motivate excellence, but ultimately the cliché about a chain being only as strong as the weakest link is correct.

Obviously, negotiated agreements will play a substantial role in an administrator's ability to retain exceptional teachers in favor of good teachers. A skilled administrator must work within a negotiated agreement to help move good teachers to positions where they can do great things, help counsel teachers out of positions where they are not great, and be patient enough to play the waiting game to eliminate teachers who are not a fit with the school's focus.

An administrator's greatest leverage occurs during the hiring practice and the first three years of that teacher's tenure in the district. If administrators will be diligent during those first three years, then the chances of creating an exceptional school are greatly increased. Obviously, this calls for administrators to spend more than one or two years in a district.

When class size begins to creep over that magic number of 24, it is imperative that a school make sure that it has not hired personnel that do not fit with its mission, or created course work that does not fit the focus. If the class sizes are at 35 and the school is still employing a considerable number of non-classroom educators like aides, counselors, and administrators, it is clear that the school needs to cut those positions.

Pitfalls for secret number two will come from within the classrooms as well as from outside of your organization. Teachers, especially older teachers, who have 20 years of experience in graded classrooms, will often start to fall back to their old ways of teaching. When a teacher starts arranging assignments in their room based upon their students' grade, it is a warning sign and the community should beware. Thought patterns like this can lead a district back to single-grade classrooms where teachers get a whole new set of students each year.

Furthermore, legislation and licensure seem to be trending toward increasing the specificity of a teacher's ability to teach. Those who seek to create and maintain an excellent school must remain vigilant to these outside forces and be part of a vocal campaign to curtail any attempts to eliminate generalists, or to make the specificity of high school teachers' licenses so restricted that they can only teach one subject within their discipline.

The pitfalls for secrets three and four are both the same. Schools and districts will be faced with decisions to cut non-instructional personnel in order to make sure teachers do not starve and that their professional development needs are met. Before a district or school hires any non-instructional personnel, it is imperative that the school be able to answer yes to the following question: "Do our teachers have all they need with regard to supplies, materials, and professional development?"

Pitfalls for the fifth secret will be never ending. Forces, most of them well meaning, will be constantly pushing you to add some new component to your existing program. Before you add anything to your program, ask yourself; "How does this fit in with our commitment to be the best school in the state at doing _____?"

CONCLUSIONS

We recognize that there are two major assumptions imbedded within our six secrets. The assumption that we have done the least to convince you of is that small schools are much more efficient with regard to delivering education than are large schools. Chapter four is dedicated to convincing you that our assumption is a valid one.

The second assumption is that multi-age instruction is a more effective way of delivering an education than are graded level classes. We have defended this assumption in this chapter; however, we plan on launching a full scale defense of that assumption in chapter five.

Chapter 4

School Size and Excellence: Is Bigger More Efficient? Or, Commonly Held Beliefs about the Benefits of Big Schools

We unabashedly support the hypothesis that smaller schools produce higher academic achievement, and they are more efficient! Additionally, nearly all secondary measurements of school effectiveness such as staff morale, student and parent involvement, student retention rate, and a myriad of other secondary benefits are positively influenced by smaller school size.

Our belief about school size is based both on our personal experiences in education, and evidence in the peer reviewed literature. In this chapter, we will examine our personal beliefs regarding school size, the literature that supports and refutes our belief, as well as provide case studies that emphasize real world experiences as they relate to school size.

Our beliefs regarding school size and academic achievement are straightforward and self evident. As we will discuss in later chapters, a pivotal component of creating excellent schools is creating a culture of excellence. The foundation of an excellent school is its teachers. Furthermore, an administrator's ability to assemble a staff composed entirely of excellent teachers is directly linked to school size.

Imagine that you are trying to outfit a science department at a 2000-student high school and you are faced with the prospect of hiring and retaining ten excellent teachers. Four of them will teach biology, one will teach physics, two will teach chemistry, and the remainder will face the dregs of the high school community in courses such as earth science and physical science.

What are the chances that you will be able to find the ten Jaime Escalantes of the scientific community at one job fair? Or will you be able to woo them from neighboring districts? Now imagine that you are going to find that teacher who is the best of the best, whose inner calling

is to teach the lowest of sciences, the earth sciences, to the most reticent
of learners.

> Aside: We absolutely do not intend to impugn the geologists of the world by
> implying that earth science is somehow a less noble field of study than biology,
> physics, or chemistry . . . particularly given that Bob's first degree is in that
> field. Rather, we are only recognizing that earth science traditionally occupies a
> lower station in the academic continuum of high schools across the nation.

We maintain that a small school stands a much better chance of hiring one
excellent teacher than a larger school does of hiring ten.

Of course all bets are off if the small school is not committed to identifying
and hiring the best possible teacher, but if all other things are equal, we
believe it will be easier to find one excellent teacher than it will be to find
five or ten. Admittedly, this approach is a "zero-sum-game" for all schools,
and some will prosper while others will falter; however, until such time that
all teachers are excellent and equal, our contention is that small schools have
a better chance of achieving the goal of hiring an excellent teacher.

Take, for example, the fictional earth science teacher that a large high
school would need to hire and the same teacher that would need to be hired
at a small school. At a large school, the earth science position is the most
unenviable position in the science teaching staff. By default the most junior
of science teachers and/or the least capable of teachers is entrusted with
the science education of the most academically challenged students in the
school.

Conversely, a small school will hire the best teacher they can possibly
attract, and that teacher will be entrusted with the science education of most,
if not all, of the students in that school. It is not that there would not be a need
for the earth science teacher at a small school; rather, it is that the earth science teacher would be the same *fantastic* chemistry and physics teacher that
those students would interact with in their junior and senior years. Again, this
supports our contention that relationships matter.

Furthermore, imagine that you are one of four administrators at a 2000-
student high school and your job is to evaluate and retain or dismiss up to
240 employees each year, 100 of whom are teachers. Your job is considerably
more difficult, by virtue of sheer numbers, than would be the job of a less
heavily taxed small school principal. With that said, how many people can
one administrator really know?

Each administrator at a 2000-student school is in charge of 500 students
and 60 employees, while an administrator at a 300-student school is in charge
of 16 employees and only 300 students. Each individual administrator has a
finite capacity for meaningful interactions with staff and students. In the end,

the small school administrator will know all of the students and employees, while a large school administrator will know only a quarter of them, and she or he won't know these as well. Further, the larger school administrator will have less contact with staff and students, which cannot help build an excellent school.

We maintain that an administrator at a small school has much greater ability to know their staff and students. Further, their knowledge will include a much richer understanding of their staff's strengths and weaknesses. Weaknesses are not inherently bad; rather they are taken into account by a good administrator. An overwhelmed administrator, an administrator who is in charge of 60 adult relationships and 500 student relationships, is less able to identify the strengths and weaknesses of his or her teaching staff and respond to them.

We think readers will agree with us, in principle, that smaller school administrators will have a greater understanding of their staff's strengths and weaknesses than their larger school peers. Given that small school principals have that advantage, it follows that small school administrators will be able to place their staff in positions to be more successful than will their larger school counterparts.

Compare a school to a basketball team; each player has both strengths and weaknesses, and good coaches place each player in positions where they are most likely to succeed. A center that can not dribble does not get the ball at the top of the key. Similarly, in football a running back that does not have good hands is not called on for screen plays. Likewise, an administrator matches kids, teachers, and subjects. This is only possible if the administrator knows both the teachers and the students, particularly the former.

In a 2000-student school, it is virtually impossible for an administrator to make the necessary connections with 60 employees and 500 students to ensure the successful marriage of teacher, students, and subject.

Furthermore, given even a low turnover rate of 10 percent, an administrator at a large school sees at least 50 new students and six new staff members in a year for a 2000-student school. Thus, the job of marrying teachers with students and curriculum is greater than 60 percent more demanding than a similar turnover rate at a 300 student school.

Other aspects of administering a smaller school are considerably easier at a 300-student school than at a 2000-student school. Perhaps one of the most important challenges that an administrator faces is that of creating a sense of camaraderie within the teaching staff. It is intrinsically more difficult to create a "we are in this together" feeling with a team of 100 as compared to a team of 16 teachers.

The challenge of getting even a divided department staff to unite and work together in a large school can be a formidable task. Assuming that an administrator in a large high school is successful in the attempt to unite one department with a common vision, the chances of uniting that department with other departments is tenuous at best.

The key to uniting departments and teachers within departments seems to us to be related to communication. How much easier is it for a school with one science teacher, one English teacher, and one math teacher to communicate about the needs of their common charges than a school with ten times the number of staff members in those disciplines? The innate advantages to communication in a small school seem to be self evident, and any school configuration that compromises communication is suspect.

We believe that there is more than one way to get to heaven, and that different approaches can lead to similar outcomes. If this is true, then it is more important to identify and pursue that common vision than it is to prescribe that one vision.

Of course, different schools in different locations, facing different circumstances will necessarily adopt different visions or approaches. It is far easier to inculcate a common vision to a small group as opposed to a large group of educators. Further, it is easier to continue to reinforce that vision and bring new staff members into the collective fold in smaller institutions as opposed to larger ones.

A staff member's agency or stake in the operation of a school is far greater in a small school as opposed to a larger school. Likewise, the member's ability to affect, influence, and guide the direction of the school climate is categorically more profound in the small school setting.

We think of the analogy of crew members on a fishing vessel. A crew of five on a near shore seine boat who work side by side to retrieve their gear and haul in the catch of the day is drastically more interdependent upon one another than is the crew of 300 on an offshore trawler that scours the sea for their own share of the ocean's bounty.

In our analogy, when one of the five crewmembers makes a particularly quick interchange of fishing tackle that results in a larger catch, the celebration is immediate, shared, and personal. A similarly quick witted maneuver on the larger, ocean-going vessel might produce a nod from a personal friend onboard the ship but not a complete celebration by The Crew.

Aside: Guess, if you will Dear Reader, on which type of boat the authors crewed?

We have attempted to demonstrate in the preceding paragraphs that the foundation of any excellent school is composed of fundamental building blocks called teachers. Additionally, we maintain that finding, retaining, administering, and communicating with a smaller number of building blocks is dramatically more efficient than larger numbers of building blocks. But the benefits of small schools extend farther than the act of finding, retaining, and communicating with staff members.

Stated simply, we believe that the benefits of a small school are nothing short of comprehensive. However, none of the benefits may be as important as the much-documented benefits of academic achievement associated with small school size.

Academic achievement is, in our opinion, the Holy Grail of education. We believe that school size and academic achievement are inexorably linked. We stringently maintain that this link is more than corelational in nature and is, in fact, causal. If all things are equal, we maintain that the very nature of small schools produces higher academic achievement than does that of large schools. Granted, we understand there are exceptions to every rule, and it is possible to produce a bad school anywhere, but we believe that students are better served by small schools.

The influential texts *Breaking Ranks in the Middle: Strategies For Leading Middle Level Reform,* and *Breaking Ranks: Strategies for Leading High School Reform* go to great lengths to demonstrate that relationships matter with regard to student academic success.[1] Relationships between peers, between teachers and students, and those between parents and the school are all critical to creating an exceptional school.

Creating relationships takes time and sustained contact to develop and nurture. Anonymity retards relationship building. Anonymity is far easier for a student or a teacher to achieve in a large school as opposed to a smaller school. In the short run, anonymity is easy, and too often people gravitate to it because of that fact. However, it is not nearly as easy in a small school.

If relationships matter to the extent that *Breaking Ranks in the Middle: Strategies For Leading Middle Level Reform,* and *Breaking Ranks: Strategies for Leading High School Reform* maintain, then we must provide an atmosphere in which relationships are fostered. This means creating small schools or manufacturing Rube Goldberg like systems to create faux small systems within larger educational settings. Small schools are free from the disruptions associated with major discipline problems that plague large schools (Langbein and Bess, 2002).[2]

Langbein and Bess (2002) talk extensively about the anonymity produced by large schools and its deleterious effects on student behavior. To combat these effects they recommend that a large school must put considerable resources into extra-curricular activities to give students avenues to form meaningful relationships. We believe it is simpler to skip the smoke and mirrors required to make a big school seem small and just build them small from the outset.

In schools where students are not anonymous, children's needs can be better identified and met. A student's needs for remediation or acceleration are both more easily recognized in a small school than a large school. Furthermore, in a small school, each student's individual needs should be placed above the entrenched hierarchy of "grade level." This approach allows progress to be addressed on a case by case basis, and the result is an improvement in the achievement of the whole.

While we have argued that some of these causal links are self evident, we maintain that the peer reviewed literature supports our conclusions. While a complete review of the literature related to school size and all the many and varied aspects of education would result in volumes, what follows is our consideration of school size and its relationship to academic achievement, economies of scale, and socio economic status.

SCHOOL SIZE AND ACADEMIC ACHIEVEMENT

To be fair, the research regarding the relationship between school size and student academic achievement is mixed. Some studies have found that smaller schools positively affect student academic achievement (Coladarci, 2006; Lee and Loeb, 2000); a few have found that school size does not effect student achievement (Tajalli and Opheim, 2005); while some argue that there is an optimal size somewhere between the smallest of small and the largest of large (Bradley and Taylor, 1998).[3]

Despite the above findings, when we review the available literature, it is clear that the literature suggests that optimal school size is far smaller than the current trend towards large comprehensive high schools and middle schools would seem to indicate.

Lee and Loeb (2000) conducted a massive study of more than 23,000 sixth and eighth grade students in Chicago K–8 elementary schools, and found that smaller schools with an enrollment of fewer than 400 students had higher student academic achievement than larger schools. Their data indicated a strong negative correlation between medium size schools with enrollments of 400–750 and academic achievement.

Further, Lee and Loeb found a small negative correlation between large schools with an enrollment of over 750 students and academic achievement. Essentially Lee and Loeb found that small schools, under 400 students, produced higher academic achievement.

Additionally, Lee and Loeb further maintain that school size has both direct effects on academic achievement like those detailed above, and indirect effects on academic achievement, both of which contribute to higher overall academic achievement in smaller schools. Some of the indirect effects that they discuss include teachers in small schools feeling more connected and more responsible for student academic achievement, as they are more likely to know those students better than their larger school peers.

It would seem clear from this research that small schools, schools of less than 400 students, are good for elementary age students. We do not believe that we will face much opposition in this assertion. There are few districts that run about willingly creating comprehensive elementary schools with thousands of students! Granted, there is a growing number of elementary schools that house more than 400 students. We think this research about school size should become common knowledge amongst district level planners who are designing new, larger grade schools nationwide.

The benefits of small school size at the elementary level are widely recognized, and consequently most elementary schools remain relatively small. Not only do most people agree that there are inherent benefits for small elementary school size, but the research continues to support the contention that there are many benefits from smaller schools.

The benefits from small schools include improved academic achievement as well as cost savings, but most research emphasizes academic results. However, we believe that the benefits of small schools hold true across all levels: elementary, middle, and high school. Even as studies seem to multiply, the total number of studies that bear on our purpose here are small given the importance of the topic.

Other researchers have not looked at the direct or indirect consequences related to school size and student achievement as Lee and Loeb did; rather they have conducted more direct statistical analysis of achievement data. Coladarci (2006) attempted to demonstrate that higher academic achievement by students in small schools, particularly by students of poverty, was a construct of statistical happenstance brought about by the smaller sample size and increased volatility of achievement data associated with small schools.

Coladarci's (2006) work with achievement data from 216 middle schools in Maine further bolstered the idea that small schools produce higher academic achievement than larger schools, particularly for students of poverty, because he determined that his increased volatility hypothesis was not supported by the data. In other words, an intense examination of the student achievement data in Maine demonstrated that the advantage in academic achievement that smaller schools produce is a legitimate factor and not a statistical anomaly.

We think that it is important to note that Coladarci began by attempting to demonstrate that small schools were not more successful at producing academic achievement, and he failed to do so. Furthermore, Coladarci was examining middle schools and not elementary schools, which is also worth noting! Apparently the research supports our assertion that it is also advantageous for middle schools to be small as well!

We do not want to be accused of only reporting data that supports our assertion that small schools are more adept at producing higher academic achievement. To that end, we want to report studies that argue against our assertion. Unfortunately, or *fortunately* from our ever so humble perspective, studies demonstrating that large schools increase student academic achievement are rare. However, at least one study by Tajali and Opheim (2005) presents a contrasting view with regard to increased school size negatively effecting student academic achievement.

Tajali and Opheim's Texas study used forward regression analysis to examine the relationship between school size and student academic achievement on the state's standardized achievement tests and did not find any statistically significant correlation between decreased school size and increased academic achievement. Tajali and Opheim did not find evidence that large schools increased academic achievement, only that it did not hurt academic achievement. Although their dissenting voice stands alone in the literature, it has been included to illustrate that research in this field is ongoing.

As demonstrated earlier, some researchers have found that small schools produce higher academic achievement; apparently only Tajali and Opheim have found the opposite to be the case. However, a third set of research studies have concluded that schools that are too big or too small both have negative effects on student achievement (Bradley and Taylor, 1998; Lee and Smith, 1997).[4]

We hope that throughout our discourse we have not caused our readers to believe that shrinking a school to its absolute minimum would create the highest academic achievement. Small schools are good, but very tiny schools are not the "be all end all" of education. In other words, we do understand that at some point becoming too small has a detrimental effect on education.

The reason we have not dwelt on the problem of "too small" is that we have rarely seen instances where large districts have fractured their student population into such diminutive populations that academic achievement actually suffered. In other words, we rarely see K–12 schools with 14 kids in large urban centers! We do recognize that at some point small can become too small and we think the following examples from the research support this assertion, as well as our previous contention that big schools are bad.

A study of nearly all secondary students in the UK between 1992 and 1996 demonstrated that very small schools and very large schools both had a negative effect on student academic achievement (Bradley and Taylor, 1998). Their research examined student performance on the General Certificate of Secondary Education examination, a test taken by nearly all students in the UK, and correlated their scores with school size while controlling for many other factors such as school type, school funding, and student socio-economic status.

Much of Bradley and Taylor's research focused on two different types of schools; 11–16 schools and 11–18 schools. Their data demonstrated that increases in school size up to 900 students produced robust and statistically significant gains in academic achievement for students in 11–16 schools. However, as population increased between 900 and 1500, students' gains in academic achievement began to flatten off and then decrease at around 1200 students. Similar results were found for 11–18 schools, with optimal school size occurring at around 1400 students.

One study of elementary schools in Kentucky by Borland and Howsen in 2003 noted a similar relationship, and found the optimal school size for student academic achievement to be around 760 students.[5] Borland and Howsen examined third-grade achievement data, ability data, economic data, teacher salary levels, and a host of other variables such as student socio-economic status and tax data from 1990.

When Borland and Howsen accounted for all variables, they found that academic achievement in elementary schools peaked at 760 students, and was lower in schools that were either larger or smaller than this optimal number.

The idea of a non-linear relationship between student achievement and school size was also demonstrated by Lee and Smith (1997). Lee and Smith used data from the National Educational Longitudinal Study of 1988 to demonstrate that high schools that were either smaller than 600 students or larger than 900 students were associated with an overall decrease in student academic achievement in math and reading.

Lee and Smith found that overly large schools, those with more than 2100 students, were further associated with an even more drastic decrease in student academic achievement than either small schools in the range of 0–600 students, or large schools in the range of 900–2100 students. Further, they found that an overly large high school with a low socio-economic status was even more at risk for producing low student academic achievement than a similarly sized high school with a higher socio-economic status.

In summary, the larger schools become, the lower the achievement of its students, assuming everything else is equal or held constant. We are not arguing there will not be students who excel at big schools. Rather, we are saying that achievement across the board will be lower; the overall amount of education delivered, retained, or achieved will be less.

SCHOOL SIZE AND THE ECONOMY OF SCALE

It is a commonly held belief that larger schools present a more economical approach to conducting K–12 education than smaller schools. One needs only to look at the size of schools, particularly high schools, being built in large metropolitan and suburban neighborhoods to recognize that when given the choice to build and operate many small schools or fewer large schools, the large school option wins out.

To demonstrate how this choice wins out, consider this example. Randy recently attended the National Association of Secondary School Principals national convention for state principals of the year. Of the 39 state principals of the year represented at the conference, 11 operated schools of fewer than 900 students, 18 operated schools between 900–2000 students, and 10 operated schools of more than 2000 students (Principals, 2007).[6]

Interviews with the principals from the 11 smallest schools represented at the conference revealed that of the 11 schools that contained fewer than 900 students, only two of them were small by choice. For instance, Corbett School District, where Randy Works, only had 225 high school age students. Corbett High was small by definition not by choice. Eight of the small schools, including Corbett, served all of the high school students in their district's and therefore were small by definition. The remaining 31 districts had the choice to build and maintain any size high school. Only 2 of the 31 chose to create small high schools rather than large high schools.

This example is obviously not a complete sample of school size across the United States. However, the sample does show us that in this random sample of districts that had the potential to create several small schools rather than a large school, only 6.4 percent chose to do so! This is particularly surprising given the breadth of literature espousing the academic and other benefits associated with small schools.

One might assume that the reason 29 out of 31 random districts country wide chose to create large high schools rather than small high schools was for economic reasons. Bigger schools produce an economy of scale that, in essence, makes each dollar buy more educational units.

Even disregarding the evidence Randy garnered amongst the state principals of the year, the commonly held belief that larger schools present a more economical approach to conducting K–12 education than smaller schools is self evident. Again, looking at the size of schools being built in large metropolitan and suburban areas, we see that when given the choice to build and operate many small schools or fewer large schools, the large school option wins out.

Because there is strong evidence, as demonstrated in the previous section, that large schools produce lower academic achievement, one would have to assume that there must be some other reason for communities to build large schools. It may be that there is an assumption, held by many, that bigger schools produce an economy of scale that in essence makes each dollar buy more educational units.

A logical path for this discussion and de facto literature review to follow would be to provide evidence in the literature supporting the assertion that such an assumption exists. However, the peer-reviewed work in this area is apparently absent. There appears to be no peer reviewed research during the last 10 years examining the concept that larger schools present an economy of scale that makes them more efficient. This lack of research bolsters the idea that, even amongst researchers, there is an assumption that big schools are more economical.

In addition to a lack of research examining the economy of scale argument; there is also surprisingly little evidence in the literature investigating the actual costs associated with operating small and large schools. Indeed, what little work has been done in this field seems to do as much to refute the argument that large schools are more efficient than it does to support the idea that they are more efficient.

We could find only three studies regarding the efficiency of operating small and large schools, of which only two have been published in the last 10 years. The oldest study, published by Walberg and Fowler in 1987, demonstrated that schools in New Jersey became less efficient with regard to student achievement as they grew larger.[7] So, it appears that even 20 years ago researchers understood that large schools were less efficient! But, come on . . . that is 20 years old! So, if we disregard the findings from the New Jersey study because their findings are 20 years old, then we are left with only two studies.

As indicated earlier, the literature during the last 10 years with regard to school size and economy of scale is sparse. The only research that has been found supporting the economies of scale argument was conducted in Wyoming by Bowles and Bosworth in 2002.[8] The research examined 17 school districts' school level data for more than 80 schools over a four-year time period. The schools ranged in size from 3 to 1500. The researchers used a least squares dummy variable model to control for different factors in each school in an attempt to analyze their economy of scale argument.

Bowles and Bosworth determined that for every 10 percent increase in student count in a school, there was a 2 percent decrease in costs associated with educating those students. They demonstrate, in table form, that this linear cost savings holds true for schools ranging in size from 70 to 429 students. Because their table only demonstrates linear cost savings for schools ranging from 70 to 429 students, it is unclear if they maintain that this linear relationship is static for all schools with student bodies of between 3 and 1500.

These results prompt us to ask if they are really arguing that a school of three is just as cost effective as one with 429 students. Furthermore, if they examined schools with up to 1,500 students, why do their linear cost savings only report the results for schools between 78 and 429 students? To put it bluntly, this represents an apparent weakness in their research.

We actually hypothesize that very small schools, schools with three people for instance, are inherently less cost effective than larger schools! Furthermore, we also hypothesize that any economies of scale that are realized for schools in the range of 429 students quickly flatten out as they grow larger than the number that Bowles and Bosworth established in their research.

Bowles and Bosworth (2002) further maintain that previous research about economies of scale dealt with district level economies of scale rather than school level economies of scale. However, it is interesting to note that Bowles and Bosworth cited only one study more recent than 10 years old supporting their assertion that large schools are more efficient. All attempts to find this article have proven fruitless.

Conversely, other researchers, Stiefel, Berne, Latarola, and Fruchter, found that there is no economy of scale associated with increased school size.[9] Their study, which focused on the economics of large and small high schools in New York City, concluded that small high schools were just as efficient to operate as large high schools.

The conclusions of Stiefel, Berne, Latarola, and Fruchter were based upon a review of 121 high schools' data on budget, graduation class, and school report card. The researchers used an ordinary least squares regression technique to lead them to their recommendation that the city of New York continue building and supporting the creation of smaller schools in the range of 600 students.

The research does not stop with budgeting and graduation rates. For example, Stiefel et al. (2000) concluded, as others have (Coladarci, 2006; Lee and Loeb, 2000), that small schools helped mitigate the achievement gap for low SES students and that they were essentially more economical to operate when balanced against overall student achievement such as graduation rate. The fact that these researchers also published a very limited number of citations, none of which were more recent than 10 years old, further demonstrates the sparse nature of the literature with regard to the economics of operating a school.

It would seem that the research supports the idea that big schools are more efficient just as heartily as it supports the idea that they are less efficient. It is noteworthy that the research in New York suggests that small schools are at least as efficient as big schools and they may be even more efficient with regard to educating students from a low socio-economic status (SES).

The literature, as we have shown, is neither deep nor definitive about the economics of small school/large school operation. Furthermore, the literature does not engage the question of dollars-per-result, just dollars-per-student, a distinction that is much more than academic. The literature is clearer when it comes to school size and socio-economic status.

SCHOOL SIZE AND SOCIO-ECONOMIC STATUS

Throughout our discussion of school size, and for that matter the rest of the book, we have thrown in occasional comments about the differences between rich kids and poor kids. We do not think that we will find much disagreement with our readers with regard to the concept that, in general, the richer kids do better in school than the poorer kids. With that assumption in mind, we want to examine the research with regard to how rich kids, kids of a high socio-economic status, compare with poor kids, kids of a low socio-economic status, when school size is taken into account.

The socio-economic status (SES) of students is a significant factor with regard to student achievement. The literature indicates that increases in student SES correlates to increases in student achievement. For instance, in 2006, Buchanan demonstrated, just as many before him had (including Bradley and Taylor, 1998; Lee and Smith, 1997; Sirin, 2005), that SES is a predictor of academic achievement.[10] While Buchanan was investigating achievement in post-secondary education, others investigated achievement amongst students in high school, middle school, and grade school.[11]

In 2005, Sirin conducted a meta-analytic review of SES and academic achievement that examined data from studies by Jimmerson and Egeland as well as Sutton and Soderstom, in addition to many others.[12] In fact Sirin analyzed data from more than 6800 schools and concluded that there was a medium to strong positive correlation between SES and student achievement.

A complete review of all the literature related to SES and academic achievement is not necessary, as it is broadly accepted in the literature as noted in Buchanan's (2006) work as well as in Sirin's (2005) meta-analysis, and it is not the main thrust of our literature examination. The citation of Buchanan (2006) and Sirin (2005) have been included here only to establish that SES and student achievement are inexorably linked. So, while it seems evident that the poorer children become, the poorer they fare academically, questions remain as to how school size influences this relationship.

Lee and Smith (1997) examined school size coupled with SES and student achievement using data from the National Educational Longitudinal Study of 1988. Their general conclusion was that the optimal high school size for academic achievement was between 600–900 students regardless of SES, based upon their examination of National Education Longitudinal Study of 1988 data for math and reading scores across the country.

The optimal size identified by Lee and Smith was even more critical for students of low SES. For instance, high SES students in a school of 600–900 students could expect to gain 15 points on the math assessment between eighth and twelfth grade, while low SES students in the same size school could expect to gain only 13 points. However, as school size increased to over 2100 students, a high SES student could expect to lose about 3 points of improvement, while a low SES student could expect to lose more than 6 points if he/she was enrolled in a school of 2100 or more.

In other words, a high SES student in a school of 2100 or more could still expect to gain 12 points between eighth and twelfth grade, while a low SES would only gain 7.75 points. Lee and Smith also found similar correlations with regard to academic achievement in school size, SES, and reading. Furthermore, as the percentage of low SES students increased in schools, the negative effects of school size also increased. As the total number of students increased above the optimal level of 600–900, the deleterious effects of large school size became even more magnified for the low SES students.

It also appears that the relationship between school size, academic achievement, and SES holds true for middle schools and grade schools. A study we previously highlighted by Coladarci (2006) in Maine analyzed the relationship between schools size and student achievement on eighth grade state tests indicated that students of poverty in small middle and junior high schools fare better than equally impoverished students in large schools.

Coladarci determined that students from small schools fared better by completing many different multiple-regression analyses of the students' test data in math and reading while controlling for school size, SES, and school volatility. The study from Maine does not stand alone in the literature regarding this relationship in schools other than high school. Increased school size was demonstrated to have a more serious effect on students of poverty than their richer peers in a massive study of 264 Chicago elementary schools (Lee and Loeb, 2000).

Lee and Loeb demonstrated that there was a positive correlation of .430 between school size of less than 400 students and student SES, while this coefficient dropped to .169 for schools between 400–750 students, and it dropped farther to a negative .008 for schools over 750 students. For those readers less statistically inclined, these numbers represent a profound difference.

The literature the authors examined to date is rich with examples of academic achievement being more negatively affected by increased school size for low SES students as compared to their more wealthy classmates in high schools, middle schools, and elementary schools. In other words, the research demonstrates that elementary, middle, and high school students, particularly low SES students, see their performance drop the larger their schools become. In short, big schools seem to be bad in general, but they are especially bad for poor kids!

To be fair, there is at least one contradictory report in the research. A study by Tajalli and Opheim (2005) did not find a strong correlation between achievement by children of poverty and decrease in school size. They used data from 7600 Texas schools' fourth, eighth, and tenth grade achievement tests and they found no increased achievement by students of poverty associated with decreased school size.

However, Tajalli and Opheim point out that they were not specifically examining the assumption that economically disadvantaged students fared better in small schools than in large schools. Their focus may explain why they gave their readers conflicting information about this topic. First, in their abstract they state that students of poverty benefit from small schools. Second, in their conclusion they tell their readers that they find no increased achievement by low SES students in small schools.

To date, the research from Texas appears to be the only dissenting, although inconsistent, voice in the literature within the last ten years with regard to the deleterious effects of increased school size on the academic achievement of low SES students.

CONCLUSIONS

We have examined three different factors associated with school size, including the relationship between school size and academic achievement, school size and the economics of school operation, and school size and SES. It is well established in the literature that there is an optimal school size for general academic achievement. To summarize, the research generally indicates that smaller schools, schools in the range of 300–900 students, are associated with larger gains in standard achievement than in considerably larger or considerably smaller schools.

The literature is less clear with regard to the relationship between school size and the economics of school operation. It appears that only two peer reviewed studies have been published in the last 10 years on this topic, and they published opposite conclusions. One study found that larger schools were more economical to operate, while the other found just the opposite.

As the final topic of research, SES appears to be one of the strongest pre-
dictors of academic achievement, especially in larger schools. Essentially,
SES by itself is a great predictor of student academic achievement. However,
if you combine low SES students with increased school size over an optimal
level of 300–900 students, academic achievement is critically influenced
in a negative direction. Overly large schools, schools with more than 2100
students, are particularly detrimental to academic achievement of low SES
students.

Research is all well and good, but there remains the almost certain belief in
circulation that bigger schools must be more efficient. We believe this belief
persists because people believe that for the same reason that it is cheaper to
purchase a 100-roll pack of toilet paper than a 4-roll pack, it should also be
cheaper to run a 2000-student school than it is to operate one of 300 students.
This belief is misplaced and unsubstantiated. What is even more important,
this belief leads to erroneous conclusions and actions.

We are willing to concede that a large school may get a price reduction on
toilet paper. However, the bulk price for paper products is more than overwhelmed by the larger systems and bureaucracy that big schools entail.

Consider small schools you may have known Gentle Reader. How many
small schools have public relations staff, how many have a Community and
Business Liaison, or a Curriculum Director? How many small schools issue
parking permits, have security officers, Human Resource Departments, or
vice principals? The obvious answer is none, which means that small schools
do not have these expenses that bigness requires. Moreover, vice principals at
big schools tend to get paid more than small school principals.

Obviously, there is some subjectivity in defining what is large and what
is small, but the authors reviewed the salaries in Oregon for the writing of
this chapter and, although we did not present it, the data is readily available.
Furthermore, we believe that any thoughtful person will agree with our conservative definitions of what constitutes a large and a small school.

After reviewing the salary tables, we found that, as expected, large high
school principals are paid more than small high school principals. What is
even more revealing is that the Instructional Curriculum Directors, positions
held by people with administrator licenses (principals) are paid more than
small school principals. Clearly, administrators benefit from larger schools
and are rewarded for being part of bigger schools.

The upshot of these points is that we are confident that there is no economy
of scale for big schools. A straight dollar-per-student examination in our state
bears this out, but it may be skewed because it is primarily a rural-urban comparison. In this case, a critic might argue that we are just seeing the cost of
living differences in rural and urban places, but we do not think so.

We think that big schools cost more to operate. The reasons are more complex than simply saying it is the same reason that it costs more to own a yacht than a canoe, or a yacht compared to 50 canoes. We think it is related to the entire process; it costs more to hire lots of teachers and maintain a system designed for the lowest common denominator. We think that anonymity and alienation, which inevitably accompany large schools, entail costs that are ultimately reflected not only on the bottom line, but also in academic achievement and quality of life.

NOTES

1. National Association of Secondary School Principals, Breaking Ranks in the Middle: Strategies for Leading Middle Level Reform, NASSP, 2006. And National Association of Secondary School Principals, Breaking Ranks II: Strategies for Leading High School Reform, NASSP, 2004.

2. L., Langbein, and Bess, R. (2002). Sports in school: Source of amity or antipathy? *Social Science Quarterly* (Blackwell Publishing Limited), 83(2), 436–454. Unless noted otherwise, subsequent references to these authors refer to this document.

3. Coladarci, T. (2006). School size, student achievement, and the "power ranking" of poverty: Substantive finding or statistical artifact? *Educational Policy Analysis Archives,* 14(28), 1–23. And Lee, V. E. and Loeb, s. (2000). School size in Chicago elementary schools: Effect on the teachers' attitudes and students' achievement. *American Educational Research Journal, 37(1),* 3–31. And Tajalli, H. and Opheim, C. (2005). Strategies for closing the gap: Predicting student performance in economically disadvantage schools. *Educational Research Quarterly,* 28(4), 44–54. And Bradley, S. and Taylor, HJ. (1998). The effect of school size on exam performance in secondary schools. *Oxford Bulletin of Economics and Statistics,* 60(3), 291. Unless noted otherwise, subsequent references to these authors refer to this document.

4. Lee, V. E. and Smith, J. B. (1997). High school size: Which works best and for whom? *Educational Evaluation and Policy Analysis, 19(3).205–227.* Unless noted otherwise, subsequent references to these authors refer to this document.

5. *Borland, M. V. and Howsen, R. M. (2003). An examination of the effect of elementary school size on student academic achievement. International Review of Education,* 49(5), 463–474. Unless noted otherwise, subsequent references to these authors refer to this document.

6. National Association of Secondary School Principals (2007). 2007 State principals of the year principals' institute. Paper presented at the 2007 State Principals of the Year Principals' Institute, Washington D.C. Unless noted otherwise, subsequent references to these authors refer to this document.

7. Walberg, H. J. and Fowler, W. J. J. (1987). Expenditures and size efficiencies of public school districts. *Educational Researcher,* 16(7), 5–13. Unless noted otherwise, subsequent references to these authors refer to this document.

8. Bowles, T. J. and Bosworth, R. (2002), Scale economies in public education: Evidence from school level data. *Journal of Education Finance,* 28(2), 285–299.

9. Stiefel, L., Berne, R., Latarola, P. and Fruchter, N., "High school size: Effect on budgets and performance in economically disadvantaged schools." *Educational Evaluation and Policy Analysis,* (2000) 22(1), 27–39. Unless noted otherwise, subsequent references to these authors refer to this document.

10. Buchanan, C. M. (2006), "The impact of race and socioeconomic status on post-secondary achievement," *International Journal of Learning,* 13(4), 69–81. Unless noted otherwise, subsequent references to these authors refer to this document.

11. Kinney, D. W. and Forsythe, J. L. (2005). The effects of the arts impact curriculum upon student performance on the Ohio fourth-grade proficiency test. *Bulletin of the Council for Research in Music Education,* (164), 35–48. Unless noted otherwise, subsequent references to these authors refer to this document.

12. Sirin, S. R. (2005). Socioeconomic status and academic achievement: A meta-analytic review of research. *Review of Educational Research,* 75(3), 417–453. Unless noted otherwise, subsequent references to these authors refer to this document.

Chapter 5

Configuring Instruction for Excellence: Continuous-Progress Model Versus Grade Level, Curriculum-Oriented Model

In chapter two we spent a bit of time talking about the common knowledge and universal acceptance of grade-level grouping as a fundament of the education system here in the United States. To refresh your memory on the topic, we were critical of the idea of grade level. Further, we claimed we knew about a method by which an educational nirvana could be attained. We maintained that our educational nirvana could be claimed much easier than the nirvana of world peace that John Lennon sang about in *Imagine*.

To quote ourselves (something we like to do and hope that you will like to do too) we promised that "we have seen schools that have traveled far down the path toward educational nirvana by utilizing the best practices of multi-age instruction, coupled with a commitment to a continuous-progress model rather than a grade-level, curriculum-based model. These examples will be detailed in later chapters." This is that later chapter.

In fact, in previous chapters we promised several times that we would address these issues ad nauseam. Much of what we talk about in this chapter will be redundant and may feel like we are beating the same dead horse of grade level and school size. However, to push the horse analogy farther, we feel like the horse died and most schools in our country are still riding it! We are not trying to beat the horse, we know that it is dead; we are trying to beat the riders. We want them to wake up and get off that dead horse! Riding a dead horse is not usually a good way to fashion an excellent school.

GRADE LEVEL

"We do not have litters of children, but we insist on educating them as if they were born in a litter." We cannot remember who we are loosely quoting, and we would love to give them credit, because that one sentence captures a bit of the absurdity known as grade level.

The single grade-level configuration is by far the most popular way of organizing schools. You do not need to do any research other than to walk into school to figure out that this is the case. Indeed, we believe that almost everything to do with education is geared toward the grade-level model. Publishers of textbooks and novels identify their books by grade level. Testing companies prepare tests according to grade level. Teachers identify themselves by the grade they teach. The list goes on and on.

We believe that this adherence to the grade-level model is accompanied by a list of assumptions that are either consciously or subconsciously held with regard to grade-level instruction. We want to detail those assumptions before we propose a new model that creates a separate list of assumptions that, we believe, will produce the educational nirvana we spoke of earlier.

GRADE-LEVEL MODEL ASSUMPTIONS

First, grade-level instruction is heavily dependent on a curriculum-based model. Certain aspects of the curriculum are reserved for different grade levels. The curriculum is articulated in such a way that students learn the necessary pre-requisites in one grade level to make a seamless transition to the next grade level. The third grade teacher will teach the necessary math, science, social studies, and English skills for the students to pick up the fourth grade curriculum the next August when school starts again.

Given the emphasis on grade-level curriculum mandates, much of a teacher's planning time is spent addressing the demands of the curriculum. They spend hours deciding how they will deliver the curriculum. After all, they are given a curriculum document and told that they need to cover all of this material before the next year. If they do not meet the demands of the curriculum, their students will be behind when school starts the next year.

Secondly, within the grade-level model there is an assumption of a particular level of proficiency required and measured for all students in all subjects. Students are expected to read and do math at the third grade level in third grade. Students can be easily sorted against a static bar. For example, a student can earn 100 percent in third grade vocabulary, or 48 percent in third grade math. Further, they can be 11 points below the third grade benchmark for the state test in science or 12 points above the benchmark for third grade reading.

In essence, at any one time 50 percent of all students in a given grade level are below the average for that grade level and the other 50 percent are ahead. This is an example of the tyranny of averages. Consider a hunter and a flock of birds that are not endangered, but are an exotic species that need to be eliminated in order to preserve habitat for threatened native, indigenous waterfowl.

We hope that we have been "over-the-top" in our effort to be politically correct, but think of any flock of birds if it makes it easier for you.

In the case of a flock of birds, the total space occupied by the flock is as much open space as anything. If the hunter shoots at the average position of the flock, he or she is likely to hit nothing. Instead, the successful hunter shoots at individual birds, no matter how large the flock or how pretty the bird. A successful teacher teaches at individuals, not at the class.

The third assumption about grade level is that students in a grade level are judged against a static bar. In short, they are expected to complete a prescribed portion of an articulated curriculum, and the tyranny of averages means that there will be some kids who are unable to meet the bar or complete the prescribed curriculum. These special students need protections from the grade-level model and its expectations. These students will need a Special Education, one different than the rest of the students in the litter . . . oops we meant grade level.

Fourth, and clearly, if some of the kids are unable to meet the bar or complete the prescribed curriculum then there must also be students for whom the bar is absurdly low and the curriculum below their abilities. These students will also need something different; the curriculum-based, grade-level model is breaking down for them. These talented and gifted students will need a program that lets them escape from the confines of the grade-level model so they can learn something worthwhile and at their own level. We should probably call it a TAG program.

Fifth, teachers become experts at teaching particular aspects of the curriculum. "How can I teach the Oregon Trail better to my third grade students next year?" or "How should I cover the unit on Electricity and Magnetism in the seventh grade Science class so they will be able to do the ninth grade Physical Science unit on Electro/Magnetic Forces?" These are examples of concerns that grade-level teachers might voice with regard to their mastery of the curriculum in a grade-level system.

The educational focus in a curriculum-based, grade-level model is directed at the demands of the curriculum rather than the needs of the students. In fact,

programs like Special Education or Gifted and Talented are aimed at supporting students so they can access the articulated grade level oriented curriculum.
Additionally, much of the resources around staff development are apportioned
to making teachers better at delivering particular aspects of the curriculum.

Curriculum articulation meetings within building and between buildings,
as well as curriculum coordinators, who tend to be better paid than many
teachers, are more evidence of the assumption that an integral part of good
teaching and learning is a commitment to grade-level expertise accompanied
by the corresponding articulated curriculum.

CONTINUOUS PROGRESS AND MULTI-AGE MODEL DEFINITIONS

We hope to juxtapose assumptions inherent to a multi-age, continuous-
progress model with those we detailed about the grade-level model. Our
hope is that you will agree that these assumptions are far more tenable
than those associated with the more prevalent grade-level model of instruction. Further, we maintain that the assumptions associated with a multi-age
continuous-progress model are examples of best practice. However, before
we address those assumptions we feel we need to clarify what we mean by
both continuous progress and multi age.

The simplest definition that we can think of with regard to continuous
progress is this:

> Continuous progress is the assertion that every student is expected to make
> progress from where he or she is in every subject to someplace further down
> the academic road.

Some readers may think that this definition is already part of a grade-level
model assumption. A person might say that of course every student is
expected to make progress down the road in grade-level model as well! We
can understand why a person might think that; however, we believe a more
accurate description of the grade-level model goes something like this.

> Grade leveling is the assertion that every student is expected to make progress
> down a pre-determined academic path known as the curriculum. Some will
> make adequate progress, some will not, some will be ahead of the curve.
>
> Those who are ahead will earn higher grades than those who are behind,
> because all people will be compared to that pre-determined pathway. However,
> these students who are ahead will effectively be held back because the curricu-
> lum does not allow them to proceed at their own pace. Special considerations

will be needed for all students who do not meet predetermined grade-level curricular benchmarks (SPED) as well as for those who exceed those pre-determined benchmarks (TAG).

Other than being much shorter and more concise, the main differences between these two definitions is that in a grade-level model, students are judged against a static bar and from the beginning it is assumed that some will be behind, and some will be ahead.

The teaching in a grade-level model will happen to focus on those in the middle and be aimed at a pre-determined curriculum. In the continuous-progress model there are no assumptions that some students will be ahead or behind; progress is not measured against a static bar. Rather, it is measured against each individual child, and since curriculum is not the focus of instruction, students can become the focus of instruction. (We will further beat this part of the dead horse in upcoming paragraphs.)

We have a simple definition of multi-age instruction as well.

Multi-age instruction is the process of teaching a common theme to students of varying ages in the same classroom.

At its root, multi-age instruction is the kind of instruction that we do in families where there is more than one child (excluding those few families where they only have two kids who happen to be twins). This harkens back to the litter idea! We are not born in litters and much of what we learn happens in a multi-age environment because our siblings are not usually our same age.

A common theme in our households might be something like "How to behave." At the writing of this manuscript we each have two or three young children learning from us, their parents (and we suppose vice versa but that does not fit our discussion right now).

A common lesson in the "How to behave" theme is the "How to clean up after yourself" lesson. All of the learners in our houses get instruction in this particular lesson, but each person does not get the same lesson at the same time. All of the learners are expected to make progress down the "how to clean up after yourself," pathway.

That path is part of a longer trail called the "how to behave" trail. Not everyone will make each waypoint on the trail at the same time, because they all will not walk it at the same rate, but they all will walk it at the same exact time in the same exact house even if they are not all walking the same exact portion of the trail at the same exact time!

Multi-age instruction alone will not produce the results we are aiming for without coupling it with a continuous-progress model. You cannot just put students of varying ages in a room and treat them as if they were still in separate grades and expect them to work on a pre-determined curriculum by which you will judge each of them. This is just a grade-level model with kids of two or three different grades in each classroom.

But, if you take kids of different ages, place them in the same room, and expect each of them to make progress from his or her starting point forward, we think exceptional results will follow. In the following paragraphs we will detail the assumptions found in a continuous-progress model and the assumptions found in a multi-age level classroom.

CONTINUOUS-PROGRESS MODEL ASSUMPTIONS

The first assumption in a continuous-progress model is that unlike in a grade-level model where curriculum is the focal point, students are the focal point. Also no aspect of the curriculum is reserved for any particular age student.

In a continuous-progress model a student might actually learn about long division in the second grade rather than the third grade, because that particular student was ready for long division at age seven instead of age eight. You will not hear a teacher in a continuous-progress model school complain that a teacher who teaches younger students has invaded some verboten curricular territory because some younger students have learned materials usually associated with older students.

There is an assumption that curriculum will be presented to students in a continuous-progress model; however, the curriculum presented in a continuous-progress model will look different than in a grade-level model. A grade-level model would present a sixth grade math unit in the following manner.

"This week we will all be learning how to calculate mean, median, and mode. I will give the entire class instruction in each of these topics, you will all pay attention because each of you will do all of the same problems even if you already know how to do them. At the end of our unit on mean, median, and mode we will take a test.

You will all be expected to pass this sixth grade mean, median, and mode test with a score of 70 percent or higher. Some of you will not pass because we will have gone too fast for you; you are now behind and will probably experience the same thing during the next unit when we learn about percentile ranking.

Speaking of percents, those of you who knew what mean, median, and mode were before we started this unit did not learn a thing. However, you probably will have earned a 100 percent on the test and we will reward you with an "A"! Your accomplishments will be lauded by all who know of them, even though you did not learn anything new in this particular unit. In fact you were probably bored."

Conversely, a continuous-progress model would present mathematics to students ages 11 and 12 in the following fashion.

"This week we will do math just like we have done every week this year. Diane and Elisa, I think it is great that you both finished the Algebra 1 book last week; the first part of Algebra 2 should be review. I think with the 12 weeks left in this year and at the pace you two are going you might be 1/3rd of the way done with it!

Zack, you and two others are working on prime factorization in the pre-algebra book. I think you should work on these problems and get ready to take an assessment about prime factorization by Friday.

Emma, you and the other four people in your group are ready to take your test over exponents today so let's get that started.

I want to meet with Tessa's group to talk with 10 of you about mean, median, and mode after I get these folks started on their exponent test.

Aurora, you and five others are just starting to learn about division and I will set aside some time for you to use some math manipulatives because I think that will be a good way for you to get a handle on what fractions really are.

Finn, I am really happy with the progress you have been making on learning your multiplication facts; I want you to keep working on those flash cards, and I will make sure we have a few minutes to play that multiplication facts hang man game we came up with last week.

My intention is that none of you become bored or swamped by your math work this week. I expect each of you to work hard and make progress forward. I will report your progress without comparing you to any standard such as the sixth grade week 21 mean, median, and mode standard imposed in that grade-level school several paragraphs before this one. "

The assumption that students are the focal point rather than the curriculum has some striking ramifications at the transition from one year to the next. Let's compare the notes that a teacher in each model might give to the teacher that will get their student the following year. We will start with the grade-level model.

"Hi, I managed to cover the entire sixth grade book just in time this year! Most of the kids did really well but about 1/3rd of them are behind.

A couple of them are really behind and I got tired of telling their parents they were failing.

Another 1/3 of them were perfectly challenged for the entire year; I felt like I really did a good job with them.

The last third of them did really well, especially Zack and Emma. They got a 100 percent on every assignment and never had homework. Actually, the top third of the students were often bored, especially Zack and Emma.

Anyhow, I covered the sixth grade curriculum; they can now move onto the seventh grade curriculum."

A teacher working in a continuous-progress model might report to the teacher who would be inheriting her kids the next year in the following fashion.

"Hi, the students made great progress this year. I want to give you a quick run down on where each student ended the year and what challenges each one faced and some suggestions about what worked for me with each of these kids.

First, Zack and Emma are both midway through the Algebra 2 book. They work well together and are largely self-directed learners. I try to give them both lots of praise as they are the type of kid who loves to please adults.

Finn came so far last year from where he started! He has mastered all of his math facts and was so proud of himself. He is a very competitive little guy and anytime I could make math into a game I did that. He thrived with competition. (The list would go on for another 21 kids with details about learning styles and individual student progress being reported.)

Anyhow, they are a great bunch of learners and I know they will all make progress like they did this year."

The first assumption, that a continuous-progress model is student centered rather than curricular centered, has ramifications with regard to communication to parents about student progress as well. We understand that another set of comparison reports might be an example of beating a dead horse. Recall however, that our blows are aimed at the rider of that horse, and at the risk of hitting them one too many times and killing the rider, here goes a comparison of a grade-level model report card and a continuous-progress model progress report. Once again we will start with the grade-level model and some examples of a grade-level report card.

"Zack . . . . 6th Math . . . . A"
Yep, that is it! It went by so fast we want to show you another example! Read slowly so you do not miss this one.

"Randy . . . . 6th math . . . . F"
Did you catch it? As a parent you absolutely know how to react to each of these report cards. "Great job Zack we are so proud of you!" is how you react to the first report card. "Randy, you need to work harder! F's are not acceptable!" is the proper sentiment for the second report card. But do you really know what happened with each of these kids? All you know is that Zack mastered sixth-grade math and Randy did not, but could there be more to the story? If Paul Harvey was reading aloud to you he might say . . . ."And now for the rest of the continuous-progress report story."

"Dear Zack's parents, as you know, Zack long ago finished pre-algebra and Algebra one. Most students do not start Algebra 2 until they are much older than his 11 years. Despite his young age, he is still doing very well with the abstract concepts found in second year Algebra. He has really been challenged learning the use of the quadratic formula. It has been great watching him learn at his own pace."

The progress to Randy's parents might sound something like this.

"Dear Randy's parents, as you know, Randy is still working on accuracy with regard to his math facts. At the start of this term, he only knew 10 percent of his multiplication facts. He has now mastered nearly 90 percent. This is good progress. He has really been challenged learning the use of his multiplication facts with regard to fractions. He is working hard and it has been great watching him learn at his own pace."

Each of these continuous-progress reports tells a parent more about what their student can or cannot do than the grade-level report card. Further, we know from these two reports that each of these students worked hard and made progress forward.

In a grade-level model, a student who was "ahead" could easily slack all term and still come out with a passing grade on the report. A student who was "behind" in that same grade-level system would still fail the course, but their parents would not have any clue if that failure was due to a lack of effort or their lack of ability. In a continuous-progress model report, a highly capable student who did not learn anything new in a given term would receive the same poor progress report that a less capable student would receive.

Our last example is a progress report written by a teacher in a continuous-progress system for two students who have not made acceptable progress for the term.

"Dear Zack's parents, as you know Zack long ago finished pre-algebra and Algebra one. Most students do not start Algebra 2 until they are much older than his 11 years. Despite his earlier successes in math, I am disappointed in his work this term. He has consistently wasted his class time and his work has not been up to his standards. I do not think he has challenged himself one time this term and I expect more from him next term."

A less talented student who was not making progress due to a lack of effort would receive a progress report that sounded very similar to Zack's. Here is an example.

"Dear Randy's parents, as you know Randy has always had to work extra hard at math. His efforts have always resulted in slow, sometime faltering progress, but he has made progress. As you know if a student works and does his best, I am a happy teacher. Despite his earlier struggles in math, I am disappointed in his work this time. He has consistently wasted his class time and his work has not been up to his standards. I do not think he has challenged himself one time this term and I expect more from him next term."

The second assumption found within a continuous-progress model is that there is no assumption of a particular level of proficiency that should be required and measured of all students. There is no static bar by which all children are judged. Let's use the example of vocabulary to illustrate the differences between a grade-level system and a continuous-progress model system.

In a grade-level system, a curriculum coordinator may go so far as to publish a list of vocabulary words that all fourth grade students should have mastered by the end of the term. All progress, of all students, will be measured against this bar.

A teacher will divided the words by the number of weeks in the year, and develop some method by which he will teach the entire class those words each week. At the end of the week, he will assess the students' mastery of the vocabulary words. They will be judged against a predetermined curricular bar. Students will receive percentage grades for each test each week, and in essence these scores can be summarized to quantify a student's year-long success, or lack thereof, at meeting the demands of the fourth grade vocabulary curriculum.

For argument's sake let's pretend that there were 1000 words in this fourth grade vocabulary curriculum. Of course you know what we are going to say about the smart kids in the class. They knew the words before the year started and do not learn any knew words despite being anointed with an "A" for the year in vocabulary.

The average kids knew 50 percent of the words going into the year, and added 25 percent more by the end of the year. They will be labeled with the passing mark of C.

Those poor dumb kids, however, are going to get an F, despite the fact that they learned 35 percent of the words! They went from knowing 0 words to learning 350 new words, beating the medium kids' vocabulary gains by 100 words, and the smart kids by 350 words! Does this seem like a good system?

In a continuous-progress model there will not be a predetermined list of vocabulary words that all of the fourth grade students will study and be tested on. Instead, each vocabulary list will be differentiated for each student; in fact you should probably have the students differentiate their own list.

Imagine that every student was reading different books at different reading levels. Each time students ran across a new word that they did not recognize, they could put it on their own personal vocabulary list. The students could do all of the same types of drills they do in a grade-level system to learn vocabulary; they would, however, all be working on different lists!

Obviously you cannot give them all the same test at the end of the week like you would in a grade-level system. But you could develop some other assessment where each student demonstrated their mastery of all of the new words they learned in that week. At the end of the year, you might find that the dumb kids, average kids, and smart kids had all managed to learn an additional 1000 words. You could report this if you wanted to put the information in a quantitative format. In this way it wouldn't matter who was average; the focus would be on learning, education, and gains.

The third assumption about a continuous-progress model that flies in the face of the grade-level assumption about progress is that there is no static bar by which all students are judged. In a grade-level model there is an assumption from the beginning that some students will be unable to meet the grade-level bar. These students will need to be given a special education. In contrast, in a continuous-progress model there is an assumption that every student will be at a different level and that every student will move forward.

In a grade-level model, the curriculum is delivered to the middle of the curve. Students that do not fall near the middle of the curve must have the curriculum differentiated for them, or modified in such a manner that at the extremes they are not even included in the class.

In a continuous-progress model, instruction is differentiated for every student so that students are only removed from the classroom in the rarest situation.

There is no assumption that anyone is behind in a continuous-progress model; there is an assumption instead that everyone needs something different. This assumption never brands anyone as a failure or a genius; rather it allows that everyone can be successful and make progress.

In fact, it demands that everyone make progress. Too often the grade-level model allows that some will not make progress either because the curriculum is too hard or too easy for the students in that model.

We do not want the reader to assume that we think there is never a situation in which students should be identified as special education students. Clearly there are some students, those who are most challenged, that need protection from the vagaries of public education so they can have the opportunity to learn at their own pace and in their own way. What we do want the reader to consider is that that the numbers of special education students will be vastly lower in a continuous-progress model as compared to a grade-level model. Why? You may ask.

It is simple; when you do not assume that people will be behind from the beginning, you do not need to identify those who are behind! Furthermore, when you assume that everyone will be at a different place academically and that you will have to differentiate for every single person, then you do not need to do anything special for the slow kids. In a grade-level system, differentiating for the SPED students constitutes something different for the classroom teacher to design and implement. In a grade-level system, the lessons are predominately designed so everyone does the same thing at the same time.

For example, in a middle school grade-level class that is learning about stained glass craftsmen from the middle ages, a teacher might assign a bit of reading at the eighth grade level, and then expect each student to answer questions about that reading.

Perhaps, if they were a good teacher, they would have the students take the information they learned from the reading and make a poster detailing how craftsmen in the middle ages created the first stained glass windows. The teacher can expect from the beginning that some will do very well, and others will not; those who do well will earn high grades, while those who don't do well will earn low grades.

From the beginning, they will know in advance that some of the kids are just not going to get it; they will have to do something special for them, or just let them fail. Even if they do something special to differentiate the instruction, how fair is it to give them a grade based on the same scale as everyone else when they do not do the same thing as everyone else?

In contrast, a continuous-progress model classroom will approach the same topic like this. Each student will be expected to learn about crafts in the middle ages. Some of the students will learn about stained glass craftsmen, while others will learn about craftsmen who wove baskets, or created horseshoes, armor, or any number of things.

Why the difference? Simple! The teacher has resources at different levels. Their resources about stained glass happen to be at the "eighth grade level" in reading, the books they have about armor are at a lower level, the books about basket weaving are much higher reading level, etc. Students are free to pick (or be assigned) a topic that fits both their interest as well as reading level.

Once the students have picked a topic to research, they will be expected to create something detailing the information they have learned. Their assignment will be a rubric detailing what types of things their poster should include; however, they will not be judged against each other or against some static bar.

When it comes time to evaluate the projects, the teacher will make a professional judgment about that student's efforts relative to his or her abilities. Students will not be compared to each other or to a common bar. Instead, the teacher will have expected each to make progress against the standard that they have previously established for themselves.

A special education student and a gifted student will all be expected to produce work that is slightly better than their previous work. In fact, all students will be expected to make progress, and all differentiation for those students will be the norm rather than something special like it has to be in a grade-level model.

The fourth assumption has already been hinted at in the previous paragraphs. Recall that in a grade-level model it is assumed that some students will find the grade-level materials absurdly easy; these kids are called gifted and talented students.

In a grade-level model, something special will need to be done for these students. However in a continuous-progress model something special is done for every student (and by the way this makes it not special but the norm). There is no reason to identify TAG students if every lesson is differentiated for every student and every student is expected to make progress from where they are forward.

The fifth assumption in a continuous-progress model is that teachers become expert at dealing with students and their needs relative to the curriculum. Recall that in a grade-level model, teachers become expert at specific portions of the curriculum. Their efforts in a grade-level model are often associated with developing the curriculum; conversely, in a continuous-progress model the teacher's efforts are more often associated with developing the student's abilities relative to the curriculum and not the other way around.

You may be thinking that this sounds hard! After all, how can a teacher know enough about each kid to design lessons that are easily differentiated for every single student?

In a typical grade-level model, an elementary teacher gets between 24–30 new students every year; in most middle schools a teacher will see more than a hundred kids per day, and in high schools it is often worse! Even if teachers were to develop lessons that were easily differentiable, how could they possibly know all of the kids well enough to differentiate the instruction for all of them? How could you compare every student to his or her own personal bar when you see all of those kids for a brief period? Good questions!

We will discuss one method in the next section. However, if you can remember back to Chapter Three, you probably know that we champion keeping kids and teachers together for as long as possible.

MULTI-AGE ASSUMPTIONS COUPLED WITH A CONTINUOUS-PROGRESS MODEL

The questions we brought up in the previous paragraph beg for another set of questions to be asked.

The question they bring to light include:

- Why in the world would you make an elementary student form a relationship with his or her teacher and classroom peers only to fracture that relationship after only one year?
- Why in the world would you make a middle school student fumble through seven or eight different relationships with teachers as well as hundreds of interactions with their peers each day if you did not have to?
- Why in the world would you make high school students form a relationship with one specialist teacher, say a science teacher, and then the next year be forced to form a relationship with another specialist science teacher?

The answers to the first question may be that after one year in grade school, a teacher has exhausted all she has to teach her elementary students.

The answer to the second question may be that by the time you get to middle school, the breadth of the curriculum is so broad that a single teacher cannot be expected to have mastery over the rigorous topics of sixth, seventh, and eighth grade English, math, science, and social studies!

And of course, by the time you get to high school, the material becomes so complex that it would be absurd to think that one single adult could possible master the curriculum in biology, chemistry, and physics; or the curriculum in US history, World History, and Government; or ninth-grade English, tenth-grade English, AP English literature, *and* AP English language!

These may be the answers, and in fact we think they are the answers that most people would give and reflect common knowledge in general circulation; however, we think they are horrible answers! Horrible answers that are used to justify the single grade-level model.

Some of the questions on which we ended our discourse on a continuous-progress model do have an answer that we embrace. Questions like; how in the world can you differentiate the instruction for 100 students a day, can be answered with one idea. That idea is multi-age education.

Imagine that you have adopted a continuous-progress model but instead of teaching third grade, you only you have a classroom of both third- and fourth-grade age students. Isn't it entirely probably that there is as much overlap in abilities between the third- and fourth-grade age students as there is difference in their abilities? In other words, the amount of overlap of the top half of the third-grade students with the lower half of the fourth-grade students is probably equal to the amount of difference between the two extremes of the two grades.

One might argue that this has made the breadth across which the curriculum must be differentiated even greater than in a single grade classroom. You are correct and this is a good thing!

The reason this is a good thing is that the grade-level model so permeates the teaching profession that even teachers who are committed to a continuous-progress model often fall back into the habits associated with the grade-level model. After all, most of their training, and if they are experienced teachers it is probable that most of their experience, will have been aimed at the grade-level model. However, when faced with the breadth of needs present in two grade levels it becomes impossible to fall back into those old habits.

So, a multi-age approach forces teachers to maintain a focus on continuous progress for every student. But are those the only reason to create multi-age classrooms? No, and we have detailed the reasons in previous chapters; however, we will recount some of them here. First, we do not think that an elementary teacher has exhausted all they have to teach a student after only one year's exposure.

Furthermore, maintaining relationships between elementary students and their teacher for more than one year allows the teacher to gain a richer understanding of each student's individual needs. It gives the teachers an incredible advantage when trying to maintain an environment that supports continuous progress of every student.

Second, we do not believe that the curriculum becomes so cumbersome and intricate by the middle school years that a teacher cannot continue to meet the needs of students of that age in a generalist classroom rather than in a series of specialist classrooms.

Once you accept that middle level classrooms can (and we think should, for reasons we have mentioned earlier) be operated by generalist rather than specialists, the reasons for teaching middle school using a multi-age approach are the same ones that we championed for using multi-age classrooms in elementary school. We will speak at length about middle school in the next chapter.

Finally, we do not believe that the curriculum becomes so cumbersome in high school that a subject area specialist cannot handle teaching more than one subject in a given discipline.

If you accept the assertion that a capable high school teacher should be able to teach several subjects within a given discipline, say science or English, we think you should adopt multi-age classrooms as well.

Imagine you have a teacher who teaches biology, chemistry, physics, and earth science in a small high school. (Of course we assume you will be making every effort to create small schools rather than large ones!) If one year she taught three periods of biology and another three periods of chemistry, she could have a mix of freshman and sophomores in biology, and a mix of juniors and seniors in chemistry.

The next year she could teach earth science to that year's freshman and sophomores, and physics to that year's juniors and sophomores. In this fashion, every student would get four years of science, they would maintain a relationship with one teacher for four years, and the amount of fractured relationships they formed with their peers would be less than in a traditional system.

Furthermore, the teacher could approach the actual instruction differently. The range of abilities in each class would necessitate a different approach to each topic. The teacher would be able to adopt a continuous-progress model with these students because she would know each of them far better than her counterparts in a traditional high school system.

The traditional system is characterized by teachers who are expert at teaching one subject in a discipline. Even in a high school of 400 students, you could have three or four science teachers, one who might teach earth science only, one who might teach biology only, etc. These teachers will not have a relationship with their students that last through time. Rather, they will teach their special subject to the student for only one year before the student is forced to move on to a different subject area specialist within the same discipline.

Multi-age classrooms in a high school are possible, and they bring with them the same benefits they afford students in younger grades. One byproduct of a multi-age high school classroom that is operating using a continuous-progress model is that from the beginning it is assumed that all of the students will not do the same exact things, but they all will be expected to make progress forward.

If you then agree to document each student's progress against his or her own personal bar rather than by a static bar by which you judge everyone, the number of students who fail will go down. Graduation rates go up and world peace becomes a reality.

Well maybe not the last one; for the last one to come true, more people would have to listen to Jimmy Buffet. Speaking of Jimmy reminds us of Margaretville, which is someplace we imagine you should head now that you have stayed with us so far. To make this possible, and to let you cogitate on this chapter, we better move on to our conclusion so you can start searching for that last shaker of salt!

CONCLUSIONS

We hope that we have piqued your curiosity in this chapter enough that you will consider advocating for a continuous-progress model coupled with a multi-age configuration in all schools.

We think it is difficult to argue that expecting all students to make progress forward without judging them against one another is a bad thing. Also, we think it is difficult to argue that differentiating instruction to better meet the needs of each student is a bad thing.

Additionally, we think it is difficult to argue that spending more time with a competent teacher is a bad thing. One of the side effects of multi-age education is that students are given the opportunity to spend more time with one competent adult. We maintain that this is a good thing. If you agree with us, perhaps you will join us in trying to move the riders who insist on riding the dead horse of a single grade-level model to a more productive approach.

We believe that if we can all get people to stop riding the deceased equines of grade level; all schools will take a giant step toward excellence. Excellence in schools is our goal for all schools. We think that it is attainable, but not without a willingness to make the changes we have suggested so far, as well as those that we discuss next. Some of those other changes deal specifically with how middle school is taught. That, dear reader, is our segue to the next chapter.

Chapter 6

Middle School: A New Approach Leads to Excellence

If we can only make reforms at one level, if we can only convince our readers to take one bit of our advice, it would be to change how middle level education is organized and structured in the United States. There is plenty of work to do at the grade school and high school levels in our country, but the most egregious practices employed in our country in education occur at the middle grades. Middle school is most often the grade level that people choose to forget, or remember with—to borrow a line from Hunter Thompson—a mixture of fear and loathing.

This mixture of fear and loathing is the impetus for our decision to include a special chapter on middle level education. In our opinion, and in the opinion of other middle level education reform experts, the middle level years are instrumental in determining the success or failure of students once they enter high school.

To put it bluntly, although we believe that there is much that needs fixing in grade school, the damage inflicted at those grade levels is far less significant than the damage inflicted at the middle level. In fact, a student can suffer through what we would call a misinformed (yet well meaning) grade-level system, and still emerge from their K–6 experience without any long-lasting, educationally significant scars.

Essentially, grade schools with grade-level classroom generalists are not nearly as destructive as middle schools with multitudes of grade-level subject area specialists. (We believe assessment data from across the nation demonstrates that student achievement falls off the cliff the same year that students begin experiencing subject area specialists. As most grade schools limit the use of subject area specialists, student achievement remains relatively high. We use the phrase "relatively high" because we believe student achievement across the board would be even higher in grade school if students spent their grade school years in multi-age classrooms.)

Furthermore, a middle level system that produces students who view themselves as lifelong learners are able to weather even the most fundamentally flawed high school experiences.

Hopefully, after reading the previous five chapters of our pontificating you can predict that we believe that middle level education should occur in small schools with classroom generalists teaching heterogeneously grouped students in a multi-age looping configuration. But perhaps you are one of those people who start reading books in the middle. If you are one of those people then you have picked a good chapter, but we want to give you a two-paragraph synopsis of a model for middle level education that we believe will lead to excellence.

SYNOPSIS OF A NEW MODEL
FOR MIDDLE-LEVEL EDUCATION

First, start with a small middle school that is part of a small district. By "small district," we mean one grade school, one middle school, and one high school. The middle school can be any combination of grades 6–9. Local conditions will dictate this arrangement, but regardless of what grade configuration you use, the instruction in the school needs to be done by classroom generalists who spend multiple years with students in heterogeneously grouped multi-age classrooms.

In other words, there will be no such thing as a seventh grade science teacher, or even a seventh grade generalist teacher. Instead, teachers would be a sixth/seventh grade generalist, or a sixth/seventh/eighth grade generalist, or an eighth/ninth generalist, etc. By generalist, we mean a teacher who teaches the same kids all day, in all subjects. (Even P.E., math, health, etc.)

Within the instructional day, things look different in our model. Bells are not needed as the students spend almost all day with their teacher. Their teacher is free to flex time each day; they may spend more time on science one day and more on English the next.

This is a bit misleading because the bulk of all instruction will revolve around interdisciplinary thematic units. A study of volcanism will incorporate social studies, reading, writing, math, perhaps even health and P.E. Much of the work produced by students will be project based. All of the work required of students will be differentiated for every single student. Just because everyone is studying volcanoes does not mean that they all will read the same text about geology, or create the same interdisciplinary project.

Therefore, traditional letter grades based upon grade-level expectations (often reported in percents) do not apply in this model. Instead every student is expected to produce the best work he or she is capable of, and feedback to parents about their student's work will judge each student against his or her own personal bar.

In a nutshell, the assessment system in our model is a continuous-progress model where every student is expected to make progress. We will expand our description of this model in this chapter, however this gives you a quick overview of the model that we believe will lead to excellence for middle grades instruction.

You may be skeptical about our recommendations for configuring middle schools. We will spend the next ten thousand words or so trying to convince you that our model is a good one. Perhaps our model's components will ring more true if we compare them with the recommendations of the National Forum, the National Middle School Association, and other significant players in middle level education reform.

With that said, we want to begin our discussion with a brief overview of the National Forum's School to Watch program, followed by an examination of how our proposed model correlates with the recommendations of the National Forum.

OVERVIEW OF THE NATIONAL FORUM AND THE *SCHOOL TO WATCH* PROGRAM

The National Forum is an organization comprised of several other professional associations to include the National Middle School Association and the National Association of Secondary School Principals. The National Forum Created a program called *Schools to Watch* in 2002. The program started with three states that represented 19 percent of the nation's middle level population, and had grown to include 60 percent of the country's middle level age students by 2008. The *Schools to Watch* program is, at its heart, a school improvement initiative aimed at creating excellent middle level schools.

Essentially, schools are evaluated against a list of criteria deemed, by educational experts, to denote best practice at middle level education. In 2008,164 middle level schools had been identified as a *School to Watch* across the nation. The power of the program is that it serves as a guide for middle level school improvement, and not just a recognition program for those schools that are excellent. Furthermore, once a school is identified as a *School to Watch*, it is reevaluated every three years to insure that it is maintaining the recommendations for middle level best practice.

Corbett Middle School was identified as the first and only *School to Watch* in Oregon in 2008. Obviously, Corbett Middle School practices what we preach, and obviously what we preach has been recognized as constituting best practice by the National Forum. However, we believe that the model we are championing, the model used at Corbett Middle School, is an efficient and easily reproducible implementation of the best practices recommended by the National Forum.

In the following pages, we will detail what the evaluative criteria of the *School to Watch* program is as well as how the program we propose meets those criteria with less modification than required in traditional systems.

School to Watch Criteria and Recommendations for Meeting those Criteria

Before a school can become a *School to Watch* it must examine itself with regard to 4 main areas. The four major areas in which a school must exhibit excellence in order to become a *School to Watch* include academic excellence, developmental responsiveness, social equity, and organization and structures. Within each of these categories there are a multitude of questions designed to help schools establish whether or not they are promoting each of the four major areas in which a school must excel in order to become a *School to Watch.*

We will examine the questions within each of the four major areas while simultaneously detailing how our proposed model of education meets the requirements for becoming a *School to Watch* without developing a vast array of "special programs" in order to meet the requirements.

Academic Excellence

Under the heading of academic excellence, the *School to Watch* (STW) program demands that *"High performing schools with middle grades are academically excellent. They challenge all students to use their minds well."*

This decree is followed up with eight questions/statements that a school to watch applicant must answer in order to become a school to watch. The statement/questions are designed to help a school determine if it is meeting the standard of academic excellence. We will paraphrase each of the statements/questions in italics after which we will describe how the model we are proposing meets the criteria for becoming a STW.

All students are expected to meet high academic standards: In our model every student is expected to meet the highest of standards. The standard is of course the best work that that individual student is able to produce. Students are not limited in their achievement by a standard that is set at some arbitrary level by which every one of their peers their age will be judged. An example from Corbett Middle School will help illustrate what we are describing.

In order to move out of the middle school, Corbett students must complete the Cardinal Three. The Cardinal Three includes a published piece of writing in a public forum, delivery of a public address, as well as a service learning project. Every student's efforts and focus on each of these three aspects of the Cardinal Three will be different for each child. Their teachers, who have spent two complete years with them, will be very capable of judging if each of the students has produced a piece of writing, a speech, and a service project that is of the highest academic standard relative to the individual child.

When the experts in the building, the teachers, decide that a kid has produced work that is considered *academically excellent* for that individual, his or her Cardinal Three is completed. The focus throughout the process is on the student, not on the curriculum. Academic excellence is expected of all; however, that bar is a relative measure, calibrated to each student.

In other schools, much of the planning around these same three topics will revolve around the demands of the curriculum and not the needs of the students. A school wanting to become a STW might design similar requirements in order for students to exit their middle school, but their focus would be different than in our model.

First, the actual requirements for the writing, speech, and service project would be far more detailed and prescribed. A school striving to become a STW would spend considerable time designing requirements that were "Academically Excellent." For instance, the writing assignment might have details like it must be 500 words in length, have zero errors, and be written at the eighth grade level such that it could pass the state's eighth grade writing assessment. Clearly if every eighth grade student were able to do this, the school must be promoting academic excellence!

Yes, it would be promoting academic excellence, just not for all students! Let us explain. Students who are academically talented or gifted will not be challenged at all in this system. They will earn their "A"; easily meeting the requirements.

Some of them may actually push further than required, but there is no expectation that ALL students will push for academic excellence. If you are smart enough and this writing, speaking, and service stuff comes easily to you, you do not have to strive for academic excellence. You can, but there is really no expectation that you must strive for academic excellence; in fact you can just phone it in.

Conversely, the slower kids are not even able to strive for academic excellence. The bar has been set too high for their individual circumstance, and unless some specific interventions are designed (an IEP or an RTI plan) they will fail. If the student is identified as needing specially designed instruction, the expectations for his or her work production can be changed. However, these changes will reinforce these students' "otherness" as they will be the only kids in the room, or perhaps out of the room in some pullout program, that are not expected to meet the same high academic standard.

We realize we are beating this to death. And speaking of death we want to explain our rationale for continuing to hammer this idea. A study about severe cardiac arrest patients' response to their near death experiences provides an example of why we feel we must continue to harp on this topic.

In the study, each of the patients had a nearly fatal heart attack exacerbated by aspects of their lifestyle. The patients were all advised that they need to change their ways if they did not want to risk another, possibly deadly, heart attack. Initially most of the patients followed their doctor's advice and stopped smoking, eating bacon and eggs, and sitting on the couch for days at a time drinking beer and eating buffalo wings while they watched football.

However, within a year, more than 50 percent of the patients had relapsed into their old ways of life, and within two years 85 percent had relapsed (if they were still alive)! All this is to say that people, once set in their ways, are slow to change. If the risk of death is not enough to get people to stop eating bacon cheeseburgers for every meal, then us asking you once to change a deeply held belief about teaching is probably not nearly enough! Therefore, we plan on continuing to drive home these tenants.

Curriculum, instruction, assessment, and appropriate interventions are aligned with high standards. We want to try and keep this description short. What could be a higher standard than expecting every single student to perform at the highest end of his or her academic register? And what could constitute a better alignment of curriculum, instruction, and assessment than differentiating every single lesson for every single kid?

We think that few people will argue that expecting all students to perform at their absolute maximum, while at the same time differentiating every single lesson, assessment, and intervention for every single kid is a bad thing. However, we are used to hearing a chorus of reasons why this will be impossible to pull off in practice. The chorus sounds to us like a list of self inflicted wounds (a title of an upcoming chapter). Here is a list of three of the reasons most often voiced with regard to our model.

"Come on, I see 130 eighth grade students a day; how in the world can I differentiate it for every kid? How would I even know how to differentiate it for every kid, I do not know each of them well enough to do that?! What about grades? How will it be fair to give two kids an "A" even if they do not do the same work?"

Our response to these three questions should sound familiar. Stop seeing 130 kids per day, become a classroom generalist, or, if you are teaching high school, limit the number of new kids you meet in a 4-year period by teaching multiple subjects within your discipline (for example, in science teach chemistry, physics, biology, and earth science on a four year rotation).

Once you become a classroom generalist, spend as much time with your kids as possible, (years is preferable), get to know them and you will be able to easily differentiate for each of them. Eliminate letter grades; they serve as a glass ceiling for achievement. If you are a teacher, you do not need a letter grade for you to understand how well a student is doing in your class. In short, stop inflicting the wounds!

The curriculum emphasizes deep understanding of important concepts and the development of essential skills. One of the heralded ways to create deep understanding of essential skills is to teach across the curriculum. In a typical system, teaching across the curriculum requires that a school go through considerable gyrations to get a social studies teacher teamed up with an English teacher and perhaps, if you are cutting edge, a science, and maybe even a math teacher. Teaching schedules are concocted so that the team of specialists can get together and design instruction that occurs around a common unit or theme. From a student's perspective, the experience might look something like this.

"First period I go to English where we are reading *Catherine Called Birdie*. We all read the same book and then answer questions about each chapter. Our teacher Miss Hyperbole talks about how the stuff in the book ties into the Middle Ages. It is kind of cool that we are reading a book about the Middle Ages while we are also learning about it in social studies with Mr. Civic. But I asked Miss Hyperbole a question about the Crusades and she gave me a totally different answer than Mr. Civic.

Of course, that was better than Mr. Beaker, my science teacher! He is teaching us about the plague. He makes it sound pretty gross how the people died during the Middle Ages from the plague, but he really did not tie it in very well to what we were learning in English. Still, now I know that the plague happened in the Middle Ages, and the plague was carried by fleas on rats.

Mrs. Abacus had us figure out how much a draw bridge weighed using unit multipliers. I asked Mr. Abacus to read my paper I was writing for Mr. Civic because I got done early with the unit multipliers stuff. I should not have asked him because he is a math guy. I am a math guy too; that is why I needed help on my writing! Anyhow, he told me to ask my English teacher."

Of course, this is a straw man that we have created, but we believe most of the straw is a legitimate representation of what a student sees when an interdisciplinary unit is conducted in a traditional system. Students see four different teachers, each with a different area of expertise trying to provide instruction around a common theme. Often the teachers view themselves as subject area specialists, and therefore unaccountable to the other portions of the curriculum that do not fall into their bailiwick. In fact, they often communicate this to their students, either covertly, or as often as not, overtly.

Further, the degree of integration across specialties is a continuous hurdle over which interdisciplinary teams must leap. In order to integrate seamlessly across the curriculum, loads of common planning/teaming time is required. The team must get together to decide how each of the specialists will bend their curriculum to fit the desired theme. Often, initial difficulties will arise when it comes time to decide whose area of expertise will trump the other four areas.

In this example, the unit was kowtowing toward the social studies end of things. It was clear to the student that the other three disciplines were being modified to reinforce the primary social studies focus. This covertly emphasizes the ideal that some people are science people, some are math, some as socials studies, and some are English people. It makes it O.K. for students to describe themselves as such; it gives them a built in excuse for not being proficient at one or more of the other content areas.

The fact that the theme was aimed at the social sciences would also be clear to the members of the teaching team. If the themes always revolved around social studies, it is possible that the science, math, or English teacher might just get really sick of always having to modify their curriculum to fit the social studies curriculum. I mean, "After all I am a math teacher, not some damned social studies teacher!"

In our model, the problems associated with creating time for interdisciplinary teams to meet, and any resultant miscommunications or misunderstandings associated with trying to get four people on the same page are eliminated. Furthermore, no message, either covertly or overtly, is sent to students that they can view themselves or others as a social studies person, or a math person.

We do not want to imply that teaming in and of itself is bad! In fact, we believe in teaming. In our model we think classroom generalists should be given common planning time to team. However, rather than a group of specialists coming together to try and figure out how they can individually modify their curriculum to fit a common theme, a group of generalist can come together to collaborate on how they each can present the same materials to cover all of math, science, social studies, and English curriculum.

We agree that four heads are better than one when planning, we just think it is even better when the four heads are planning commonly about aspects of an interdisciplinary unit they all will deliver in its entirety rather than each one of them planning separately to try and weave their individual presentation into an overarching theme.

Instructional strategies include a variety of challenging and engaging activities that are clearly related to grade-level standards, concepts, and skills being taught. Dear reader, if you are still with us you can imagine how we bristle at the idea of grade-level standards.

However, we think that the STW folks really can embrace the idea that instructional strategies include a variety of challenging and engaging activities, concepts, and skills that are clearly the most demanding that every single student can be expected to accomplish!

As for variety, what better way to encourage variety than to add a plethora of engaging activities into a curriculum and to establish a cross curricular system where student learning around broad themes is differentiated for every single learner? If every lesson is differentiated for every student, will you not have as diverse a variety as your population? Further, won't the odds of every lesson being interesting and engaging for every student be considerably higher if every lesson has been differentiated for every student?

The odd part, and the best part of our model, is that when the idea of grade level disappears, students are free to exceed the expectations associated with grade level! In fact our experiences at Corbett have demonstrated that this model creates student achievement that far exceeds the state average for eighth grade students. We believe this occurs because students are far more interested in lessons that have been differentiated for them, and they are far more interested in attempting work when they are going to be evaluated against their own personal abilities.

Traditional systems can only hope to approach a fraction of the level of differentiation, and therefore engagement, of students through providing a discrete menu of possible ways in which a student can demonstrate grade-level proficiency at any given curriculum. The hobble of grade level prevents traditional schools from maximizing both differentiation and achievement.

Teachers use a variety of methods to assess and monitor the progress of student learning. Teachers in our model and teachers in traditional models will, and do, both use a variety of methods to assess and monitor the progress of student learning. Teachers are free to use rubrics, tests, projects, and any other assessment device to monitor students learning in both systems. The main difference will be that in a traditional system, at some point, the assessment results will need to be quantified and given a grade based upon a pre-determined passing score. This fact alone limits the variety of methods by which a teacher can assess and monitor the progress of his or her students.

The faculty and master schedule provide students time to meet rigorous academic standards. We believe we have shown that asking every single student to perform at their best on every single assignment is the most rigorous bar for academics that a school can set for students. At issue in this question is the time allotted for students to meet rigorous academic standards.

Strictly speaking from a utilitarian standpoint, the amount of time that a middle school student spends learning is greater in our model than in a traditional model where students are switching classrooms every 45–60 minutes. Our model eliminates passing periods as well as the transition times associated with every passing period. In a seven-period day, with four minute passing periods, students will miss twenty-four minutes per day. In a 170-day student contact year, students will miss more than sixty-six hours of instruction, ten days, darting back and forth between classes!

However, the real power of our model comes in the freedom it affords teachers to use large blocks of uninterrupted time for students to investigate rich, personalized curricula. Proponents of block scheduling recognize the importance of large chunks of time. Our model has this advantage of block scheduling in spades. If a teacher decides that they need four hours in a day to work on some specific science content, he or she is free to flex time from day to day and from week to week.

Students are provided the support they need to meet rigorous academic standards. The key aspect of this requirement to becoming a STW is "support." Traditional schools have many ways of trying to provide additional layers of support for students to meet rigorous academic standards. Schools can make special homework labs, or design pullout for groups of students, they can implement peer tutoring programs, planners can be instituted for every student, adherence at the school level to positive behavior support systems can be a school goal, advisory programs can be used so every student has an adult touchstone who keeps track of the student's progress, and the list goes on and on.

These things are not bad in and of themselves. Rather, they are symptomatic of a system where adults do not know their students at a personal level. Instead, school wide programs are created and interventions as prescribed in a cookbook/checklist fashion.

In our model, teachers know their students to a degree that is impossible to achieve in a traditional system. Rather than academic supports being delivered in a shotgun catch-all manner, they are delivered in a sharpshooter personal manner.

Conversations focus on; what can we do for "Jim," as opposed to what can we do for the "Kids in the eighth grade"? A teacher in our model spends five hours per day with each of their kids for two years. They know what the kid has learned, they know what they need to learn, they know the difficulties that child has with learning, and they can individualize supports for that student. Support programs in traditional schools can only loosely approximate the degree of specificity that student support looks like in the model we are asking you to consider.

The adults in the school are provided time and frequent opportunities to enhance student achievement by working with colleagues to deepen their knowledge and to improve their standards-based practice. Every school model can manipulate the schedule to afford time for the teachers to collaborate and deepen their knowledge and improve their practice. However, in our model teachers have identical teaching assignments.

Imagine how much more powerful it is for teachers to sit down and compare notes, brainstorm activities, and strategize about the next unit. Furthermore, every single one of the best ideas that a single teacher comes up with can be immediately transferred to all of the other staff members as they are all doing the same thing. In a traditional system, cross-curricular team planning can produce a situation where a science teacher has a great idea about how to teach the importance of disease, especially as it relates to the plague; however, he has no one to share his great idea with. No one else can try out his new idea.

To be sure, there is a power in different people with different expertise coming together in a multi-disciplinary team, and in our system we embrace this power as well. Recall that in the ultimate expression of our model a middle school will be located directly next to a similarly sized elementary and high school. Once you have a K–12 institution, teachers can be afforded time to work with colleagues from the grade school and the high school.

We maintain that it is more powerful from a K–12 perspective to have teachers across the entire spectrum meet to enhance student achievement. In other models there is often as much, or more, discord and disharmony between the elementary, high school, and middle schools in a district than there is cooperation or a commitment to enhancing student achievement.

A sense of a K–12 commitment to education on the part of all of the teachers in a district leads to enhanced student achievement. Imagine how powerful a staff meeting can be when a teacher who is teaching a tenth grade student English can talk directly to the student's seventh/eighth, fifth/sixth, and third/fourth grade teachers. That tenth grade student will benefit from the knowledge that his previous teachers pass directly on to his new teacher.

The model is all the more powerful because at the same time future students in high school will benefit because their elementary and middle school teachers understand that they will be directly questioned as to each student's abilities, strengths, and needs. Essentially, once you are a student's teacher in our system, you are their teacher until they graduate!

Once a school has successfully answered these questions with regard to academic excellence, it can move onto the second portion of the STW criteria for becoming a STW. The second strand of questions revolves around the idea of delivering services to middle level students that are developmentally responsive.

Developmental Responsiveness

Under the heading of developmental responsiveness, the *School to Watch* (STW) program demands that a high-performing middle school be sensitive to the unique developmental challenges of early adolescence. This section has ten statements that a school must respond to, in a positive fashion, in order to be considered a STW. Once again we will look at each of the STW criteria and contrast the difference between how our model fits these criteria with the more common traditional grade-level subject area specialist model.

The staff creates a personalized environment that supports each student's intellectual, ethical, social, and physical development. To borrow a phrase from Bob Dunton the Superintendent of Corbett Schools, "We don't begin with a large impersonal institution and create personalized enclaves or oases of caring." Imagine how intimate the community becomes when each student spends 5 hours per day, for two years, with the same teacher and the same cohort of students with whom they entered seventh grade. Relationships are not fractured at the end of each year, or even the end of each period.

We can imagine no better way to personalize the student's intellectual, ethical, social, and physical development than to utilize a multi-age, looping, classroom generalist model.

If you were in a large, impersonal school with multiple subject area specialists spending a fraction of an hour out of a student's five or six hour contact day, then you should strongly consider creating personalized enclaves or oases of caring. Advisory programs, mentor programs, and recognition programs are all examples of these enclaves or oases of caring. It is far better to staunch the bleeding caused by the impersonal nature of traditional system by using bandages such as mentor programs. But, we advocate for stopping the hemorrhaging all together by adopting a model that does not lead to an impersonal environment.

Teachers foster curiosity, creativity, and development of social skills in a structured and supportive environment. If you have kids as we do, you have seen how adept they are at playing both parents against one another. If Dad says no, ask Mom and hope for a different answer. Middle school students, in a traditional system, get to play that game six or seven times a day, depending on how many teachers they have. A student can exhibit inappropriate social interactions first period with one teacher, second period with the next teacher, and so on throughout the day.

Socially appropriate skills are honed much more quickly in our system; a student's track record of behavior is known from the beginning to the end of every day, every week, and every year during their middle school experience.

For example, there has been a 10-fold decrease in disciplinary referrals since Corbett Middle School adopted this model. Think about how striking this statement is. A system that used to generate 300 suspensions per year now generates less than 30. There was no significant demographic shift in the population of the kids; the kids essentially did not change. What changed was how the adults in school interacted with the students.

Dear reader, we want you to further realize that no special behavior program was purchased, no time was spent training staff in the hot buzzword program of the day, such as Positive Behavior Support or some other program. Essentially no band aides were created; instead, the source of the problem, subject area specialists, was removed.

As for fostering curiosity and creativity, interdisciplinary thematic units are the mainstay of our model. Few people can argue that a good way to foster curiosity and creativity is to allow students the freedom to explore a theme from a cross-curricular perspective. As we have argued previously, our classroom generalist model leads to the most seamless integration of curriculum across the disciplines.

The curriculum is both socially significant and relevant to the personal and career interests of young adolescents. One of the key ingredients in creating a learning environment where differentiation is the norm for every student is the inclusion of student choice into a student's everyday experience. When students are free to choose how to meet the requirements of a thematic unit that includes math, science, social studies, and English, they are also free to create their own learning opportunities that are both relevant and personal.

A teacher, one who knows their students intimately, can counsel their students into exploring aspects of the thematic curriculum that are both socially significant and directly related to possible career interests of their students. In our system, that counseling will occur at a far more personal level than in a traditional system.

Teachers use an interdisciplinary approach to reinforce important concepts and skills, and to address real-world problems. Of course you know what we will say about the power of classroom generalists as it applies to an interdisciplinary approach to instruction. It ROCKS!

But, there are ramifications of this approach that we have not discussed. Consider the use of textbooks. Suddenly the extent that textbooks drive instruction has been minimized.

If the instruction is interdisciplinary and differentiated for every student, then the text book becomes less defining; it does not command the same power with regard to what each student will read or learn. Conversely, real world resources are more often used for instruction. Students will use filtered internet search engines, an array of specific theme-related texts that the teachers provide, as well as other resources to investigate a given theme.

Other systems will always struggle to create a fluid interdisciplinary approach to instruction. These struggles will by necessity undermine the school's efforts at reinforcing important concepts skills and addressing real-world problems.

Students are provided multiple opportunities to explore a rich variety of topics and interests in order to develop their identity, learn about their strengths, discover and demonstrate their own competence, and plan for their future. The structure we are proposing accomplishes this task as a matter of course.

Within nearly every assignment, there is an emphasis on choice, differentiation, and integration, leaving students free to discover and demonstrate their own competencies. Throughout a student's two-year experience in a multi-age, looping classroom, his or her generalist teacher is free to provide a wide variety of topics through which the student can continually grow as a learner.

Furthermore, that same teacher provides a consistent voice of mentorship and guidance for students beginning to explore plans for their own future. Their teacher serves as a personal guide at the academic, social, and long term career interests and goals. Discussions about high school and beyond are a consistent talking point in our system, not just because it is looming on the horizon for the student, but also because the teachers are so personally invested in the success of their students even four years after they leave the middle school.

As we have discussed, traditional schools can only approximate the kind of personal attention given toward each student examining and discovering their own competencies and interests as in our model. We are not arguing that the teachers in those models care less than our teachers; indeed, Randy was one of those teachers. It is just that the model itself precludes the type of personal attention that our model affords students.

All students have an opportunity for voice. Imagine that you are at sea alone in a life raft and you decide to set sail in a given direction because you think the nearest shore is in that direction. Essentially, you have all of the voice in the raft. Next, add another castaway to your small craft; your voice has been cut in half. As you add more and more of your shipwreck peers, your voice, your percent of influence decreases linearly. Eventually you have between 24 and 30 people in the raft all advocating for a different heading in 12 degree intervals.

The scene seems pretty desperate, but with time and communication the group of 24 people (or perhaps as many as 30) might be able to come to a consensus as to which way they should sail. Heck, it might even be a good learning experience to learn how to communicate with the other 23 people in your raft. In fact, if you spent enough time in the raft with them you might even form some pretty substantial and meaningful relationships. In fact, the more time you spend with them the more voice you will gain back after the initial division by 24.

Unfortunately, the shipwreck was worse than we first described; there are 50 or 60 other life rafts, and every 45 minutes you have to switch boats. Your voice has been even further curtailed. And, even if you spend two years in this flotilla of life rafts, the chances of your voice growing amongst the cacophony of other voices is slim.

Sure, maybe one of the boats will be labeled the leadership boat, and a few lucky kids will be placed in the leadership boat. They will speak for all of the muffled masses hopping back and forth between the rafts. Maybe every morning you spend 15 minutes with a lesser number of kids in an advisory raft before you begin the endless flipping and flopping between crafts throughout the day. But even so, that is only 15 minutes per day, and nothing compared to all day every day that you had when there was only one boat adrift with 24 hapless shipwreck victims.

We have used this analogy before. We hope it further illustrates how a stable, multi-age, generalist approach gives every student more voice.

The school staff members develop alliances with families to enhance and support the well being of the children. A traditional single grade-level area specialist teacher in a large middle school can easily have 250 different students in a two year period. If each of these students has two parent figures to deal with, then the teacher meets an additional 500 people in a two-year period with whom they need to develop alliances relative to the 250 students. WOW! Good luck connecting with every single one of them.

Conversely, in our small school, multi-age, generalist model a teacher will meet 25 new kids in a two year period, along with their 50 parent figures for a total of 75 people with whom they must develop alliances to support the well being of the 25 children. This is still a hard task; it takes time and effort. However, it only takes 1/10 the time and effort that is required in the other system!

Staff members provide all students with opportunities to develop citizenship skills, to use the community as a classroom, and to engage the community in providing resources and support.

Let's say you are a teacher and you have a great idea to take your students from your classes down to do an invasive species removal and indigenous species reintroduction project at a local estuary. The idea is a great one; it is actually using the classroom as a community! Furthermore, the bureau of land management loves the idea of getting 25 or so middle level students at a time and getting them engaged in a community service project while at the same time educating them about invasive species.

However, you are a teacher in traditional school; you see 125 students per day in 45 minute blocks. How in the world will you travel the 20 minutes to the estuary and the 20 minutes back, and have time to accomplish anything worthwhile during the 5 minutes you are there? Sounds impossible, but you are committed to the idea because after all you are the science teacher, and invasive species are a huge problem so you are going to move mountains to make this field trip happen.

You begin by coordinating with all of the other teachers who see your 125 eighth grade science students. This means you have to talk to 18 other teachers because you are lucky and your school only has about 800 kids in grades seven and eight. Of course they are none too happy about your idea of taking each of your five classes out for half a day, mainly because that means there will be a few of their kids missing from every period in which they teach English, social studies, health, P.E., etc.

But you are passionate about it, and you convince everyone it is a good idea and you will make sure the kids know they have to catch up on the curriculum that is being delivered that day.

Meantime, you have made sub plans for 2.5 days. This is a real pain because while you are away with 25 kids from one period, the other kids you see each day continue showing up at your room every 45 minutes. You persevere in writing the sub plans, try to make them something that any idiot can deliver, and you try and make them somehow attached to invasive species (at the eighth-grade level of course . . . I mean how in the world would you differentiate sub plans for every single one of your 125 students!).

Anyhow, the sub shows up. They do a good job of managing the situation. You spend the next 2.5 days hustling kids back and forth to the estuary and it is a success. The BLM loved having the kids and the kids liked being out in the community working. In fact they loved it so much, and you saw them learning so much, you wish you could do it more often . . . . . . but come on, this one field trip nearly killed you! Still, if you have a year to recover, and you continue to soothe the ruffled feathers of your fellow eighth grade teachers, you might pull it off again next year.

Now, imagine you are a classroom generalist and you think it would be a great idea to work with the BLM teaching the kids about invasive species at the local estuary. You call them up and arrange a half day field trip for your 25 students. You take the kids there and focus on the service and science of the project while you are there, but when you get back to the building you have the kids integrate what they have learned into their writing journals.

Furthermore, you tie in the entire invasive species thing into your Oregon Trail discussion as that is where all of these species came from. Suddenly, a trip to the estuary has aspects of science, social studies, and English mixed in.

Everyone loved it so much you go back once a week. Soon, you are doing bio mass calculations, which sound pretty mathematical. Since you are a dependable source of volunteer labor, the BLM begins giving you longer projects that require students to walk over a mile there and a mile back just to get to the riparian zone; man all that exercise sounds like P.E.!

Students are collecting data each week, and in fact that data can accumulate over years! Each individual student can watch the data collection process for two years with their own eyes, and the partnership is so effective that it can last basically as long as the estuary is flowing and the classroom generalist teacher keeps loading his seventh and eighth grade students on the bus each week!

Co-curricular activities. Almost all schools have them. In a school of 150 seventh and eighth grade students with two girls' and two boys' basketball teams, 50 students can play, or one third of the population. Their classroom generalist teachers will absolutely know every student who plays basketball and can communicate with each of them about their favorite co-curricular pastime at a very personal level.

In a moderately large school of 800 seventh and eighth grade students with 4 girls' and 4 boys' teams (seventh grade basketball and eighth grade basketball. . . . yes the specter of grade-level grouping even applies to sports), about 100 students can participate. One eighth of the kids, about 12 percent of them, will participate.

A teacher in this system will have a couple of them in each period; she may not know that they play basketball, but she knows that sports are important so she keeps up on the team and mentions it now and again when the team loses or wins! This keeps her connected and lets kids know she cares . . . . about the team! Of course she cares about the kids, but she has way too many kids to know what each of them is into each season.

If a school can develop methods to ensure that students are treated in a developmentally responsive fashion that recognizes the unique needs of these young adolescents, it can go farther into the STW application and explore the STW criteria about social equity. We think that our system has met the first two requirements: academic excellences and developmental responsiveness, with less jury rigging than in the traditional, single grade-level classroom specialist models. Of course we think the same is true for the requirement of social equity; we hope you agree.

Social Equity

In order to become a STW, a high performing school with middle grades must be an institution where the environment is socially equitable, democratic, and fair. We think if you looked up a picture of this description in a dictionary, you would find something that looks very similar to our model. Once again we will examine the 10 statements, associated with social equity, in which a school must provided evidence of supplying in order to be considered a STW.

To the fullest extent possible, all students participate in heterogeneous classes with high academic and behavior expectations. Isn't a mixed-grade classroom more heterogeneous than a single grade classroom? Within that mixed-grade classroom, isn't it more socially equitable to expect every single student to perform at the highest academic standard relative to his or her own abilities?

How socially equitable is it for a grade-level area specialist to expect every student to complete the exact same work at the exact same time, say work that is at the seventh grade reading level. This just sounds unfair to us! After all, all of those seventh grade students are not reading at the seventh grade level; isn't it a little bit like torture to expect a person who reads at the "third grade level" to read a seventh grade level test?

Others have thought that that situation sounded unfair and so their solution was to track kids. They make a slow class, a regular class, and the fast class. This sounds less mean at an individual kid level. You stop asking your slow readers to read materials that are way over their heads, but at the same time you are now being unfair at the group level. Invariably, the fast kids' class gets more of the "good stuff" than the slow kids' class. The good stuff can be the good teacher, the fun activities, the field trip to the estuary, etc.

The idea of grade level is socially un-equitable, and any system like our model that minimizes the stereotyping of grade leveling is therefore more socially equitable.

Students are provided the opportunity to use many and varied approaches to achieve and demonstrate competence and mastery of standards. Who will have a greater arsenal, or breadth of resources, to assess a student's mastery of standards then a classroom generalist? It would not be unheard of for a classroom generalist to incorporate P.E. into their discussion of the Civil War, perhaps via a reenactment, of the battle of Gettysburg. This is a single example of the freedom a classroom generalist enjoys with regard to the ability to provide instruction with "many and varied approaches."

Further, if everything is differentiated for every single student, couldn't a teacher in a generalist model also differentiate the opportunities for students to demonstrate their competence and mastery of the materials?

Additionally, teachers are free in this model to assess not only the mastery of standards, but also a student's efforts at vastly exceeding those standards. Often, in the fervor to assess standards mastery, no one takes time to assess the degree to which the most academically advanced students have exceeded the standards. Isn't it more socially equitable to assess every student's efforts, even those who had attained mastery of the standards even before they started that particular grade level? We think so.

Teachers continually adapt curriculum, instruction, assessment, and scheduling to meet their students' diverse and changing needs. If we were going to describe how a classroom generalist should approach the teaching day, a good spot to start would be to use the previous italicized sentence. The simple fact of the matter is that continually adapting the curriculum, instruction, assessment, and scheduling is much easier to pull off in a classroom generalist model than in a grade-level specialist system. Why not do it the easier way?

All students have equal access to valued knowledge in all school classes and activities. In Corbett Middle School, where they employ this model, 97 percent of the students are mainstreamed 100 percent of the day. The other three percent have a total number of pullout hours of four hours per day combined. Is this just because the teachers in Corbett are amazing? They are amazing, but the simple fact of the matter is that when the curriculum is differentiated for every learner, there is no need to pull the vast majority of students out of class.

If they are all in class together and grouped heterogeneously, and if all of them are expected to perform at their maximum academic abilities, suddenly everyone has equal access to valued knowledge in all class and activities!

In a traditional model, there is an assumption from the outset that some students will not be able to keep up with the rate that the valued knowledge is delivered, and that some will be ahead of that pace. Special programs are developed for each of these types of students in order to try to combat the effects of the grade level wound from which the school is suffering.

Students have ongoing opportunities to learn about their own and others' culture. This actually sounds like a curricular focus question. It is not inconceivable that both a traditional model school and our proposed model could incorporate a commitment to learning about the various cultures of that school's students. In a school of 800, there could easily be a wider range of student cultures represented in the student body.

However, would the students really know each other well enough to learn about the different cultures when they are busy jumping from classroom to classroom every 45 minutes?

We think that any loss of diversity a student may encounter by spending the majority of the day with the same 24 students in the generalist classroom will be more than made up for by the depth of the relationships formed with those other 23 students.

In other words, they will have a real opportunity to learn about the culture of their classmates rather than briefly peruse the culture of fellow school mates who happen to occupy the same giant building in which they all happen to spend each day. Essentially, we are advocating exploration of a lesser number of cultures in a mile deep fashion, rather than a greater number of cultures in a mile wide fashion.

The school community knows every student well. If you create classrooms, such as those we are proposing, where everyone knows one another, and if you create schools that are a reasonable size rather than the giant behemoths that are prevalent across our country, the chances of actually knowing the occupants of the building and its classrooms are much increased. In larger schools, special programs are necessary to try and make sure the school knows every student well.

The faculty welcomes and encourages the active participation of all of its families, and makes sure that all of its families are an integral part of the school. If you were a teacher at a large, grade-level, subject area, specialist school, and you went to a student-parent teacher conference, what do you suppose the chances are that you would see 100 percent of your students' parents? In fact, if you are a parent and you go to a conference night like that, it can sometimes be difficult to visit your student's six or seven teachers.

Imagine how amazing it would be if the teacher saw 125 kids' parents, given that it is hard for one parent to see seven teachers! Further, let us say parent-teacher conference night is eight hours long, 480 minutes of time in which you can garner the active participation of every family of every kid you teach. There is only a little less than 4 minutes per kid, if every transition between families goes perfectly smoothly.

Instead, in our model, each teacher could call their 25 parents and set up a time for them to come in and discuss their student's progress. Sure, calling 25 people is a bunch of calling, but it is possible—unlike calling 125 students' parents! Given the same parent-teacher night of 8 hours, the conference would last closer to 20 minutes. You could probably get past the introductions in 20 minutes—something that is almost impossible in the other model.

Essentially, big schools with lots of grade-level specialists are the exact configuration of a system you would build if you wanted to alienate parents and take them as far away from the educational process as possible.

The school's reward system is designed to value diversity, civility, service, and democratic citizenship. Actually, the thought of a "rewards system" brings forth horrifying images, in our opinion, of an extrinsic school wide system. A system where children are Skinnerized to behave for rewards such as gold stars and a chance at having their name drawn from a hat to win a special eraser for their pencil. We think that rewards systems, like those used in many Positive Behavior Support systems, treat students more like pigeons that are being trained than it treats them like real humans whose diversity, civility, and democratic citizenship is valued.

However, that is not the only rewards system against which we shall rail. No, there is a much more pervasive system that permeates our traditional grade-level system. That reward system is the letter grade! Does a letter grade system really value the diversity of the special education student or the gifted student? Does it promote a sense of democracy whereby every person has the opportunity to perform at his or her individual maximum and be rewarded for their efforts? We think that it does not.

So, what reward system is there in our proposed model? The rewards in our system are each student's ability to participate in a classroom community and a school community where they are valued and known on a personal level. Participation in a community where everyone is treated civilly, and where their academic as well as social diversity is respected is a reward in and of itself.

Staff members understand and support the family and value the backgrounds of their students. An argument as to numbers of parental interactions that you can honestly expect any teacher to maintain in a year comes into play once again. Suffice it to say that it is far easier to gain an understanding of the family values and backgrounds of 25 students every year than of a number five times that large.

The school rules are clear, fair, and consistently applied. All schools can establish rules that are clear and fair. It is the application of those rules that often becomes a stumbling block in larger schools.

First of all, consensus about what the rules actually should be amongst the adults in a school can become an issue with larger institutions. Even if consensus is attained, you have the issue of enforcement given that no one person in the school actually feels a sense of ownership for a kid from the beginning of the day until the end of the day. I mean the rule says _____ and teachers are often happy to enforce that in their own classroom; after all, that is their domain. However, once that kid leaves their classroom he or she is out of the teacher's domain. In our system, the kid, not the room, is the teacher's domain.

There is only one portion of the STW application left to review. The last section of the STW application process has nine questions that are designed to establish whether or not a school has created organizational structures and processes that will continue to create a high performing middle level school.

Organization Structures and Processes

The last set of hurdles that a school must cross in order to become a STW revolves around the idea that "high performing schools with middle grades are learning organizations that establish norms, structures, and organizational arrangements to support and sustain their trajectory toward excellence." We will examine the nine statements associated with this idea in an effort to further demonstrate that our suggestions will launch a school on a trajectory toward excellence.

A shared vision of what a high-performing school is and does drives every facet of school change. Randy worked in a large high school with over 70 teachers. It was difficult to fit the entire teaching staff into the school library for a staff meeting. Given that it was hard to get all of the teachers in one room, you can imagine how difficult it might be to get them to share a vision about what it would be like to turn that school into a high-performing school. The same is true for large middle schools.

We maintain that if you keep the school small, and fill it with classroom generalists who are all doing the exact same job, then your chances of creating a shared vision that will drive every facet of school change goes up immensely.

The principal has the responsibility and authority to hold the school-improvement enterprise together, including day-to-day know-how, coordination, strategic planning, and communication. In a small school, one with only one administrator, he had better have the authority to hold the school-improvement enterprise together. In fact he needs the authority to hold the entire thing together. A small school principal will have much know-how about how the buffer works, when the bus schedule runs, how to fill in for a teacher, what it is like to be a counselor, how to answer the phone when the secretary is at lunch, how to ring the fire bell, and the list goes on and on.

The power of the small school is that of course the principal will have the authority to manage the entire school improvement process. He does not have other administrators with whom he can share the load and the blame when something goes wrong. The buck literally stops with the small school principal.

The school is a community of practice in which learning, experimentation, and reflection are the norm. In a system like the one we are proposing, each of the teachers in the small school have an identical teaching assignment. If you have a middle school with multi-age, self contained generalist classrooms, then all teaching staff will have a similar experience upon which they can share what they have learned about working to differentiate every lesson for every student. Teachers are free to experiment with different methodologies and strategies in their classroom; further, they are able to reflect upon their experimentation with one another as peers with identical experiences.

In a traditional system, it is true that teachers can experiment, but with whom will they share their results? They are not free to reflect upon their experiments with twin brothers and sisters in education; the closest they can come is a conversation between cousins.

For instance, if you teach eighth grade science, you can talk to other eighth grade teachers, but one will be an English teacher, the other a math teacher, a social studies teacher, etc. Conversations happen between educational cousins, not twins. Teachers can share reflections about kids in general, but not specifically about how to teach every subject to eighth grade students.

The school and district devote resources to content-rich professional development that is connected to reaching and sustaining the school vision and increasing student achievement. We do not want to propose that any school could not devote resources to content-rich development that is dedicated to sustaining and increasing student achievement. In fact, all schools could, and we think should!

In our system, those professional development resources can be applied to all staff. You will not find professional development activities aimed at the social studies teachers or the English teachers. Rather, professional development activities are equally available and applicable to all teachers.

The school is not an island unto itself; it is a part of a larger educational system. Consider the island analogy/concern in this prompt. In most districts, schools are islands and the bigger the district, the larger the gulf between each of the islands. Rarely are schools located geographically close to one another within a district. More often than not, a district will have schools established in a ration of three or four grade schools per middle school, and two or three middle school per high school.

As the district grows, the numbers of feeder grade schools and middle schools expand as does the number of giant high schools. More often than not, there is a difference between the students attending each of the different schools. One area of town will have a lower socio-economic standard than another part of town. Differences between schools have the potential to build rivalries and sometimes contempt. Schools become islands within districts; there is no sense of community.

In a small school, in a small district, a true sense of community can be achieved. If there is one feeder grade school and one feeder middle school for each high school, then students, parents, and teachers alike can identify with all levels of the education system.

We have talked before about the power of a high school teacher speaking directly with a student's seventh/eighth, fifth/sixth, third/fourth, and first/second grade teachers; this power speaks directly to the idea of forming a middle school that is part of a larger education system. Further, we have talked about the power of teachers K–12 sitting down to discuss the delivery of reading instruction, math instruction, etc. There is power in small district, and paradoxically it leads to the construction of a larger educational system.

The school staff holds itself accountable for the students' success. Consider the one room school house of Laura Ingles Wilder. In that situation, who would be accountable for the success of the students in Laura's school? Could a student's failure or success in mathematics be attributed to someone other than the person with whom you would credit their failures or success in reading? Would the student's failure or success in elementary school be credited to someone other than the person whom you are also crediting with the student's success or failure in the middle grades? Of course not; the teacher in the single room school bears the accountability for all.

As a school and district grow, and as a teacher becomes more and more of a subject area specialist rather than a generalist, the teacher begins to hold less responsibility for a student's successes and failures.

Size and specialization are the prime reasons why schools struggle with inculcating a sense of accountability for students' success. In big schools and in big districts, subject area specialists become more disconnected from the grand picture of student success. It is essentially a "forest for the trees" conundrum. Teachers in a large system are just individual trees in a large forest; they are unable to see the entire forest. At best, they can see the immediate grove of trees around them.

District and school staff members possess and cultivate the collective will to persevere, believing it is their business to produce increased achievement and enhanced development of all students. The vast majority of all teachers want what is best for their students. They want their students to achieve and develop academically, socially, and emotionally; however, schools are often too large, and teachers are often too specialized to view their work as an incremental part of a larger effort.

Increased size and increased subject specialization breeds anonymity and an abdication of responsibility to be accountable for the achievement and development of every single student in a school. In our model, where middle school teachers spend all day every day with students in a small school setting, no such anonymity or abdication of responsibility is possible.

The school and district staff work with colleges and universities to recruit, prepare, and mentor novice and experienced teachers. There is no magic associated with smallness or a classroom generalist model that would allow a school like the one we are advocating for to work more or less closely with a college or a university than a school that uses a more traditional approach to middle level education.

However, consider the opportunities a student teacher could enjoy in our system as opposed to a more traditional system. In most teacher licensure programs, students must spend some number of weeks in one setting, say an elementary setting, and a greater number of weeks in their primary student teaching area, say middle school. To pull this off, student teachers switch schools part way through the year. The culture they have just become comfortable with in their first practicum is quickly lost in their rear view mirror as they drive across town to spend 12 weeks in a totally new school, with new administration, and new . . . . . . well everything else!

Just as students benefit from a long lived identity as a member of a K–12 program, student teachers benefit from a longer term placement in a stable K–12 environment.

The school includes families and community members in setting and supporting the school's trajectory toward high performance. Once again, we come back to an argument for smallness. It is far more likely that you can include families and community members in setting and supporting a school's trajectory toward high performance if you have hundreds of parents to work with rather than tens of thousands, or—in the case of really big districts—hundreds of thousands of parents! In fact, we do not think it takes an appeal to the peer reviewed research to state that the larger institutions become, the harder it is to incorporate the input and support of the members of that institution.

CONCLUSIONS

This chapter has drawn on a bit longer than we had hoped. However, we hope we have convinced you that our multi-age, looping, classroom generalist model, when coupled with small school and district size, correlate nicely with the parameters established by the National Forum to become a School To Watch.

If all middle schools were on a trajectory to become a STW, imagine what it would mean for all of their feeder high schools. We think that our model will lead to excellence. We do say lead to excellence because the work we advocate for in the middle school will be wasted unless reforms are initiated at that level as well. We will share our opinions about high school reform in the next chapter.

Chapter 7

High School: Excellence in the Spotlight

For those of you in K–8 education, think of all of the conferences, programs, techniques, experts, configurations, brain research, and innovations that are launched each year with the expressed goal of improving achievement at the third grade, fifth grade, eighth grade, etcetera, benchmark. There is an endless cavalcade of such initiatives each year. With those in mind, ask yourself the question, "What is or has their combined effect had on high school achievement?"

We have thought about this question and our research reveals something startling, at least in the state of Oregon. Specifically in Oregon and, as far as we can determine, in the nation generally, the impact is negligible. During the last ten years in the state of Oregon, countless millions of dollars have been dedicated to reform at the lower grade levels, (as well as at the high school level), and yet high school scores on assessments have remained stubbornly low and virtually unchanged!

We do recognize that each round of the newest and greatest programs may have a temporary effect on the test scores at the grade school or middle school level, but this has not manifested itself in achievement at the high school level. Furthermore, when you read newspapers or watch news commentary, most of the critical focus about education is consistently aimed at high schools. No one seems to stop and consider that all of the millions of dollars of educational reforms and programs aimed at grades K–8 have manifested little or no change at the older grade levels.

These reforms and programs may have temporarily produced blips of achievement at grades three, or five, or a given grade level. However, the programs aimed at eking out a few points on state tests at the younger grade levels will never, and have never, produced lasting results that persist through the higher grades.

There are two lessons we want to illustrate in these opening paragraphs. First, even though most of the programs and interventions aimed at producing gains in achievement at the younger grade levels will not help develop sustained achievement through the high school years, few critics will recognize this, and they will continually criticize high schools; essentially high schools will always be in the spot light. Second, the job of fixing high schools is manifestly more difficult than it should be, precisely because of all of the wrong-headed programs implemented at the lower grade levels.

However, we do not want to cast all of the blame relative to high school performance, or the lack thereof, at the feet of the K–8 system. No, there are plenty of problems that can be addressed at grades 9–12 as well.

In a perfect world, if you are striving for excellence in high school, ideally you first, or simultaneously at worst, need to implement the changes we have proposed in the previous chapters in grades K–8. Whether that option is available to you or not, the remainder of this chapter will focus on changes that are necessary at the high school level to redirect the spotlight of criticism to focus on the fundamental changes required to make an excellent high school.

Even if you are not in a position to affect change in the younger grades of your district, all hope is not lost. Meaningful improvements can be achieved in any high school. The goal needs to be to redirect the spotlight to highlight excellence in high school rather than to illuminate the vagaries of that institution.

By this point in the book, we recognize that we may be guilty of reemphasizing points we have made throughout the text; however, neither of us tire of listening to ourselves, and we understand that what we are proposing represents a paradigm shift in the educational norms that permeate our country. You do not convince people to alter the very fabric of an institution as ensconced as education by telling them one time! No, it takes more persistence than that, and we are nothing if not persistent.

COMPREHENSIVE HIGH SCHOOLS:
HURDLE NUMBER ONE

The number one hurdle you need to overcome if you want to create an excellent high school is the notion of comprehensiveness, as in a comprehensive high school. If you are striving for excellence, you need to focus. A comprehensive focus is an oxymoron at best, and an impossibility at worst! It is not reasonable to expect a high school to be excellent at everything, and yet comprehensive high schools have, at their root, an assumption that they will be just that.

Comprehensive high schools offer everything imaginable. Occasionally, a particular area, like the robotics program or the agriculture program, may shine brightly in a comprehensive high school. Most often the particular high school with a shining star program is one with a client base of the highest socio-economic status.

Sometimes, a particularly gifted educator, the Jamie Escalantes of the world, can produce bright spots in comprehensive high schools where the clientele is not so financially gifted. But both of these situations are rare, and you never see a comprehensive high school that is exceptional in every area. If you want to create an excellent school, abandon any aspirations of being comprehensive and focus your efforts on one area.

Once you have relinquished any pretense of comprehensiveness and have embraced a single-minded focus, it will become even more painfully clear that large high schools are an impediment to excellence. There is no need to have a high school of 2,000 if you are not trying to field an agriculture program, an AP math program, a jazz ensemble, a DECA program, a Spanish program, a French Program, a football team, a lacrosse team, 22 other sports teams, and so on, to name but a few. In fact, if you pick only one of these areas and focus in on it like a laser, having 2,000 students in the building will make maintaining that focus more difficult.

Excellence, and the focus it requires, demands an institutional commitment, which includes all teachers and students; it is much more difficult to achieve this with a larger organization, especially when one person's impact on the whole is miniscule.

SCHOOL SIZE: HURDLE NUMBER TWO

Yes, we are proposing that you stop building giant high schools and make every effort to reconfigure those that you currently have standing. What we are proposing represents a colossal shift in how capital improvement resources are used, as well as a shift in how existing infrastructure is used. First, every district, particularly large districts, are constantly in the process of building new schools.

If a district wants to create schools that have the potential to become excellent schools they must make a commitment to building more schools that hold far fewer students per building rather than fewer schools with an absurd number of students. This strategy, given enough time, will change the educational landscape across America. We cannot overemphasize the need for the nation to embrace this strategy, but the decades it will take for this strategy to begin to have substantial effects on education nationwide demand that a second strategy be employed as well.

Our second strategy can be implemented much more quickly. Each large district has at its immediate disposal numerous buildings. For example, some are designed for 600, 1,200, or even 2,000 students. In most large districts, the buildings with the lowest capacity are currently used as grade schools, the middle size buildings for middle schools, and the giant buildings for high schools. Usually the district's buildings, particularly the smaller and medium size buildings, are evenly distributed across the geographic footprint of the district.

A district should evaluate all of these buildings as possible locations for K–12 schools. Granted, a building designed to hold 2,000–3,000 is still too large to be an effective K–12 campus, and the removal of these buildings will require implementation of the first strategy, but the bulk of the buildings in large districts will most often be of a size more conducive to establishing reasonably sized K–12 institutions. The implications for such a change are profound, and range from creating a much stronger sense of connection for students with "their" school as well as shortening bus routes and lessening bus time for students.

Implementation of this second strategy can alter the face of a district in a relatively short span of years. Instead of a district with two, three, or four giant comprehensive high schools, a district can be the home of dozens of smaller K–12 institutions, each with its own identity and laser-like focus.

The facility that had the incredible track, soccer, and football fields, which was probably an old middle school, might choose athletics as its focus. Another building with a great stage and auditorium might have as its focus a commitment to the performing arts. Another school may have college prep academics as its focus.

The intricacies and nuances of selecting the focus of each K–12 school cannot be described here, as these are the types of decisions that are best left to the local school community. Of course, we will always default to a laser-like focus on academic achievement. We do not propose to revisit the construction of magnet schools, but instead to encourage every school to focus and excel.

Why would you want to attempt such a mammoth task? You would attempt this type of restructuring to shift the spotlight of criticism so often aimed at high schools. Currently, when newspaper articles, books, web pages, and TV programs talk about education, they separate their commentary into three levels because that is how they are separated geographically.

An article about failing high schools rings true to non-educators as well as educators in elementary schools and middle schools because American society sees the institutions as separate from high schools. Perhaps that is why no one ever questions the billions of dollars spent on educational reforms at the younger grade levels that never produce persistent academic change in the older grades. However, this will change as more and more schools become

K–12 schools! The spotlight will focus on education as a whole, not on arbitrary grade-level divisions such as high school.

A change to thinking about education as a K–12 venture will help teachers at all levels to begin to picture themselves as part of a system that produces graduates! Currently, only high school teachers and other staff members associated with high schools spend much of their time thinking about graduation rates. For example, typically when a grade school implements a new program very little thought is ever given to the effect that program will have on those same students' graduation rate years down the line.

Grade and middle schools do not look to examine the impact of their decisions on graduation rate, because the grade and middle schools are only focused on moving the students on to the next level. For grade and middle school teachers and administers, the way they are evaluated has nothing to do with the ultimate education of their students, only the interim steps.

Imagine judging a portion of a car-making company based solely on the first ten steps in the manufacturing process, thinking nothing of the ultimate product. Instead of long-term results, these people teaching at lower grade levels are more focused on questions such as "how will their students fare on assessments six months or two years from now," but not usually six years or twelve years from now.

On the other hand, if a school is a smaller K–12 campus with only a few administrators, every decision about program implementation will be viewed through the lens of achievement at both the younger and older grades. Essentially, the administration of such a building will ask questions like; "Why would we continue to use this "ACME reading program" in grades 3–6 if it does not ultimately produce sustained achievement in grades 9–12?"

Creating K–12 schools will refocus all of the educators in the system on the end product, producing well educated graduates. Furthermore, this reconfiguring will foster deep, rich, and powerful relationships between educators across all grade levels and between students through the temporal portal of time, as they will identify themselves as members of "A School" rather than members of several different schools, and it will foster those same deep, rich, and powerful relationships between students and teachers. Those relationships and their creation are the subject of the third key area we want to address with regard high schools.

RELATIONSHIPS: HURDLE NUMBER THREE

Whether or not you have been able to create a small school with a laser-like focus, you can always address the relationships present in a high school. The most critical relationships in any high school are those formed between teachers and students. Harkening back to our list of secrets from chapter 3, if you wish to create an excellent school, you hire exceptional teachers and let them spend as much time as possible in contact with a small group of students.

Regardless of the size of your high school, changes can be made immediately to create richer, deeper relationships between teachers and students. The first strategies you can use include changing how teachers are assigned to classes as well as how students are assigned to classes.

If you have departments in your building with multiple teachers teaching in the same discipline, analyze how those teachers are assigned. Are your most senior teachers, or most skilled teachers, given first choice over which courses to teach? Are your best veteran teachers teaching your high end students only, leaving your youngest staff members to teach lower and entry level courses?

If the answers are yes to any of the above questions, consider what this practice creates with regard to meaningful relationships that last for more than one year or one term. Essentially, this approach precludes students and teachers from forming the relationship that are most critical in producing excellent schools. By simply changing how teachers are assigned to courses, you can create systems where teachers can spend multiple years with the same students. For instance rather than having teachers who only teach freshman English, and three other groups of teachers who teach sophomore, junior, and senior English, create a cadre of English teachers who teach 9–12 English.

By making the described change, teachers can spend multiple years with the same group of students. Furthermore, since more teachers will share the same teaching assignment, think of the peer resources you will have created by giving all of your teachers in each department similar assignments. This restructuring of personnel can be implemented in all of the disciplines in which you have multiple teachers teaching in the same discipline.

Will this be easy to accomplish? Of course such a change will not be easily done! First, you will have the inherent difficulties associated with any change. Additionally, you will have issues of competence and licensure to deal with. Some teachers may simply be incapable of teaching the breadth of curriculum you will ask them to teach. It is entirely likely that this will be the case, since in many instances your worst teachers will have been relegated to positions where they are in charge of your most incapable or disinterested students.

The teachers' weaknesses will be highlighted when they are forced into teaching a wider range of curriculum to a wider range of students. Their weaknesses will need to be addressed in one of two methods. The first method requires working within the constraints of negotiated agreements. Administration will need to remove the most incapable of teachers rather than allow them to continue hiding in plain sight in those low-level classes.

The process described here is far from pleasant; however, as often as not poor teachers will quit when faced with realities of teaching outside of their comfort level. In short, it becomes painfully obvious to the teacher, their teaching peers, students, and parents that the poorest of teachers are incapable of doing the job for which they are being paid. Given this realization, most of the problems will remove themselves from the equation.

The second method involves working with the teachers who do not have the expertise to teach the new expanded curriculum; however, they may possess the skill to teach effectively. For these teachers you will need to invest considerable resources into training them and providing professional development opportunities so they can develop the curricular expertise to match their teaching skills.

To understand how professional development can help, consider that a school may have a very capable biology teacher who had been teaching biology for 20 years. However, this biology teacher's expertise in physics may have become a bit rusty. The school and the district must provide the resources necessary to bring that teacher's expertise in the subject of physics up to snuff. Rest assured, this expenditure will pay for itself in the relationships it fosters between teachers and students.

Licensure issues will also come into play when a school attempts to change the way it assigns teachers. Licensure in many states is becoming more and more restrictive. It has not reached the absurd level of requiring English teachers to be specially certificated to teach freshman English, sophomore English, etcetera, but it appears to be headed that disheartening direction.

Our answer to this phenomenon comes in yet another two parts. First, campaign against licensure reform that calls for an increasing level of specificity with both regard to subject and grade level. Second, recognize that you are caught in a game in which an increase in the specificity of both grade-level and subject-area licensure requirements is a reality, and do whatever you must to insure that your teachers have the licensure to teach across grade levels and subject areas.

Our approach will require a commitment to having your teachers take extra course work as well as pass screening exams such as subject area praxis tests. Once again, the monetary resources you spend on this endeavor will be repaid when teachers spend multiple years teaching the same students.

Much of what we are proposing costs money! Retraining teachers and paying for them to take coursework so they can teach across a given discipline rather than in just one subject are not trivial expenditures. Where is a school or district to come up with these funds? The answer to this question is the fourth hurdle that must be cleared in order to refocus the spotlight on high school in a positive fashion rather than the typical spotlight of negativity that is so often aimed at high schools.

MINIMIZE ALL NON-TEACHING POSITIONS: HURDLE NUMBER FOUR

Harkening back to our list of secrets from earlier in the book reveals the answer to fiscal challenges associated with providing enhanced professional development for teachers. The answer is simple; minimize all expenditures on personnel that are not teachers. In the State of Oregon more than 50 percent of the employees in schools are not teachers. This makes little sense to us. The most fundamental unit of education is the teacher.

At the most basic level teachers provide instruction; with instruction comes learning, which presumably is the goal of education and the purpose of schools in the first place. If you increase the number of teachers relative to the number of learners, you can increase the amount of learning, and you come closer to meeting your goal!

Any addition of non-instructional personnel will reduce a school's or district's ability to meet its goal of increased learning. Furthermore, without teachers the other 51 percent of the employees in schools are not needed. By reducing non-instructional personnel, you can afford to purchase more teachers, and pay for increased professional development needs associated with making the changes we spoke of earlier.

We have not suggested that you eliminate all non-teachers. To be sure, there is a need for janitors and even principals and the like. We just believe the needs for these types of employees are often exaggerated. Some may argue that in a big school and a big district there are increased needs for non-instructional personnel. After all, in a district of forty thousand students not only will you need SPED teachers, you will need SPED directors, and SPED administrators, and SPED support staff for the SPED administrators who work in the district office.

People may further argue that not only do you need extra personnel in your SPED program in large districts, but you also will need extra personnel in every program in the large district. We agree! And, we have come full circle to another great way to save money so you can invest it in hiring and providing for professional development opportunities for the most important units in the educational endeavor: teachers. Specifically, the way to do this is to build smaller schools and districts.

ELIMINATE PROGRAMS: HURDLE NUMBER FIVE

Along the lines of minimizing investments in your non-teaching staff comes another idea on how to refocus that ever critical spotlight. Simply stated, the idea is to avoid spending dollars on anything that is called a "program." Programs are usually created in response to self-inflicted wounds, or they are intended to "people proof" an aspect of education. We need to explain.

Advisory programs are a good spot to start. Advisory programs in high school are built so that every student has a touchstone, an adult, and/or a group of relatively stable peers that they can relate to on a regular, usually weekly or sometimes daily, basis. Furthermore, advisory programs are built so that teachers are forced to care about students; they are built to be people proof. We realize that we are breaking some unwritten code of polite public discourse by bringing this up. But behind closed doors, conversations about the start of advisory programs go something like this:

> "No one knows any of these kids. Teachers in our giant school do not know the kids and do not try to get to know the kids. They do not see the kids as their problem, so we can make the teachers care about the kids by starting this advisory program! That way they will see these same 25 kids for four years and they will at least have to care for those 25 kids."

Of course, the conversation goes on much longer than this but somewhere at the heart of every advisory program is a deep understanding that teachers in giant schools do not have time to care for every kid! It is not that teachers are uncaring. If you have read this far, you must know that we maintain that teachers are the most important of all the employees in the educational system.

Emphatically, teachers in giant schools want to care, it is just impossible to care for each student on an individual basis. As an example, when Randy worked in a large high school of 1,600 students for five years, he had over 1,100 students in that five-year time period. How many of their names do you suppose he remembers? The answer is very few. If you can not remember their names, how rich, deep, and powerful can the relationships be between the teacher and students?

Educators further recognize that students, in order to do their best, need to feel cared for on an individual basis. Since teachers have the inclination to care but not the time to care, and since students need to feel cared for on an individual basis, advisory programs are created because they sound like a great solution. Unfortunately, these programs are just band aides on the self-inflicted wound of size. An advisory "program" would not be necessary if the school were not so large that no one knew the students in the first place.

A critic might well argue that the reality is that many people are stuck in a big school. Given that they are stuck in a big school, is it not better to invest in an advisory program or something similar, even if it is a band aide? To be sure, a band aide is better than nothing, but if the wound keeps bleeding and bleeding even after you put the band aide on it, you had better figure out how to stop the bleeding. If a district cannot build a new school or move students within schools in your district, there are other ways to address the specific issues advisory programs are concerned with.

Just as we have argued earlier in this same chapter, a giant high school could restructure the teacher's teaching assignments so students would see the same teacher in math, English, social studies, and other core subjects for several years running. This would require that those people designing schedules for students do a little extra hoop jumping to make sure kids had the same science teacher year after year.

This approach would also require a commitment by the people who design teacher schedules to make sure teachers were treated more as generalists rather than as specific subject area specialists within a given discipline. Additionally, this approach requires that the people in charge of licensure compliance issues, as they relate to teacher work schedules, spend time and dollars providing the training that teachers need to teach across a wider array of subjects within a discipline. Nevertheless, in our opinion it is worth it to invest these resources.

The upshot of either restructuring the use of a district's school buildings or restructuring teaching assignments to embrace a generalist approach toward each discipline is that students will have access to that same touchstone with an adult on a daily basis over several years as is accomplished with an advisory program.

We think it is instructive that nobody thinks third graders or sixth graders need advisory programs. A big part of the reason is that they already have a strong, intact relationship with a single teacher. Furthermore, in our preferred arrangement, a student can have meaningful relationships with several adults over their high school career rather than just one as in an advisory program school. It is entirely possible, indeed likely, that they would have the opportunity to become connected to all of their core teachers.

Even if the student under consideration did not hit it off well with one teacher, his or her other core teachers would still have the opportunity to form those meaningful teacher student relationships. In an advisory program, if a student did not hit it off with that one adult in charge of the advisory class, his or her chances of forming a meaningful relationship that lasts years could be totally annihilated.

Like advisory programs, behavior programs, TAG programs, reading programs, in fact every program we can think of, share several common- alities. Programs are intended to correct problems associated with school size, with a commitment to grade-level configuration or a response aimed at "idiot proofing" instruction. Any program that is designed so that "anyone can do it," should send up warning signs if you are considering using that program!

If you decide to use a behavior support system because even those lousy sixth grade teachers can pull it off, you have a much bigger problem on your hands. The problem may not be that your have discipline problems in your middle school; rather it may be that you have lousy sixth grade teachers! If you are using a program because it is idiot proof, consider removing the idiots rather than paying for the idiots to learn how to use the program!

Another example of a self-inflicted wound, as well as a hurdle that needs to be crossed in order to refocus the spotlight on high school success, is the practice of using programs that emphasize grade-level benchmarks and stan- dards. These programs can be found at all grade levels including high school.

The prime examples of programs are grade-level texts in reading, math, and science, as well as protocols of instruction aimed at students meeting grade-level standards in those same areas. This hurdle is growing in height with the ever increasing influence of federal legislation such as No Child Left Behind, (NCLB). The combined effect of federal and state legislation relative to NCLB has been to cause schools and suppliers of educational materials to produce programs that are aimed at meeting specific, grade-level standards across the core curriculum.

The most destructive part of this hurdle is the name itself. Who could argue against a program that does not want to leave children behind while at the same time establishing benchmarks of achievement at various grade levels? No one wants to argue against it because it either sounds either like you are whining, or that you are against the education of all children. However, enough has become enough. More and more educators are voicing their dis- satisfaction with NCLB and the reforms that states have enacted in response to that federal legislation.

Most educators recognize that it is not reasonable to draw a line in the sand at a given grade level and expect 70, 80, or 90 percent of all students to cross that line by a given year without regard to any extenuating circumstances. They will argue about the specific cases that point to the absurdity of the legislation. Cases such as an immigrant from Mexico who arrives in the US during his or her sophomore year unable to speak English and yet expected to pass the tenth grade benchmark in English are often used to point out the disconnect between the law and reality.

Those same people who understand that it is unreasonable to expect that student from Mexico to pass that test will go out and purchase A PROGRAM designed to get him to start reading at grade level. The absurdity of NCLB and accompanying state laws, as well as the absurdity of programs aimed at grade-level benchmarks is the very notion of grade level itself!

Part of NCLB is a measurement called Adequate Yearly Progress, (AYP). Like NCLB, AYP is one of those names that you can not imagine arguing against. Who would argue that there is not a certain amount of progress that each school should make relative to student achievement, and presumably learning, in a given year? Certainly we would not argue this. Schools should make progress each year toward teaching their students. Although we cannot imagine how you might measure such adequate yearly progress, we do know that the current measurement system is fundamentally flawed.

Every year, the state departments of education give each high school, along with every other school in the district, a rating based on how it has done relative to making AYP. The AYP rating is a high stake rating because if a school does not make AYP for enough years in a row, it is deemed to be a failure and is taken over by the state. Schools do not want to earn a failure on AYP and will go through considerable gyrations to avoid the stigmatizing brand.

As the requirements for AYP are ratcheted up relative to the NCLB legislation, more and more high schools nationwide are failing to make AYP. (As an example, despite Oregon consistently posting some of the highest scores on the SAT in the nation, about 65 percent of the high schools in Oregon failed to make AYP in the 2007–08 school year.) The problem with AYP is not necessarily that more and more schools are failing to make AYP; it is the method by which AYP is measured.

We do not want to pick on Oregon relentlessly, but the method by which AYP is calculated for schools in Oregon illustrates beautifully one clear fault with the evaluation system as well as a second fault that is much more devastating although it is hidden in plain view. The first fault is that each year, high schools and the other schools give tests to different grade levels in math and reading. The next year they test a different batch of kids at those same grade levels and compare one year's tenth grade scores to the next year's tenth grade scores.

The laws expect each school to make progress at each grade level from year to year. The obvious flaw is that you are not measuring the progress of individual kids because the test that a student takes in eighth grade does not equate to the test that the same student takes two years later in tenth grade. In essence, the testing system is not designed to measure the growth of each child, so they are left trying to measure the growth of one cohort of students relative to another cohort of students.

In small schools, like those we are advocating for, one cohort can outperform the previous cohort not because of any change in their instruction, but because of the law of average associated with small groups. The simple truth is that one group might just be more gifted academically than the other group.

Even setting aside the difficulties associated with comparing cohorts to cohorts, rather than measuring the progress of individuals through time, the tests are continually changing. They are constantly in a state of flux, so not only are cohorts being compared rather than individuals being examined for growth through time, but the very instrument that is being used to do the comparing is not consistent from year to year. You can imagine how these difficulties draw criticism from the 65 percent of high schools that fail to make AYP in the state of Oregon.

But those difficulties are the obvious and least destructive of the two flaws found in the AYP ranking system. The largest flaw is, yes you guessed it, the notion of a grade-level standard or benchmark.

Imagine you are in a high school where nearly 100 percent of your students are living below the poverty line and do not speak English. When they enter your school, they are well behind "grade level." You work mightily with these students, placing them in contact with exceptional teachers for years at a time.

Throughout their time at the school, these students, you, the school, and the teachers focus intently on a given area of instruction that your school has decided to embrace as a best fit for the staff and students, working hard to differentiate the instruction for every student, and your efforts are rewarded with incredible growth at the individual level. The average student entered your high school four years behind "grade level" and graduates from it only two years behind "grade level." Furthermore, you have been working these miracles for years.

This scenario outlined above will result in this school failing to make AYP. The students are behind grade level; it does not matter that individual students are making amazing growth. They started behind grade level and they ended behind grade level, so they do not make AYP. Additionally, your school has a track record of students not measuring up to "grade-level" standards and is ripe for a take over by the state.

The point is that AYP is not a measure of progress at the individual level. Average yearly progress does not embrace the philosophy of a continuous-progress model although the name suggests that it might. Most people gloss over the notion of grade-level standards and do not stop to consider how damaging and damming the grade-level assumption can be.

If you are stuck in a school where the entry level population is behind this arbitrary mark we call "grade level" you are doomed to fail to make AYP. Furthermore, since everyone is running around assuming that grade level is an actual organic level and not a man-made construct, programs spring up everywhere to help those poor districts and their incompetent teachers meet grade-level expectations. What is worse is that in our experience, those programs often do not represent best educational practices.

Our whole point with this particular jab at NCLB and AYP is that programs aimed at grade-level anything are suspect, just as programs aimed at fixing problems associated with size and incompetent staff members are also suspect. Every program we can bring to mind is either aimed at either grade-level expectations, mitigating the detrimental effects of overly large schools, or idiot proofing instruction.

If there were a program that embraced a continuous-progress model of education, we would support it, although it seems a stretch that such a program can exist. Programs come with a checklist and a set of rules designed for a mythical archetypal student with a specific profile. Since students are not usually clones or exact twins, programs aimed at any given profile are inadequate.

A continuous-progress model, on the other hand, is not aimed at any particular student profile; rather it assumes that all students are different and that they have different needs, abilities, starting places, and end goals. The list of rules and the check list associated with a continuous-progress model are short. Treat each student as an individual, meet them where they are, and move them forward.

CONCLUSIONS

Our list of areas that you need to concentrate on in order to create an exceptional high school and refocus the spotlight on that exceptionality has grown, but we think it is manageable.

The question for educators and concerned citizens is this: what are you to do after you have decided to abandon a comprehensive approach and have focused on one area, reduced the size of your school, changed how you assign teachers to classrooms, eliminated all unnecessary non-teaching personnel, and eliminated the use of all programs that are aimed at bandaging problems associated with school size, incompetent teachers, or grade-level and standards-based assessments that are aimed at grade level? Which should you do first? Should they happen all at once?

Manifestly, the answers to these questions need to be provided at the local level and should fit local circumstances.

Every school site and every community has special needs and resources. We have purposefully created a list of a reasonable length that speaks in broad enough terms that it can be applied equally broadly to the vast majority of high schools in the nation.

Unfortunately, the broader that one creates recommendations, the less likely they are to be a perfect fit for every single school. Our recommendation is that administrators, teachers, board members, parents, and interested parties examine their school's individual needs and resources and determine how our five recommendations can be refined to form a perfect fit with its individual circumstance.

Without a clear understanding of your individual situation, we cannot make more specific recommendations. For us to do that, we would have to spend some considerable time visiting and examining how your school operates. We both have busy schedules, but call us and we will see if we can fit you in!

Chapter 8

Creating and Maintaining a Culture of Excellence

Creating an excellent school is not a one-time achievement; rather it must be an ongoing pursuit. Perhaps this is obvious, but because the need is self-evident does not make it a common activity.

To support the point, borrow an allusion from athletics; good teams continue to practice. They continue to refine their plays and to pay attention to what other teams do. Businesses do not stop advertising a successful product, and they continue to search for new ways to maintain sales. Likewise, they continue to do research and make improvements. Henry Ford's Model T was a huge success, but he had to continue to improve, seek innovations, and incorporate new methods and technologies. So, too, must an excellent school strive to maintain that performance.

To maintain an excellent school demands self-reinforcing standards and approaches that support the core goals. In short, an excellent school builds an internal culture that helps transmit the approach, rules, goals, and norms to new teachers, students, and administrators. The culture of a school (another name for culture may be its atmosphere), the unspoken rules, the taboos, and the acceptable. However, culture does not develop from alchemy, but from deliberate decisions; it is important for anybody seeking to create an excellent school to pay attention to the idea of a school's culture.

With the need to create, as well as to maintain a culture of excellence, the balance of this chapter focuses on meeting these goals. Earlier chapters discussed the rules for making an excellent school, but they emphasized the mechanics of creating a school and its policies. This chapter moves through what the authors regard as the six core rules for building and maintaining a culture to support an excellent school. These principles include the following:

- Do only what you can do well
- Recognize the behavior or accomplishments that you seek to encourage
- Make sure actions align with words
- Avoid new jargon, trends or fads
- Hire only the best teachers, and then believe in and sustain them with training, materials, equipment, and moral support
- Set high standards and maintain high expectations

DO ONLY WHAT YOU CAN DO WELL

A too frequent problem for people, institutions, businesses, and schools, is that their efforts become diffused through any number of situations. Sometimes as entities grow, they attempt to move into new fields, markets, or areas and overstretch themselves. For example, because a company makes great camshafts does not mean that it has what it takes to make great pistons or whole engines.

In a world of specialization, it should be no surprise that it is increasingly difficult to master multiple fields or activities. As physicians specialize and become more and more expert on a single anatomical system, say the renal system, they simply cannot be equally knowledgeable about the neural system. Just as individuals cannot do all things well, neither can schools.

The simple, albeit sometimes unpleasant, truth is that schools must individually make choices. To have to choose whether to major in mathematics or chemistry, for example, may be a hard decision to make, but barring unlimited resources the individual must make it. So, too, must schools.

Consider someone starting any other business. Who in the world would go to investors or a banker and pitch a business proposal to do multiple or contradictory things. For example, an entrepreneur proposing to manufacture airplane tires and violins would have a tough job to sell a connection and reason to combine the two things. If one prefers professional services, who could find investors for a company to provide childcare and package delivery? A more prudent and logical course would be to pick a single focus and be very good at that thing or service.

A person may well have the ability to make airplane tires and violins, but the resources to set up two factories will be much harder to find and the resulting production lines will be much harder to manage. Unfortunately, resources are finite and, wish as one might, this is a truism that cannot be imagined away, no matter the power of dreams.

The observation that resources are limited is not a remarkable one. Anyone associated with American schools and their limited resources knows that this fact forces hard choices. Often the worst thing a school or an individual can do is to avoid making choices. The act of not making a choice is in itself a choice, and the authors believe it is the worst one possible. Worst because it may allow people to believe that they do not have to make choices, and worst because it retards or inhibits the creation of an excellent school.

We as the authors do not advocate the universal creation of any one focus for schools. A school can decide to pursue a curriculum that emphasizes any number of things, but no school can manifestly do them all. To do it all requires a school of unparalleled size and we have already established that large schools are counter-productive.

We certainly do not advocate eliminating academic programs outright, but we do believe that it is critical to make choices. A high school cannot, for example teach ten foreign languages, and do that along with the core of science, math, English, and humanities, without becoming unwieldy. Picking one language and focusing on excellence in that one is infinitely preferable. Moreover, it will be much easier to find one or two excellent teachers who fit with the culture and personalities of the school than it will be to find ten.

THE CHALLENGE OF GOOD IDEAS
IN THE WRONG PLACE

Most schools are blessed with caring parents and community members with passions and ideas of their own. Often times these individuals champion new programs, approaches, or classes and are even willing to provide direct support. The challenge for a school comes in culling these ideas and proposals so that they fit with what it is already doing.

The business schools of America are replete with examples of companies that opted to diversify and go into new arenas and found themselves out of their depth. Some companies, such as GE, do manage to be diversified conglomerates, but many more find themselves selling off units or brands that simply do not fit with the core company.

The same circumstances businesses face are true of schools, except that there is no way to sell off a welding shop or foreign language program. The refusal or inability to admit defeat or to return to a more focused curriculum then becomes an albatross around the collective necks of the students, faculty, administration, and ultimately the entire community.

The news that a school cannot do everything should not come as a surprise, yet many still continue to attempt to do everything and offer every program from teaching aeronautics to ultrasound technicians. While the authors do advocate pushing limits, they also recognize their very human limitations and suggest that such recognition is not inherently bad. Trust us, if you knew the authors, you would quickly recognize their limitations too.

An example of the good idea gone wrong and an organization overreach itself comes from extrapolating one author's consulting experience. This example combines several real experiences into a hypothetical example. A nonprofit organization identified a grant opportunity from the Office on Violence Against Women to support a domestic violence program in a rural, underserved county. The nonprofit saw an opportunity to extend their services into an adjacent county. The adjacent county was rural, had evidence of a high rate of domestic violence, and no domestic violence service programs.

In this example, the nonprofit was an eligible applicant and the county government tacitly supported the application and agreed to provide an office for the program staff person. After review, OVAW awarded the grant funds, and that was when the problems began. The nonprofit did not have an office in the county and there was no one in the region interested in staffing the position. Therefore, it was months before someone could be recruited.

Once a staff person was in place, the county provided an isolated office, as the program did not fit in any existing department or office and there was no avenue to introduce the new program to the residents. The nonprofit could provide little direct support as their offices were in a different county and they had only cursory experience delivering any services in the county.

In the end, the staff person ended up with doors slammed in her face, had a difficult time performing outreach, and never found a way to bridge the suspicions and perception of a program controlled by outsiders. Furthermore, there were few if any supporting ordinances. When the grant funds ran out, the program died without much comment.

The example had many things working against it, but it was a program imposed on people without an investment in the outcomes, and done by an organization that tried to expand without the institutional support and structure. The same thing happens when schools decide to add programs without ensuring they can do so exceptionally, not just serviceably. Indeed, why bother to add an average or mediocre program? Instead, the goal should be: be excellent, and any activity that compromises that excellence does not belong.

The caveat to this rule is that following the rule cannot become an excuse for not taking advantage of truly good ideas and opportunities. For example, the Athena-Weston High School band specializes in bagpipes and drums; it was something that fit with the community, and there was a staff person with the ability and interest to make it happen.

Another example is the Robotics Program at Corbett High School in Oregon. The small school had a staff member with an interest in teaching robotics and was able to integrate it into the science curriculum in a way that augmented the learning environment. The highlighted programs were good ideas that took advantage of the available resources. Moreover, the program implantation was done in such a way that they fit with the culture and goals of their schools.

RECOGNIZE AND ENCOURAGE THE
BEHAVIOR OR ACCOMPLISHMENTS YOU WANT

Granted, this principle can be found in Psychology 101 texts around the nation if not the world. The question remains why so many people do not follow the maxim. Children, dogs, and horses to name three, all know exactly what you do and do not reward or punish, and they respond accordingly.

Who among us has not shaken their head when they see a parent in a public place tell a child not to do something and then let them do it? This is training, pure and simple, which teaches that the parent can be ignored. This principle to recognize and encourage behavior you want should be self explanatory, if not self evident. Unfortunately, all too often organizations and schools fail to pay attention to what they tacitly reward and discourage.

Adhering to this principle demands planning, careful evaluation, and a willingness to take a hard, cold assessment of what happens at a school. Good teaching must be recognized and rewarded. There are certainly a precious few who will be self-motivated and not require rewards to do well, but the vast majority of individuals tend to take the path of least resistance. When the easiest course is to be mediocre, then that is what will result.

Instead of tacitly encouraging mediocrity, an excellent school must create a culture that expects and rewards excellence. This approach requires teamwork and it must invest everyone in achievement, so that the goals of the school are collective goals, not ones imposed from the top or from the outside. Indeed, the seeds of failure of legislation, especially federal standards, are borne by their very nature. Outsiders can rail and demand whatever they like, but unless the goals are internalized, they are meaningless.

The federal government attempts to address this by tying money to achievement and it is successful to varying degrees, but ultimately those standards are too easy to dismiss as coming from the "outside" from "the feds," from "politicians" who simply do not know what is going on. The critique is all the more powerful in that it is usually valid.

NUMBERS

The authors both have a good friend who is an engineer and works for a large manufacturing corporation who tells the following abridged story. The company in question identified 50 priorities it expects its employees to address and emphasize. Every few months the company reshuffles this deck to re-order the priorities and attempts to rally the people to reorient themselves: now priority number 17, becomes number 1, for example. The story presents two morals and they spring from two equally ridiculous situations.

The ridiculousness of having 50 priorities cannot be lost on a thoughtful person. How can anyone seek to do 50 things well? Perhaps a person can pay attention to a dozen, but even that seems more likely to overwhelm than guide. The thought of memorizing 50 priorities seems daunting, and it is instructive to note that there are only 10 "commandments," 9 reindeer if you count Rudolph, seven deadly sins, seven dwarfs, and just three Musketeers, (ok, four). Lists with more entrants than ten become unwieldy, and so, too, is it with priorities.

Combine the 50 priorities with the quarterly reshuffling of those priorities and you have a recipe for derision and ultimately for ignoring the whole exercise. As the engineer points out, the manufacturing process and mechanical engineering does not lend itself to quarterly changes, the timeline is much longer. Instead, reshuffling priorities ultimately tells employees that there are no real "priorities." Indeed, when supervisors really want something done, they do not order two or fifty things done, they order that one thing which is their real priority.

The upshot of this story and its application to schools is the rejoinder to focus on only a few core goals or priorities and to stick to them. Nobody at an excellent school has to think hard to figure out what the goals are. Nobody at an excellent school is concerned with gimmicks like rotating priorities or a long list of principles; they are invariably too busy producing results.

MAKE SURE ACTIONS ALIGN WITH WORDS

This principle is closely related to the previous one, but deserves articulation here. Historically, the command: "Do as I say, not as I do," has not been very effective. Similarly, forbidding some action, say leaving work early, and promising swift punishment, then doing nothing when someone does leave early tends to encourage people to leave early. Nothing so undermines authority as non-enforced rules, and nothing so encourages disregard for those same rules.

Everybody has personal experience with someone whose talk does not match his or her actions. Eventually such people are tuned out and nobody listens to them anymore. As an interpersonal strategy, this is poorly considered. As a plan for creating an excellent school, this course of action is doomed to failure.

An extension of aligning words and actions is the injunction that nobody cares what you know until they know that you care. An outside expert with no stake in the outcome or investment in the school will have little chance of effecting meaningful change. Instead, a reluctant staff, student body, school board, or community will find it easier to rally against the non-invested expert than to bother to listen or use the advice.

Asking people to follow, to make changes, to alter their patterns is an activity fraught with anxiety. A leader who is inconsistent, inconsiderate, and uncaring is destined for failure. We do not argue for faking it, for not being true to one's self or personality, but instead, that changes be made with an articulated and honest investment in the outcome. That investment can only come by demonstrating ability and by creating genuine connections that matter to those involved.

Consider an example from the realm of athletics. It is easy to identify coaches who are calm, cerebral, and disciplined, while other coaches are boisterous, passionate and animated. Both types of coaches can tally wins and championships. Either approach can be wrong or right; the challenge is to fit the approach with the person and the culture.

Generally, people are quick to spot a fake, especially in a supervisory capacity, be it administrator, coach, or teacher. It is difficult, if not impossible, to force a calm and cerebral coach to be animated and passionate when it does not fit his nature. Moreover, people can tell when a person is not genuine. Someone play acting will not only fail in that specific instance, but this failure it will erode their credibility and undercut their ability as a coach or a leader. Truly, little more needs to be said beyond the admonition to walk the talk.

AVOID NEW JARGON, TRENDS, OR FADS

Jumping on new bandwagons or trends is tempting, to say the least. The whole fashion industry, from clothing to furniture, to what colors are popular, are all built on the expectation that people will embrace something new and dismiss the old. Trends and fads support consumption as much as necessity.

More importantly, leaping at new trends or embracing new jargon, especially jargon out of context, suggests a lack of fidelity. How committed can a person be to their program or plan, so the question goes, if they are willing to grab at the first new thing coming down the pike? The question is a fair one; it serves to undermine the confidence of staff and students, if the educational regimen or program is under constant threat of upheaval and replacement by the next big idea.

The challenge of avoiding new jargon and fads is particularly acute in the field of education. Even a cursory review of the literature of the field is replete with the remains of new acronyms, methods, and approaches. The carnage of educational maxims, paradigms, and new methods begs the sage rejoinder that "just because you can do it, does not mean you should do it."

Changing methods demands careful planning, enlisting support, and demonstrating effectiveness, just as creating an excellent school does. For anyone involved with a school, convincing staff, board members, and students to follow them and adopt a new approach is a monumental test of faith, ability, and good will. A wise person will not squander these resources and will only act when there is a high degree of certainty of success.

A corollary to this principle is to pick your methods carefully and stick to them until it is clear they do not work, or there is a better option.

HIRE ONLY THE BEST TEACHERS AND THEN BELIEVE IN AND SUSTAIN THEM WITH TRAINING, MATERIALS, EQUIPMENT, AND MORAL SUPPORT

The reader may find admonition to hire only the best to be repetitive by this time, but the authors do not think they can over emphasize the time. The ultimate ability and responsibility for educating children lies with teachers. A great building, excellent administrators, and involved parents cannot substitute for good teachers.

Teachers typically face challenges from students, intentioned or not, and challenges from parents; there is no good reason to add to the burden through unhelpful relations with the administration. This means that the culture and environment in a school must focus on teachers. Teachers must be appreciated, valued, rewarded, and given opportunities to achieve.

Much attention has recently been given to continuing education and training for teachers by the initiatives of the Bill and Melinda Gates Foundation. These initiatives are wonderful and will undoubtedly produce benefits, but if the schools cannot find a way of sustaining the investment, of keeping the focus on the teachers, then the long-term impact will be minimal. As remarkable as the Gates Foundation funding is, there are places where their millions in grants still will not bring the recipient schools up to the per-teacher spending levels on professional development in excellent schools.

How is it possible that some schools manage to spend so much more on teacher education than others? The answers are complicated and are rooted in the recognition of the critical importance of teachers. If a school is able to retain teachers, then it spends less on recruiting, background checks, and hiring teachers to replace those who leave.

If a school is able to attract and retain the best teachers, then it becomes more effective, more people want to put their children in the district, and it has more resources. If a school is able to attract and retain the best teachers then it has fewer discipline problems, needs fewer support staff and fewer administrators, and has more money to spend on teachers. Creating a positive environment for teachers invariably is reflected in the students, and an excellent school is able to create a feedback loop that supports the process and the outcomes.

Worth noting here, is that excellent schools are also willing to adopt mechanisms to reduce costs and provide benefits without an out-of-pocket or institutional expense. For example, in Corbett, where Randy works, there is a four-day school week. The guaranteed weekday off allows teachers to schedule medical appointments or attend to personal business without taking a day off. This reduces the cost of substitute teachers and increases the budget available to support teachers' education directly.

The four-day school week reduces the transportation budget, eliminates classroom time lost by coaches, and eliminates the need for substitutes as well. The four-day week also eliminates lost classroom time for athletes, band members, and pep squads, improving the overall effectiveness of the school. The four-day week also allows staff to take a three-day weekend when they wish without having to lie about why they need a substitute, which is normal if not common elsewhere.

As important as teachers are, they are human too and they need the proverbial pat on the back and evidence that they matter. Working to provide a dependable budget for equipment and training is one way to provide that evidence. Even better is a teacher-controlled budget for equipment so that they have ownership of the decisions and the responsibility as well as the freedom to make crucial decisions. These are basic ways to create agency, "empowerment" if you prefer the current vogue term, but they are important.

ROLE OF THE ADMINISTRATORS

At the core of emphasizing teachers and giving them the tools to succeed, is creating an organizational structure in which the administrators work to support the teachers. This approach turns traditional hierarchy on its ear, but not only does it work, it makes sense. Clearly, a school can function for days and even months, without a principal, but this is not true of a school without teachers. The fact that a school needs more teachers only emphasizes their importance.

As a challenge to confirm the approach above, ask 10 or 100 teachers what would make their jobs easier or them more effective: a principal who teaches them new things; or a principal who helps them get the tools they need? Ask them if a principal who stands and tells them what they should do would be most helpful, or if they would rather have a principal who listens and helps them solve problems as they arise? Such a survey might yield one teacher who wants to be taught and talked at by their principal, but probably not.

SET HIGH STANDARDS AND MAINTAIN HIGH EXPECTATIONS

The authors believe fundamentally, that within a reasonable range, people tend to rise or fall to expectations. A person who can make 20 widgets an hour will happily make ten if the standard expectation is nine. Human nature typically overcomes any in-born desire to excel, especially when there is no incentive to do so. This is why the authors believe teaching to standards or tests is ridiculous and does not serve students. Students and schools should be aiming much higher.

In an example close to home and one that readers may someday tire of, Corbett Oregon elected to put all students into AP courses. There were very real concerns that some students would fail and, in doing so, lose interest and self-esteem.

Thus far, after years of operation, the results demonstrate that students are far more resilient and able than usually given credit. Students not only did well, but some who never would have forced themselves to take an AP class have been given the opportunity and tools to achieve. More to the point, they have done it. Moreover, for college bound students there are financial benefits. Along the way, students easily cleared the state testing bar because they never noticed it at their feet, aimed as they were at the much higher standards.

To be sure, setting, maintaining, and focusing on higher standards is more work for everyone than not. Teachers and staff also respond to the challenge, and the outcome breeds pride and satisfaction that can only be earned from a job well done. Doing a mediocre job satisfies very few people, even fewer honest ones.

In the case described above, the school is rewarded with rankings and recognition, students are rewarded with passing scores on AP tests, and more importantly, they learn much more than they would learn in a less rigorous class. The teachers are rewarded by having outstanding students, appreciative parents, the prestige of a ranked school, the camaraderie of shared achievements, and a supportive administration.

CONCLUSIONS

To be sure, all of these principles interact and support one another, which is just as important as any one principle. As people push together toward a shared goal, they create momentum that helps sustain the activity. There are no perpetual motion machines, but there are some that run more smoothly, with less friction and better results; an excellent school is one of these.

Truly, we hate to belabor the obvious, but there are so many examples of schools and institutions that ignore the culture within a school. We do not expect all schools to look the same and we believe they should not. What resonates with one community will not work with a different community. However, estrangement will not work anywhere. Students and teachers who do not care will not yield excellent schools; neither will an environment in which teachers and administrators are at loggerheads.

Everyone within a school system must be working toward common ends and with a common purpose. However, a common goal is not enough; there must be some agreement on method, on the route to excellence. Unless teachers, students, parents, and administrators can agree on the route and work together to push in the same direction, efforts, resources, time, money, and potential will be wasted for no good reason. The academic research is fairly consistent in arguing that in education, time is of the essence. For example, children need to read well by the third grade or they are likely to be behind forever. Time spent away from teaching the youngest students to read is time lost, no matter how high-minded the goals.

Schools that fail to take the above stated principles into account will risk failing, and they will risk it in a dramatic fashion. The goal of education is too important to risk failure. At the same time, the successful work of creating an excellent school generates more than enough credit to satisfy most egos.

Chapter 9

Tailor School, Schedules, and Approaches to the Local Community

Thus far we have argued consistently that a body of common knowledge dictates how American schools are designed and operated, to the detriment of learning and achievement. These pieces of common knowledge push schools toward meeting a set of standards and, by extension, toward uniformity. Given the level of oversight and regulation that dominates education, it is not surprising that in the quest to meet these standards, schools would embrace common methods.

Embracing common methods is an approach that has many benefits. For example, this approach deflects criticism, and a failing school can reasonably say, "But, we're following standard best practices." This approach not only provides a measure of cover, it creates ready scapegoats and makes it easier to fault teachers or even the students. In this case, a school can then argue that "if the approaches and standards work elsewhere, they should work here, and the fault is not with the methods or the leadership."

We believe that as tempting as it is to use a "one size fits all" approach to operating a school, it is imperative that communities tailor their schools to fit the local circumstances and needs.

The injunction to tailor schools to fit local circumstances is not all that remarkable, given other evidence. For example, one common piece of advice is to look for and exploit "teachable moments," which are by definition the result of local events and occurrences. Teachable moments may or may not be planned, but good teachers take advantage of them. Planned or not, a school that does not take advantage of the resources and opportunities around it is plain foolish. We think that this injunction must extend to other factors beyond specific lessons.

Speaking plainly, the argument we are setting forth is that the options available to individual schools and districts to tailor themselves are both broader and deeper than typically envisioned. For example, the school day and school week present profound opportunities to improve schools and help students achieve at no net cost. Quite the contrary, we believe that there are many opportunities to save money and allow schools and districts to shift dollars to the critical functions we have described above.

Some of these savings and opportunities are detailed in Chapter Seven among other places. Changes to reduce costs and free funds to be used differently are great. At the same time, we know that there are budget-neutral changes that districts can make to shift the focus from simply creating the infrastructure for a school, to activities that are part of the curriculum and learning for students.

As schools consider ways it can tailor their activities, operations, and policies, the range of opportunities is considerable. What we propose here is not intended to be in any way comprehensive. Instead, the balance of this chapter expands on these ideas; some will no doubt be obvious, if not familiar, while we hope others will offer inspiration to administrators, teachers, and parents as they work to create excellent schools.

Significantly, the ideas and materials discussed here are emphatically not exhaustive. Local schools will likely be able to identify other initiatives that will make sense for them and their local circumstances. This is the way that it should be, and nobody will know a local school better than the local school. The options may be limited, indeed ultimately they are limited by law and ability, but by little else.

As we have argued, common knowledge too often retards innovation and makes districts unnecessarily conservative. Change is as inevitable as the new seasons, and an excellent school will not only be excellent today, but prepared to make targeted, strategic changes as opportunities and circumstances warrant.

As we have repeated ad nauseum, we believe small schools that are well staffed and focused on results will be best able to make the quick course adjustments required by the modern educational environment. Moreover, small and excellent schools will have the institutional will and ability to take calculated risks and experiment to the benefit of their students and community.

We know that there is no magic formula or incantation to ensure success, but we do know that thoughtful planning and the creation of an excellent environment will stand the best long-term chance of success. Schools can and will do things that improve or erode those chances for success and we believe that by taking the steps below, for the reasons articulated, will improve every school's performance and achievement.

TAKE CALCULATED RISKS AND EXPERIMENT

Students today live in an environment that is very different from that of their parents and oftentimes even the environment of their siblings. Clearly, the preceding sentence states the obvious, but common knowledge too often ignores the fact that schools must change. Of course, some educational methods or approaches or specific lessons may never change, but others must. Given that change is a constant and that a thoughtful administration and school board knows that change is inevitable, then it makes sense to build mechanisms that facilitate change.

The only way to make most people comfortable with change is to make them familiar with it, including the process and the results. Once again, it is imperative to note that nothing here should be construed as permission to violate any of the six secretes articulated in Chapter Three. In particular, we must remind the reader not to violate Secret Number Five: decide what your school is going to be the best at and focus on that goal like a laser.

Within the constructs of the Six Secrets, an excellent school must be prepared to experiment with its approach and respond to the educational environment. As difficult as it may be to envision, an excellent school must create an environment that allows for experimentation and new approaches, coupled with a willingness to evaluate the results in a cold and analytical fashion.

A school must embrace what works and discard what does not. This is a central problem with common knowledge. Slavish adherence to common knowledge tends to result in a school system that is unable or unwilling to eliminate what does not work. Indeed, this is at the core of what we are asking school districts to do, namely stop doing what does not work. Taking this type of an approach may result in some false starts, but in the long run it will help keep the staff engaged and the students achieving, which is, after all, the primary goal.

As any district approaches this topic of taking risks, we hope that it will be with the full acceptance of our earlier advice about hiring the best possible teachers and letting them teach. Taking risks must be done in a calculated manner that maximizes the chances of success, not just in the short term, but in the long term as well. Just as purchasing stocks may entail a risk, a smart trader will do research, understand the market, understand the company, and recognize the variables. In this case, what looks to an outsider like a risk may in fact be a very wise investment.

Experimenting and taking risks must be done in the context of the community and staff. For example, your high school may think it wants to offer an environmental science curriculum as an elective. However, if you have taken our advice and have a small school with an excellent science teacher, it may have a science teacher with a burning desire to teach robotics. We believe that in this case it is appropriate for the school to take the risk and offer robotics.

In our robotics example, the school has done all that it can to minimize the risk, is acting in a way to take advantage of its strengths and is giving the teacher an opportunity to apply his or her passion. Not only will students respond to passion and help ensure academic results, the teacher will invariably find his or her work more rewarding than when forced to teach something of less interest. All of these things result in helping to make an excellent school and sustain it.

In our example above, teaching robotics may be a risk, as it is novel and there are few models to follow. However, it is an experiment that can pay profound dividends with very limited downside, especially if a good teacher is involved. Obviously we are not advocating that a school chase every whim or facilitate every wild hair. However, deliberately creating an environment that allows teachers to pursue their interests and develop offerings based on their skills and reasonable criteria can only make the school a more satisfying place to work.

An approach that allows teachers to pursue interests can and should extend to team teaching, collaborative efforts, and cross-grade or cross-classroom work that allows as many students as possible to take advantage of a school's staff and resources. Again, this is not a radical suggestion, only the logical extension of the principle that schools maximize their resources.

All of the following ideas could constitute significant changes for a given school or district. Implementing any of them will put stress on a district and could be undermined by active or passive resistance. Even the best possible new program can be neutered by resistance, and thus the first thing a community must do is create an environment that allows for productive change and the chance for change to succeed.

THE SCHOOL SCHEDULE, BY YEAR AND BY WEEK

The school schedule at first blush may seem like one of the most basic constructs. Common knowledge dictates that a school year consists of 180 days encompassing 36 to 38 five-day weeks minus standard vacations, in-service days, and snow days in some places.

Now the obvious question: why five-day weeks? Why a one-week spring break, why a spring break, why a 3-month summer vacation? Why indeed? Already we know that at least to some degree many school districts schedule their year based on local needs. School districts in communities with colleges or universities in them, usually have a spring break that coincides with the university; to do otherwise would be asking for discontent. However, why not take that further?

In the authors' home state of Oregon, a small but growing number of school districts have adopted a four-day school week. The schools schedule teacher in-service, teacher conferences, and holidays to take place on the one weekday that school is not in session and add minutes to the school day, and they find that they can have students in their seats more minutes per year than schools with a five-day week. Even more importantly, the benefits from the four-day week are immense and they translate directly into dollars. These benefits include the following.

- Teachers can schedule various appointments without missing school.
- Staff can take care of critical personal business from banking to attending to their children without missing work.
- Teachers find they love the arrangement and retention rates go up, lowering recruitment and hiring expenses for the district.
- As teachers miss less school, the cost of substitute teachers decreases.
- Students traveling for athletics miss less school.
- Transportation costs go down.
- Overhead costs for utilities go down slightly.
- More time is available for maintenance and repairs during the regular business week.
- Reduced costs from hourly employees, such as those working a set number of hours per day.
- Remarkable albeit intangible benefits in terms of teacher morale, reduced burn-out, and increased personal flexibility.

Adjusting the weekly schedule clearly can pay remarkable dividends without altering the most important consideration, that of student achievement. Ask any administrator or school board member if they would like to know how to reduce their variable transportation costs by almost 20 percent and their fixed costs by 5–10 percent at no educational cost, and they are likely to jump at the chance. The above scenario makes this possible and it comes with additional savings as well.

There are considerable possibilities to make important adjustments to the annual schedule along with the weekly schedule, but American schools have been much slower to embrace them. The summer break is so deeply ingrained that advocating more, shorter breaks throughout the year may be the proverbial tilting at windmills. Nonetheless, it is worth noting that many educators believe that the long summer break creates an undesirable situation in that considerable reviewing time in the fall could be better spent focused on new learning.

We hope that some readers and some far-thinking districts will help lead this effort.

DAILY SCHEDULE

The daily school schedule is a relatively sacrosanct pattern, and there are many altogether good reasons for this, especially in elementary school. If the reader takes our advice and uses a generalist model, where students spend multiple years in multi-age blended looping classrooms, then it will be true for middle school as well. A single teacher can adjust the daily schedule to take advantage of natural lulls and higher energy time periods to his or her best advantage. However, when students get to high school, the daily schedule tends to lock students and teachers into advantageous and disadvantageous time periods.

The chemistry student who has class immediately after lunch. That mid-afternoon time slot is anything but the best spot for focusing on chemical formulas and valances. Indeed, anyone who has taught at all recognizes that some time periods are simply more conducive to learning than others. We do not mean to suggest that schools simply not teach during these sub-optimal times, but we do believe that there is no intrinsic reason to lock one class into the same time slot every day.

We are aware of schools that have used a rotating schedule to great effect. In the examples known to us, the schools adopted a set first period for all students and classes, but from that starting point, classes rotated every day. Classes, for example might run: 1,3,4,5,6,2 one day, then 1,4,5,6,2,3. The rotating class schedule may or may not be appropriate for a given school, but it represents an option that has worked for some schools and should be considered.

FOOD SERVICE

Every school in the United States offers meals to students and staff. The unfortunate truth is that school represents many students' lone daily opportunity for a healthy meal. At the same time school meals are routinely bashed as bastions of fried food and poor nutrition. We believe, indeed know, that there are opportunities within the realm of food service to improve the school and educational attainment, and save money all at the same time.

There is no reason that meal preparation, food service, and related functions cannot augment the curriculum. Students can be involved and prepare food under the direction of a teacher. In our experience, moving to an educational model for food service results directly in significant savings and unforeseen benefits.

Our most concrete example comes from Corbett, Oregon, where the district hired a teacher to oversee food preparation. Students participate in cooking and serving as a regular class and in addition to the mandatory Food Handler's Certificate, the students can receive an entry level chef certificate from the National Restaurant Association. The results at Corbett have been nothing short of remarkable. The district saved money, does not use a deep fryer for food preparation, and no longer uses packaged or processed food.

Whereas parents almost never used to join their children for meals, now it is a regular occurrence, and the district yields a small profit from this. More significantly, staff morale improved. At least one teacher at Corbett put off retirement and cited the lunches as a big factor.

We do not expect that a good school lunch can overcome problems big or small, but we do know from experience that it makes a difference. Combined with other thoughtful and strategic decisions, things like a gourmet school lunch program, coupled with a four-day school week and an environment that values teacher input dramatically improves staff retention and makes recruiting the best teachers much easier. The school lunch program is a tangible benefit of being at a specific school or district, and it is a foolish administration that ignores this powerful incentive.

RELATED APPLICATIONS AND IMPLICATIONS

The above discussion about food service argues that an important, auxiliary function at a school can be an opportunity for class work and student learning. There is no reason that the approach of using qualified teachers and students cannot work for other auxiliary functions, including maintenance and custodial work and technology infrastructure. For schools working to create or retain vocational education programs, it is harder to imagine a more real world application of skills and vocational education training than the real world of maintaining a school or providing Information Technologies services for a school.

Again, we know of schools that use certified teachers to provide Information Technologies services for the district and use the provision of services as an opportunity to teach students. Students not only learn the intricacies of running wires and making physical connections between hardware systems, but also learn how to troubleshoot software and other related skills.

The end result of the student involvement in IT services has been not only a small savings for the district, but a new learning opportunity and coursework that would not otherwise be available. Although we will continue to rail against big schools, the benefits for larger schools would be even more dramatic than for small schools as the budget is that much larger.

Using students and teachers to accomplish core functions may bring scrutiny, and we do not advocate aggravating insurance agencies. However, there are many opportunities to integrate essential functions into the curriculum. If staff members have the required skills and interest, this is the type of experiment that a school must be willing to take if it wishes to create an environment that creates and sustains excellence.

LOCAL OPPORTUNITIES

Any school district is going to be faced by unique local circumstances, and these entail opportunities and challenges. A school in an agricultural community will have potentials to marry food science, agricultural science, 4-H, or similar offerings. The authors' home town of Cordova, Alaska for example, was a fishing community, and consequently marine biology was a very popular offering. More than that, the school also aligned its schedule with the specific fish runs. School ended relatively early in May to allow students to participate in the Copper River Red Salmon fishery and it began after the traditional end of the summer pink salmon seining season.

Another example is the western community of Pendleton, Oregon. In Pendleton and the surrounding region the school year begins later, to allow young people to complete harvest, and then stops for the better part of a week to allow students to participate in the Round-Up. There are countless similar and unique local events, and a school district benefits by embracing them.

Another good example of local communities bending their schedules to fit local conditions is found in towns that host colleges or universities. For these communities the lecture series, performances, and visiting luminaries provide additional opportunities for the local schools. We cannot and do not mean to anticipate all of the local possibilities, but we can and do exhort schools to take advantage of them.

STAFF AND OTHER LOCAL RESOURCES

For many chapters now, we have extolled the virtues of small schools and hiring the best possible teachers. We hope that you, gentle reader, are convinced. If not are not convinced then the only thing that will probably work is direct experience. Either way, we hope that we can assume that you recognize the need for excellent teachers. Just as excellent teachers are critical in creating an excellent school, they are just as important in maximizing a school's potential. Every school faces limited resources and, while those limits are different, they are no less real or imposing.

Given these limits, a successful school must be willing and able to take advantage of the unique skills and interests that its teachers bring to the fore. As we noted earlier, a talented science teacher who is interested in teaching robotics should not just be given a chance, but encouraged and rewarded for taking the initiative.

We make these recommendations with the expectation that readers will remember and adhere to our injunction to move deliberately and with care. Nothing is as potentially draining as following every well intentioned idea. A school must continue to stay focused on the thing that it intends to do well. Schools must still adhere to Secret Number Five to decide what their school is going to be the best at and focus on that goal like a laser. However, within that injunction, there is and must be room for experimenting and taking risks. There must be room to respond to the ideas and abilities of a schools staff.

We believe that teachers and any professional will welcome the opportunity to grow, take on new challenges, and have a diversified teaching slate. A school that takes advantage of its teachers' interests and abilities will not only retain talented teachers, it will also result in higher student achievement.

Chapter 10

Funding Excellent Schools

School funding, here is a topic that has probably led to the spilling of more ink than anything short of love and war over the last few decades. As much as we would like to offer brilliant insights about how to get more, school funding is ultimately tied to state and federal legislation, legislatures, and the inherently messy realities of politics.

Our purpose all along has been to focus as much as possible on things that schools, districts, and even individuals can control. Consequently, there is little to say specifically about influencing the legislative process. Leaving the state and federal lawmakers behind does not, or should not, end the conversation.

We will begin this chapter by discussing those things we can control with regard to funding—namely, where excellent schools spend the money they are allotted for the purpose of education.

WHY YOU SHOULD MOVE MONEY TO THE CLASSROOM

The purpose of a school, a district, an educational service district, and departments of education across the nation is fundamentally to teach students. Strip away all of the social services, administration, oversight, the meals, the sports, the activities, the clubs, and competitions, and the one thing left is the classroom. From one-room schools to comprehensive high schools serving thousands of students, the classroom is, or at least should be, the focus of the entire endeavor.

Beginning with local school board comprised of volunteers, the American public education system has grown to include a host of high paid specialists who never see a classroom. We believe, emphatically, that this is a problem and does not make sense.

The budget must focus on the classroom; the classroom has to be the place where the budget is expended. This means funding first and foremost for teachers, for classroom materials and for the physical structure. We know that we have hit this point before and we will continue to do so because it is so central to the effort to create an excellent school. Every dollar spent elsewhere must be scrutinized.

In earlier chapters, we advocated cutting the number of administrators, aides and specialists and we are about to do so again. As usual, we will qualify the statement to recognize that specialists are needed in some cases, and this is where educational service districts (ESDs) make sense. We think paying for another teacher who will spend hours with young people is more cost effective than hiring a guidance counselor who will see an individual student for an hour or two a year.

Twenty years ago when information about schools and their application procedures were less available, it might have made sense to pay someone to maintain a library and counsel students about careers, but this is now available on the Internet. Pragmatically, schools are not evaluated on their college matriculation rates; they are evaluated via standardized tests that focus on classroom education. The classroom is the place where young people learn, are challenged, and grow. This is where the resources must go.

We agree that in a perfect world, it would be nice to have a health clinic in the school, staffed with nurses as well as mental health experts. Further, it would be nice to have staff to help young people fill out college applications, identify vocational opportunities, and apply for jobs. In an ideal world, schools would have abundant para-professionals, aides, and specialists to meet any or all needs.

Unfortunately, the ideal is not what schools work with. Resources are scarce and this requires choices. When confronted with these choices, we insist that the classroom, the teachers, and education receive priority.

Ultimately, an individual or a society gets what it pays for. If an individual pays $3,000 for a car and then spends $10,000 for extras such as a stereo, air conditioning, leather, seat-warmers, and fuzzy dice, what they have is still a $3,000 car. We think that with this analogy, it is better to spend $13,000 for the car and forego the fuzzy dice. In the end, an individual will get more miles and better service out of that $13,000 car.

Just as we recommend the $13,000 car compared to the cheap car with lots of add-ons, we recommend spending as much as possible on the teachers who perform the critical functions in any school, to say nothing of the excellent one.

HOW TO MOVE MONEY TO THE CLASSROOM

Absent new sources of funding, the only way to move money to the classroom, the proper focus of a school, is to take it from other sources. Let us say in advance that we are sorry for hurting anyone's feelings.

We recognize that counselors of all types, para-professionals, administrators, food service employees, and support personnel, to name a but a few of the groups we are likely to offend, are important and contribute mightily to the quality of life and goodness in the world. We think there are fruitful and valuable roles for many of the people and functions we will talk about below; we just do not think that it is necessarily in public schools. With that apology that will likely satisfy nobody, let us forge ahead.

Para-Professionals

Briefly, an excellent school minimizes or eliminates para-professionals. Some special-needs children will require a para-professional, but the fewer the better. We know of limited instances in which a para-professional has made a critical difference, but at the same time, we can cite personal experiences where the biggest thing that came from their presence was the highlighting of "otherness."

The idea of highlighting "otherness" pertains to students as well as to staff. No student wants to be singled out as being different, requiring something special, and this is what having para-professionals in a class does. Yes, sometimes it is unavoidable, but it should be the exception, not the rule. Furthermore, para-professionals are not teachers, and they introduce new and often unhelpful dynamics into the organizational culture. We believe it is preferable to have excellent teachers in direct contact with students rather than people with less training, less investment, and ultimately less accountability.

Reduce SPED Rolls to Reduce Aides

As we have discussed in several other chapters, we like the SPED approach so much that it ought to be extended to every student. Using multi-age looping classrooms with continuous-progress models in place of age or grade level curriculums can go a long way toward reducing SPED rolls. If everyone is on what amounts to an individual education plan, then there is no need to single anyone out for special attention, as everyone is getting special attention.

We think this approach also helps eliminate the "otherness" that SPED classrooms and aides create. We cannot think of any inherent good that comes from being singled out as "different." We do recognize that everyone is special, just like everyone else.

By shifting funding from aides to teachers, excellent schools can reduce student-teacher ratios, improve learning for everyone, and ensure greater progress. We continue to believe that progress is more important than hitting a pre-determined minimum standard. Teachers bear the ultimate responsibility and have the authority, gravitas, and ability to influence learning and progress far more than the best aides, and we believe that it is better to hire one more excellent teacher than two aides.

Kitchen and Food Service

For most schools, excellent or otherwise, food service is a revenue center, thanks to federal funding and specifically the USDA school meal programs. Because food service is conceived this way, it is often sacrosanct when it comes to budgeting and funding. However, in an effort to be consistent, we the authors believe that food service must be focused on learning and teachers.

We described earlier how the Corbett School District brought in a teacher to oversee the meal program and used students to help prepare and serve the meals. Rather than reprise this discussion, we would rather remind you that it worked. Furthermore, not only did the change work, but it resulted in an overall reduction in costs, an improvement in quality of food prepared, an improvement in morale, and the addition of another teacher to the staff. Fundamentally, it is possible to transform meal programs from an ancillary service to a classroom.

At the risk of patting Randy on the back too much for pointing to this successful experiment, we believe that this innovative thinking is critical to creating excellent schools. Every school in the country serves food; why not make it part of the educational experience? Indeed, why not serve excellent food at an excellent school?

Facilities Maintenance and Operations

The food service model translates directly to other operations associated with running a school. For example, every school, regardless of size, employs personnel to repair and maintain facilities. It is not unreasonable to transfer portions of those resources to the instructional venue just as we recommend that you do with food services.

In many schools, vocational departments are already in place. It seems odd that a school would employ a teacher to give instruction in repair and maintenance of vehicles, or maintenance of buildings, while at the same time they employ a non-certified employee to actually repair school vehicles and maintain school buildings! Couldn't a highly educated vocational arts teacher assume much of the responsibility for building maintenance just as a highly educated culinary arts teacher can do in the food services?

Finally, isn't real world experience more valuable then the simulated vocational experiences offered in some vocational arts classrooms? We think the answers are a resounding "YES"!

Further, many schools have long ago cut their metal and wood shop programs while still maintaining non-certificated maintenance personnel. By shifting portions of the maintenance program into the realm of academics, you will have gone farther toward moving dollars into the classroom.

Information Technology Services

You can probably predict what we advocate with regard to IT services. Just as schools currently employ non-certificated food service and maintenance personnel, they often employ non-certificated IT technicians. Even in a district the size of Corbett (around 800 kids), the cost for IT services can exceed the salary and benefit package of a teacher. Why can't a highly qualified educator teach the necessary skills for students to develop expertise in IT services while simultaneously maintaining a school's IT system?

Granted, the IT teacher's classroom, the maintenance teacher's classroom, and the food service teacher's classroom may not look like an English teacher's classroom. Perhaps the IT teacher only has three or four students with whom they work each period of the day. However, even if it is only one student, there will be more dollars being spent on students rather than on non-certificated employees. At the very least, the inclusion of even a few select students in IT, Food Service, and Maintenance classrooms will have a net positive effect on reducing overall student to teacher ratios.

The extent to which any given district moves IT, food service, and maintenance dollars to the classroom will be governed by the landscape of each school. There is no universal formula for deciding what percentage of each of these areas should be moved to the classroom. All we can say for sure is that the more dollars you move into the classroom the greater the likelihood that you will create an excellent school.

Recall that one of the secrets to creating an excellent school is to focus like a laser on what you do best. The bulk of our instructional laser focus will always be directed at core academics. However without regard to what a school's individual laser-like focus is, we recommend moving food service, maintenance, and IT services to the classroom provided the move supports educational excellence at the local level.

We would not advocate having students and teachers spend time learning to cook, clean, or repair the computer network simply for the experience of the act. However, even in a district like Corbett where the focus is clearly on college prep academics, there are enough students whose individual needs warrant the inclusion of food services, maintenance, and IT into the realm of classroom expenditures. We believe that if Corbett has found a value add by including these three areas in the academic spectrum, most other schools will as well.

Administrators

As a rule, the authors tend to like administrators as much as most people. One of the authors is one and the other would like a cushy job too. All joking aside, administrators, like many other functions, are necessary; we would not advocate running a school without a few. However, we do think that there is an optimal number, which is lower than most districts actually use.

In general, we tend to be suspicious of vice-principals, principals in charge of discipline, or other subsets of school operation. Indeed, this is a measuring stick for determining when a school is too large. Multiple layers create bureaucracy, separation, and ultimately alienation. Far better, we believe to have a single principal, who can know the teachers and students, than to divide functions and build barriers. In addition, administrators cost more than teachers, and administrators at big schools cost more than do those at small schools.

In Oregon, for example, the average small high school principal makes considerably less than the average principal at a large high school with more than 1,100 students. According to the Oregon School Board Association's *2007–2008 Survey: Salaries and Economic Benefits for Administrators in Oregon School Districts and ESDs*, principals in districts with more than 4,000 students and more than 1,100 students in the high school had an average salary of $104,000 per year. That same year principals in districts with a total student population of between 500–1499 students and less than 499 students in the high school earned an average of only $78,000 per year.

Of course this data is misleading, because while a principal of a giant 1,100 student school spends all of his or her time just being a principal, the smaller school counterpart may also wear several other hats. Those hats include job descriptions such as counselor, SPED director, lunch room supervisor, study hall teacher, district sub, human resources director, public relations/information officer, student and support services manager, deputy superintendent, assistant superintendent, superintendent, and often principal of their district's grade school, middle school, or both. So much for the economies of scale that large school proponents tout.

Even in larger schools, we believe that a district is money ahead by eliminating administrative positions and hiring excellent teachers to reduce the student-teacher ratio. Excellent teachers have fewer discipline problems and require less oversight. Excellent teachers also build teams and supportive networks amongst each other that serve as bulwarks that eliminate the need for administrators.

Team leaders among teachers can be amazingly effective at providing limited administrative support without the expense of a vice-principal. To once again point at Corbett, the grade, middle, and high schools all have teachers with administrative credentials; providing them with additional duties and compensating them accordingly allows them professional development while keeping the school focused on teachers, rather than on administrators.

When a school has vice principals and other administrators, it always means that no one knows all of the students and all of the teachers. Never in our experience has the potential of being unknown, alienated, and marginalized been a positive feature in a prospective job. Why, then, would it make sense to create educational systems that foster such an environment? One answer is that it allows administrators to be paid more.

We can already hear the knives being sharpened. Stop for a moment however to consider the decision-making process when it comes to building a new school. School boards are comprised of volunteers—competent and able we are sure; however, they rely on paid professionals to advise them and carry out policy.

Those paid professionals are the administrators. Universally, administrators are paid more and carry more prestige when they administer big schools or districts. Administrators are rewarded for presiding over big schools and it is in their economic interest, to say nothing of their reputation, to create big schools. Big schools create more jobs for administrators too.

Four new high schools with 400 students create jobs for four principals. A new 1,600 student high school creates a principal, at least two vice-principal jobs, a vice-principal in charge of discipline, and a curriculum specialist job, all of which pay more than the 400 student high school principal job. These positions do not include the two or three guidance counselor jobs, the human resource position, the public relations directorship, and other jobs that do not exist at the small schools.

We are not making accusations of maliciousness, nor of deliberate wasting of public resources. We are even willing to concede that there may be an economy of scale in constructing the building, but we would argue that the small schools don't require the same administrative overhead that the large one does. No, we think that administrators respond to economic pressures and rewards like any human does, and that the system is geared to favor larger schools and to discourage any consideration of options, let alone a cogent cost-benefit analysis.

The upshot is that these conditions do not encourage or support excellent schools; they encourage mediocrity, the segregation of students by age and ability, and ultimately impede the educational process. Yes, children are educated, (learned if you prefer) but not as well or as effectively as they could be if decisions were better thought out and excellent schools were the overarching and guiding goal.

School Week

Nothing in any legislation of which the authors are aware requires a five-day school week, or a 40-week school year. As discussed in the previous chapter, a growing number of school districts have moved to a four-day school week. Seat time has not been a problem for these districts and the change translates directly into cost savings, to say nothing of morale improvement among staff.

Switching a district to a four-day school week should save 20 percent of the variable costs associated with transportation. This cost is especially relevant given the dramatic increase in fuel costs in the last years of the Bush Administration. A proactive building heating and cooling plan should also help reduce energy costs. Teachers tend to be especially appreciative of the change; at Corbett it has helped reduce the use of substitutes, as well as reduce turnover and the associated costs of hiring new staff.

Regularly in the US, if not frequently, the subject of a long summer vacation is revisited. Some educators argue that shorter, more frequent breaks would serve the educational process better, require less time spent reviewing, and keep everyone engaged.

Such a fundamental change is likely to be long in coming, but other countries operate without the three-month break and it seems inevitable that some districts will experiment with the change. Using the breaks judiciously to meet local needs as well as to schedule the breaks to coincide with the most expensive operating periods could provide some of the same benefits as a four-day school week.

Counselors

Just as we like administrators, we like counselors. Some of the authors' best friends are counselors, but excellent schools just do not need many of them, if at all. Plenty of schools, especially small, rural schools, operate without a counselor, be they guidance, career, or mental health counselors.

Many counselors at large schools are better described as referral specialists, which is nice, but hardly as relevant to providing an education as a teacher. Moreover, trainings and directives about identifying problems and referring students beset most teachers. All teachers are mandatory reporters of child abuse and other problems. Consequently, we believe that scarce resources are better allocated to teachers than to counselors who spend, at most, a few hours a year with a student.

Funding and Reporting

When is a gift not a gift? Among the many possible answers that could be correct, the one the authors are fishing for is when it costs money to accept. An effective and time-honored gaffe is the old con where to claim your prize; you need to send $10, $100, or $1,000 or more to handle the administration. No matter who runs the con, it is still a con and an excellent school will do everything possible to avoid being taken.

The authors have a single example to illustrate this short section and it comes with the rejoinder to scrutinize everything, even money that comes as a gift. In the early 2000s, the superintendent and Randy decided to look at ways to reduce administrative costs. A hard look at the costs revealed that the district was spending approximately $35,000 in direct costs to comply with federal reporting requirements that came with the $45,000 they received from the US Government.

The $35,000 expense reflected a hard, direct cost required by the reporting process. These did not include the time of the superintendent, the principal and administrative assistant who were invariably involved with collecting data, overseeing, and reviewing the reports. A modest and conservative estimate of these costs quickly demonstrated that the district would ultimately save money by not taking the federal dollars.

Not taking funding may seem a crazy way to save money, but ultimately it was. Most likely, the exchange works only for smaller districts in places where the standard of living is neither remarkably low nor high; further, a decision such as this demands a careful analysis of true costs and benefits, with an understanding of economies of scale.

FUNDING SOURCES

Rather than discussing federal funding and state formulas, all of which vary to some degree, we propose to point out a few additional sources and then move budgeting within a school or district. Some of the chapter will reinforce our themes and secrets, and hopefully will offer some alternatives and serve as a foundation for innovative thinking based on local circumstances. Whether or not money is really at the root of all evil, it is a critical component in the effort to create an excellent school.

Recovery Act Funding

As of this writing, the 2009 Federal legislation: The Recovery Act has committed approximately $780 Billion to stimulate the American economy and encourage economic activity. Some of this funding has been allocated to assist education. Notably, the Recovery Act and budgets associated with President Obama's budget include programmed funding for Special Education (SPED) and Title 1. To access these funds, schools and districts must use existing processes and paperwork used to access the funds. Significantly, the paperwork burden is increased, however.

The amount of money currently allocated by the Federal Government under President Obama to SPED and Title 1 funds is approximately twice what it was at the end of George W. Bush's presidency. Most schools and districts will jump at the opportunity to double their funding for these programs, particularly given the current economic crisis that most if not all states are facing in 2009. We want to offer a word of caution with regard to these funds.

Title 1 and SPED funds come with a tangle of strings attached. Before accepting all or even some of the funds, a district and school should carefully examine those strings before signing on the dotted line to receive this programmatic funding from the Federal Government. Make sure you are not agreeing to take funds that will jeopardize any of the six secrets we have shared with you; make sure you are not inflicting a wound you will have to bandage by taking the funds.

An example may prove worthwhile. Some of the stipulations on Title 1 funding include making sure that no Title 1 funds are spent on non Title 1 students. Often districts or schools will hire personnel to deliver Title 1 instruction. That person can not instruct non Title 1 students while on the Title 1 clock. The easiest way to accomplish this task is to assign the Title 1 instructor a Title 1 class and *pull out* the Title 1 kids from their normal class room. You can imagine how skeptical we are about a pull-out program aimed at only one segment of the population.

We believe it would be far better if Title 1 funds could be used to support every teacher, all of whom are classroom generalists. If each portion of a teacher's salary could be apportioned to Title 1 based upon how many Title 1 students were in their class, we would jump on those funds without hesitation.

We are not suggesting that, given the current economic realities, these funds be summarily dismissed. For instance, if nearly every student in your school qualified for Title 1 funding, it would be absurd not take the money. In that situation, you essentially could distribute the funding equally between all of your classroom generalists, all of whom also were Title 1 instructors.

Even if you are not a Title 1 school, we can imagine situations where you would take these funds. (In fact Randy has restarted Title 1 at his school after a two year hiatus given the increased funding levels.) Our cautionary advice is just that, be cautious; don't take funds that will cause you to endanger your quest for educational excellence.

Along with the programmed funding, the Recovery Act also created new competitive opportunities for schools, districts, and local education associations. The competitive programs tend to require significantly more work and a compelling reason to award the applicant. Typically, the competitive programs also require support documents, evidence of planning, demonstrated need, and a clear plan whose implementation will address the identified need.

The Recovery Act competitive programs announced to date for schools, districts, and local education associations have tended to emphasize cooperation and evidence of collaboration. Many have targeted high-need populations, such as Native Americans, Latinos, rural or urban districts, and low-income individuals. The targeted nature of the Act means that the competitive programs are not likely to fund general operations or ongoing programs.

An obvious caveat to the above statement is that few people can accurately predict what the Federal Government will do, and the next round of funding opportunities may contradict the trends observed to date. Therefore, we recommend monitoring the Federal Registrar and signing up for email notifications of new grant opportunities. Grant writing does demand capacity, but there are opportunities to contract for services.

Worth noting here under the discussion of grant writing is that federal law prohibits using grant funds to pay for activities already completed. Therefore, a grant recipient cannot use grant funds to pay for the grant writer, unless specifically allowed. Likewise, federal funds cannot usually be used to pay down debt or reimburse expenses already incurred.

As stated above, the Recovery Act represents a unique event in federal funding, and districts able or willing to experiment with new approaches may well find this an ideal opportunity. Furthermore, Recovery Act grant programs have thus far, tended to require less. Whereas a traditional program for transitional housing, for example, required a thirty-page narrative, the Recovery Act has seen those requirements shrink to fifteen pages. Recovery Act programs have also tended to not require the use of online submission systems that are, in our judgment, cumbersome and needlessly difficult.

To summarize, given the unprecedented expenditure of funds, we recommend that districts do the following.

- Inventory needs, priorities, opportunities within the district or school
- Be prepared to act if an opportunity presents itself
- Register on www.Grants.gov to receive notifications of funding availability (NOFA)
- Review past grant guidelines to identify information and paperwork necessary for submissions. For example, does the district have a negotiated "indirect funds rate?" If so, that agreement needs to be scanned in and available for submission.
- Have approval process ready for submission of an appropriate grant. Recovery Act programs have had a shorter than normal "open" period, so be ready.
- Check Department of Education website for grant notices, as well as other relevant federal agency websites.
- Pay attention to the number of expected awards. If there is only one award expected, it is probably an earmark and as good as dedicated to someone else. Do not waste time and resources on these opportunities.
- Lastly, if you do not submit an application, it will not be funded. Many other districts or schools will not be positioned to take advantage of the opportunities so be prepared to be the one that does.

Grants

Funding excellent schools must be about more than government spending. Alternatives to government funding are regrettably few, and those that do exist tend to be available to districts with lower socio-economic residents. When most people in non-profit enterprises think about funding, and schools certainly are non-profits by any logical definition, they turn to "grants." The reasons for this reaction are based on history and the fact that private foundations and government agencies do indeed provide grant funds for many different purposes.

Unfortunately, grant funding is inherently unreliable, based on appropriations and the subjective scoring of evaluators. Another practical factor is that grant funding comes with performance and reporting strings. Moreover, writing a grant is a time consuming exercise that has no guarantee of success. Between them, the authors have written more than a hundred federal grants. US Department of Education grants may well be the most difficult, convoluted, and redundant of all. Even without the need to keep up with and parrot the current acronyms and jargon, the DOE grants are a challenge.

Of course, a school seeking grant funds is not limited to Department of Education funding, depending on the purpose of the grant. A school wishing to start a science program around the creation of biodiesel, for example, may have opportunities to seek funds from the Department of Energy, or the National Science Foundation. Similarly, vocational programs may seek funding from Housing and Urban Development, or others.

Most states are home to private foundations and many support innovative educational initiatives. The challenge with such support is the question of sustainability, but for a school wishing to experiment with new approaches, private foundations are a good potential source of funding for the short term.

Businesses and Local Funding

Ultimately, the best source of funding for a school, other than state allocations is the local community. The people of a community can support schools in many ways, not just by voting for bond measures. Tapping these funds has been a long-lived focus of many districts, but they tend to emphasize sponsorships for events and purchasing equipment. These are necessary, but they do not go as far as a district should.

Throughout most American school districts there are local representatives of large corporations. Most corporations have corporate giving programs or grant programs. Access to the funding comes via the local manager, and many times the local manager is unaware of the opportunity. Banks, tire dealers, retail operations, and beverage distributors are all potential sources of funding. The funds are likely to be modest, a few thousand dollars; however, consistent requests and gifts can add up and make a real difference.

Endowments

A frequently overlooked potential source of funding is the endowment and legacy gifts. Institutions of higher education make extensive use of endowments and they actively build them. Colleges and universities do solicit endowment funding in annual campaigns, but the most fruitful approach for many is to target the estate planning process and being "remembered" in wills. There is no reason that local school districts cannot take the same approach.

Targeting legacy gifts is fairly easy and straightforward and does not require as much work as it might seem. Instead, a district needs to do two things:

1. Be committed to the goal of building an endowment and give it consistent emphasis;
   a. Create a concise case for support
   b. Develop a simple brochure
   c. Distribute the brochure and solicitation to the district and alumni homes at least once a year
   d. Publicize the results of a growing endowment to keep it relevant and in peoples' minds
   e. Make the endowment part of a strategic plan aimed at developing a measure of self sufficiency for the district.
2. Take the campaign to every funeral home, attorney, CPA, and estate planner in the district and discuss the goals and purpose;
   a. Revisit funeral homes, attorneys, CPAs, and planners on a regular basis

The reason for focusing on funeral homes, attorneys, CPAs, and estate planners is that they are the people in the position to advise individuals about memorials, trusts, and disposing of assets.

The variations are almost endless when it comes to the specifics about how those gifts are names or used. A person could endow a teaching position such as the "Trani-Irvine Science Teaching Chair," if they wished. A person could endow the library, a sports team, or just about anything that he or she desired. The upshot for the school is that a position or activity would be funded independently, thereby providing significant budget flexibility.

Other

Anyone with even a modicum of experience with schools will quickly be able to think of fundraisers that they have seen. Some work, some do not, but almost all schools attempt them. The list of foci invariably includes: bake sales, car washes, spaghetti feeds, "something" a-thon, art sales/ auctions, can drives, or pledge drives.

These are all good approaches and we have only two thoughts. First, there should be a minimal return on investment to justify the work that goes into such an effort. Spending $900 worth of staff resources plus volunteer hours to make $1,000 does not seem like a good investment. Second, the fundraiser should fit the community and the school.

Aside: For years, Corbett Elementary used a walk-a-thon to raise funds and kids sought pledges, with individual awards or incentives for kids who raised a certain level of pledges. The event yielded modest results and was popular and consistent.

When Randy arrived as the principal, he convinced the PTA to make one change. That change was to eliminate the stepped incentives for raising pledges and replace it with the following incentive. At each grade level, the student who raised the most money from the class that raised the most money was allowed to throw a pie in the face of the principal.

With this one change, the fundraiser netted three times the amount that it had in the past. The moral is that the incentives need to be a valuable reward for the recipients and must mean something. In this case, the chance to hit the principal in the face with a pie was much more motivating than was the chance to win a toy, a book, or a certificate.

Furthermore, it was less expensive for the school, helping to increase the net, as the aggregate cost of the stepped incentives previously used to motivate students was much more than the cost of a dozen cream pies.

Finally, people who give to schools do so with the awareness that as taxpayers they already give. Making the school a personal investment requires communication and a willingness to listen the community. As any good manager knows, often all anybody wants is the sure and certain knowledge he or she has been heard. The political equivalent is the cynical phrase "I feel your pain," but it is no less true for the cynicism. Developing such funding requires people to feel connected to and invested in their local schools, and nothing helps this so much as being an excellent school.

Chapter 11

Preventing Excellence: Bandaging Self-Inflicted Wounds

After ten chapters, we thought that most readers probably expect to find some discussion of incorporating current or vogue reforms into an excellent school. This would let us collaborate with other people trying to sell a reform and maybe increase sales. However, this is not to be; we believe that most of the reforms and "new" programs are simply bandages on self-inflicted wounds.

As the two authors are themselves slow learners at even the best of times, we recognize the need to be able to adroitly bandage self-inflicted wounds, lest we hemorrhage and bleed to death. Nonetheless, in the end we came to understand that a more successful approach and certainly one that is less messy is to quit inflicting those wounds on ourselves. We think the lesson applies to a larger realm than just our carpentry.

We certainly understand how attractive bandages are, especially for single individuals or small groups. A teacher can certainly identify the flood of problems associated with alienation of students in a large school, where many are unknown, and can create a mentoring program to combat the problem. In this case, the lone teacher is doing all he or she can do in the face of the overwhelming cataract of estrangement and isolation in a school with thousands of students.

Unfortunately, the mentoring program can reach only a handful of students at best and it does nothing to address the underlying problem. Understandably, this lone teacher may well decide that it is better to do something and help some students, rather than expend the same energy fighting the administration and school board to make fundamental changes to the structure of a school.

As much as we sympathize with this hypothetical teacher—and who would not sympathize with that teacher?—we believe that district and school resources focused on such a program are ultimately wasted. The bandages are fine, but meaningful change requires a cessation of hostilities; as a district and a society we must quit inflicting wounds on our educational process.

By insisting on building large schools and remaining focused on grade levels as well as curriculums rather than students, American education is nothing short of a danger to itself and others. We believe that the situation warrants intervention, quickly and decisively.

As we hinted above, the two basic and oft repeated self-inflicted wounds facing American education are large schools and the insistence that schools focus on grade levels as well as curriculum-based education.

> *Aside: We should stop here and note that our assumption continues to be that the point of having a school is to educate students as well as possible. We were occasionally reminded that not everyone shares this assumption.*
>
> *Recently, Randy attended a conference of principals from throughout the United States. As he is wont to do, he extolled the virtues of small schools and focusing on individual students. Finally, a principal from a large southern state stood up and said: "you have to have at least 2,000 students in a high school; otherwise how can you field 22 excellent ones for a football team?" The question was met with applause and Randy slumped, silenced, at least momentarily, but not defeated.*
>
> *For those of you who are more focused on football than education, we wanted to include something radical but well researched to make the purchase price worthwhile. Therefore, we point you to the thoughtful and cogent arguments advanced by Brookings Institute Fellow, Gregg Easterbrook.*
>
> *Mr. Easterbrook argues in his column "Tuesday Morning Quarterback" that teams would be better off going for it on 4th down rather than punting. He cites voluminous research to back up his arguments, but we have not followed his footnotes much further than that. However, if we wind up coaching another football team, we intend to eschew the punt and think you should too.*

We realize that ascribing a bulk of the current jargon and reforms to nothing more than bandages is a strong argument, but we think that a thoughtful look at the bulk of the trends and reforms will support our contention.

The discussion that follows is not exhaustive. Further, there are countless permutations to each of the types of reforms. Were we so inclined and if the reader were willing to endure it, we could go on for hundreds of pages, but we are confident that most readers will grasp the central argument and only continue on to other sources if they are determined to prove us wrong. Our purpose here is to identify the major types of reforms and to discuss why we think they distract schools from encouraging excellence, rather than supporting it.

PULLOUT PROGRAMS: INCLUDING
TAG AND SPED PROGRAMS

Perhaps one of the longest-lived types of programs aimed at addressing the inherent failings of the traditional grade-level approach to education are the pullout programs. These programs identify students for whom the regular classroom is moving either too quickly or too slowly.

Pullout programs are disruptive and reactionary; they attempt to improve things by removing the students who are a "problem" rather than addressing the basic educational approach. By definition, programs that remove students from their assigned grade level to accelerate or slow the curriculums are curriculum and grade-level focused.

A better way to address the needs of students is to adopt a looping continuous-progress model. With a continuous-progress model, there is no need to pull kids out of a class, because they are already getting an individualized education program. With an excellent teacher paired for as long as possible with no more than twenty-four students, the teacher has the ability to know his or her students and to adjust the educational process to meet their individual needs.

This is a much superior approach compared to segregating students by their performance relative to an arbitrary benchmark set by grade level. Ultimately, pullout programs devolve into individual education programs—and why not give every student the benefit of this approach?

Not only are pullout programs reactionary and homogenizing, they highlight the "otherness" of the participants. For good or ill, the message that pullout programs send is that the students are different. This highlighting of otherness fosters either elitism or defeatism, neither of which is good for the individual students or the class as a whole. Heterogeneous classes create the best environment, and this means heterogeneous by race, ethnicity, sex, culture, socio-economic status, and ability.

If a school were not married to grade level instruction, curriculum, and assessment, it would not need to pull children out of their classrooms and disrupt the educational environment. How can pulling children out of a classroom be good for them and their classmates? To state what must be obvious by now, we do not think it is a good idea. In sum, pullout programs are nothing short of a self-inflicted wound caused by the insistence that schools have to be focused on grade level and prescribed curriculums.

We would like to be clear on one point: pullout programs are better than leaving children in a class in which they are either bored or hopelessly behind. Again, the tyranny of averages is imposed by a curriculum-centered education.

As discussed earlier, teaching at the average student may mean that a teacher really aimed at nothing. The circumstance is reminiscent of the old joke about how at one time the average family once had 1.7 cars and that 0.7 of a car sure was tough to drive. Well, in this case try finding an average family. Nobody really had 1.7 cars, and in the same way, there may be no average student.

Our question then is why bother to construct an educational system around a student who does not even exist. To free schools and, more importantly, students from the tyranny of averages, we as a society must insist on addressing the core problem, rather than bandaging the wound by operating pullout programs.

Tracking

Tracking Programs are related to SPED and TAG programs in their impact and the wounds that they are created to salve. In short, tracking programs work to identify students who are working below or above grade level. These students are then treated specially. The net result is to pull kids out of their classes and to homogenize the learning environment for everyone. Kids doing better in a subject are grouped with like performers, while kids deemed behind are lumped together, and the middle kids are anointed as the norm and get the least attention.

Tracking requires a curriculum-focused learning environment and does not make sense without it. With a student focus, all students are essentially "tracked" but they are not removed; instead they are kept in a heterogeneous classroom, which is the most effective learning environment. A student-focused approach further allows for differential progress by individual students; sometimes students make tremendous progress and then slow down. Other students may be great at math but progress more slowly in reading. A curriculum-centered approach that tracks students does not adjust well to these real-life occurrences.

THE INDIVIDUAL WITH DISABILITIES EDUCATION ACT (IDEA)

If ever there were a high profile and expensive bandage created to staunch the flow of blood from the self-inflicted wound of a grade-level and curriculum-centered educational environment, this is it. The act is manifestly the result of legislatures trying to mitigate the disastrous impact of curriculums and grade levels on students who wind up the farthest behind the proscribed norm.

According to the National Resource Center on AD/HD, a service of CHADD (Children and Adults with Attention Deficit / Hyperactivity Disorder), the purpose of IDEA is as follows:

> The Individuals with Disabilities Education Act (IDEA) is a federal law enacted in 1990 and reauthorized in 1997. It is designed to protect the rights of students with disabilities by ensuring that everyone receives a *free appropriate public education* (FAPE), regardless of ability. Furthermore, IDEA strives not only to grant equal access to students with disabilities, but also to provide additional special education services and procedural safeguards.[1]

Manifestly, the purported benefits of IDEA are aligned with those of a continuous-progress model. Instead of changing the foundation of schools, the legislation scabs additional structure onto the traditional approach. Rather than fix the problem, IDEA creates new bureaucracy, new reporting requirements, and additional administration. The intent is noble, but the results shift resources away from the classroom, homogenize the learning environment, and work against creating an excellent school.

Trust us, no school, excellent or otherwise, has people standing around wishing they had more paperwork to do. Every new piece of legislation adds to the administrative burden for schools, and ultimately we do not think that this is helpful.

If anything, IDEA and the arguments for it support our contention that there is a fundamental problem with the grade-level approach. Obviously, IDEA exists to fix at least one of those problems, namely that some students are left behind, but it does not address the reason that kids are left behind. The problem lies with the fact that some students are left behind from the beginning, precisely because grade level inflicts the tyranny of the average on all kids.

The grade-level approach works fine for the average child, if such an animal exists, but those on either side of the bell curve are poorly served. Rather than adopt expensive, sometimes random, bureaucratic and top-heavy bandages, schools and society would be better off stopping the infliction of the wound of grade level on itself.

RESPONSE TO INTERVENTION/ACADEMIC INTERVENTION SERVICES

In the eastern part of the country, the vocabulary and dominant acronym is AIS or Academic Intervention Services. The same idea in the western part of the nation is deemed RTI or Response to Intervention. These programs are another bandage slapped on the educational system to stop the academic bleeding caused by a fixation on grade-level and curriculum-based learning.

A school or district uses the RTI or AIS approach when a student is failing, or appears to be headed in that direction. The approaches place a premium on documenting special intervention attempts that did not work to bring the student up to grade level. Ideally the intervention works. A teacher may decide to take better notes, seek additional resources from a specialist, or create a behavior modification plan. However, when it does not work, the RTI or AIS approach leads to a SPED designation for the student and all of the problems associated with that designation that are discussed above.

ADVISING AND COUNSELING PROGRAMS

Most, if not all, advising programs are built around the idea that students need specialized attention to address some issue or idea. The assumption is that no teacher knows the student well enough, or has the training to provide such oversight.

We think this poppycock is the direct result of a big school, in which students are allowed to become anonymous, or struggle because of a focus on grade level to the detriment of the individual students. While both conditions lead to the adoption of advising or counseling programs, pure bigness tends to be the more prevalent culprit. Consequently, such programs become more prevalent as students get older and schools get larger.

From our perspective, one of the most frustrating phenomenons is the adoption of these bandages by small schools that ought to know better. The popularity and widespread use of advising and counseling programs has resulted in their proliferation, regardless of the true need for them. Indeed, from what is available in the literature, schools seem to adopt the programs because other schools have.

Certainly, in an ideal world, with unlimited resources, schools could employ dozens of specialists to counsel students in a number of areas. However, as we are confined to a world where hard choices have to be made, we see advising and counseling programs as bandages on the injuries caused by big schools where students are known to no one.

To be fair, small schools also manage to inflict wounds from a strict adherence to a grade-level, curriculum-centered approach that advising and counseling can bandage. However, the bandages are always more expensive and less effective than a concerted attempt to fix the underlying problem, which speaks to the fundamental environment in a school.

For those schools in need of a bandage, there are many fine programs; no doubt much thought went into conceptualization of each one. Unfortunately, they are what they are: namely advisory programs that attempt to solve the problem of anonymous students at big schools, whereas we believe a school ought to solve the underlying problem instead.

Wise authors might pause here to remind the readers that we are generally quite fond of counselors and think they do good and valuable work. Authors more circumspect than we are might not have said anything so provocative. Authors more concerned about agreement would certainly not court the inevitable criticisms that will come with the assertion that counselors and advisors are bandages on self-inflicted wounds. While we may be neither wise nor circumspect, we do want to point out that the counselors do not inflict the wounds.

We are not arguing counselors do harm, only that the resources would be better employed elsewhere. Indeed, counselors and advisors can be effective bandages and they have made a real difference in the lives of thousands of individuals. Nonetheless, we continue to insist that the resources spent on counseling and advising students would be better spent on teachers and on creating a supportive, student-centered environment in which students are able to focus and learn.

Obviously, no excellent school can overcome profound problems at home, or serious mental health issues. At the same time, no school counselor is going to do that either. A school counselor therefore often becomes a referral specialist, and this is a job that teachers could do as well.

Remember, we believe it is imperative that communities, districts, and schools face up to the hard choices that come with operating schools. Too many schools make decisions by going with the norm. The norm is to hire advisors and counselors and, not surprisingly, the norm produces average results. Creating an excellent school requires doing more, especially facing up to the unpleasant realities that programs such as advising and counseling have become ensconced despite the fact that they divert resources from the classroom and the core purpose of a school.

As a lone concession, we are prepared to agree that counseling may be an appropriate service for ESDs to offer, primarily in a consulting capacity. When faced with extreme conditions and a need to respond according to best practices as well as legal requirements, a mental health counselor may be in order. The reference to legal counsel is deliberate, as every school district has need of legal counsel, but that does not mean they employ a lawyer full time; they buy one when needed and get along just fine most of the time without one.

The same is true for other types of counselors and advisors. They would be nice to have on hand, but they divert scarce resources away from where they are most needed, namely to perform the primary function of a school: to educate students. Indeed, we recognize that there is a teaching component of what counselors do, but teachers should be able to perform that role.

FORECASTING AND STUDENT SCHEDULING

At some point every year, middle and high schools have to decide which classes each student will take the following term or year. The most common approach is to ask students what they want to take and then forecast forward what classes need to be scheduled and what teachers are needed.

This approach also leads to a free-for-all approach to cafeteria scheduling, where students vie to get into certain classes. This approach is manifestly both a bandage and yet another self-inflicted wound; further it even looks like one when it takes place. We think it is remarkable that students are allowed to make these decisions. In our experience, high school students only occasionally make decisions based on educational considerations and certainly not for the good of the whole.

Using forecasting and self-scheduling on the part of students is a strategy that big schools must employ, because nobody knows the students well enough to do anything different. Of course, student preferences should be figured into the mix of scheduling, but it is the responsibility of the schools to ensure that each child receives a solid education. Letting students avoid, opt out, or just skirt specific classes leads invariably to mediocre performance. We believe it is far better to challenge students and to have high expectations.

Significantly, we know that such an approach can work. Falling back to our ready example of Corbett, students do not schedule themselves and all high school students take Advance Placement (AP) classes. No one has been left behind using this strategy; instead students have been motivated to meet the higher standards, and along the way young people who would never have voluntarily taken AP classes find themselves passing AP tests and earning college credit. The powerful lessons are not lost on the students or their parents who come to better recognize ability and the rewards of hard work.

Scheduling students, as opposed to allowing self-scheduling is only possible with small schools. At Corbett a single administrator does the scheduling, therefore a single matrix can suffice. Large schools cannot do this, and in response, they inflict a sizeable wound on themselves and ultimately encourage average performance.

MINING DATA TO INFORM INSTRUCTION

Like so many trends and reforms in education, this idea "mining data to inform instruction" has a great title; it is catchy and seemingly scientific. Who indeed could be against informing instruction with data? Arguing against it would seem to be advocating ignoring data, relying on dogma and random methods. As dynamic and progressive as the title might be, we think it is nothing more than another dressing, applied to staunch the flow of blood from the self-inflicted wounds of bigness and grade fixation.

The problem with data mining is that it focuses on the aggregate and in so doing relies on understanding the hypothetical "average" student at any one point in a grade or curriculum. Moreover, the data is lagged; information about the seventh grade class one year is used to inform the instruction of the seventh grade class the next year.

Mining data to inform instruction is a fine idea given the givens; it is a good bandage for schools that do not know enough about the specific students to use individual data to inform instruction. However, we cannot help but wonder if this is the way that society or an individual community wants to proceed? Why not skip the mining process and focus on individual students and their needs, rather than trying to apply what happened last year to a different bunch of kids to this year's crop?

Take the approach of mining data to inform instruction to the medical field. Does anyone want their doctor to treat them as an average patient, with the average cough, or do they want to be examined individually and treated based on their particular condition? Does anyone want to be treated for the most common problem last year, or have the medical regime predetermined based on what worked for last year's aggregate of patients?

We think that people want to be examined individually and, by extension, we think that it makes much more sense to look at the specific needs of a student, rather than a group of students. Again, this is only possible when students are precisely that: individuals who have specific strengths, weaknesses, needs, and preferences, known to their educators.

To be fair to the champions of data mining, simply having a small school is not enough to offset the attractions of this approach. No, an excellent school will take advantage of its smallness to keep students and teachers together for as long as possible and it will foster long-term relationships so that students are known to the faculty and administration.

By using the approaches discussed earlier to teach elementary school, middle school, and high school we believe we have eliminated the need for data mining to inform instruction. In an excellent school, teachers that needs to know the test scores of their students in order to know what to do are poor teachers. Similarly, a school that only knows how it is doing based on test scores is one that is hopelessly out of touch with its students, teachers, and the very purpose of its existence.

Evidence-Based Decision Making

Lest a topical and trendy reform be forgotten, we thought it prudent to include the idea of "evidence-based decision making" as another bandage that became increasingly popular in response to No Child Left Behind. Federal legislation during the Bush Administration has emphasized testing and data gathering and, not surprisingly, school practice has attempted to use the data to direct the application of bandages. Once again, as with data mining, evidence based decision-making focuses on collecting and sharing test data to make decisions about programming and curriculum.

As seemingly rational as it may be to use data to make decisions, the result of evidence-based decision making is to shift the focus away from individual students and toward the collective. In a legislative environment that does not care about progress, only raw test scores, the emphasis in average and mediocre schools, devolves to the aggregate, the mass of kids, and the averages.

An excellent school could undoubtedly make use of evidence-based decision making, but the temptation is to think about the program, the curriculum, and the grade level, rather than the individual students. When this happens, when the focus is on an arbitrary benchmark or average performance, then the results of applying this bandage will be more of the same.

CURRICULUM COORDINATION, CANNED CURRICULUMS, AND CURRICULUM ARTICULATION

At the risk of being accused of flogging a dead horse, again, we believe we must address the proliferation of curriculum-based bandages that various educational reformers tout. The idea behind curriculum coordination or articulation is to ensure a smooth handoff of a curriculum from one teacher to another or from one grade to another or from one school in a district to another.

As an aside here, two different reviewers read the last sentence and tried to correct us, "surely you mean to "ensure a smooth handoff of the student from one teacher to another," the readers remarked. If only it were so, no we mean exactly what we have written, the coordination is focused on curriculum; the individual student is almost irrelevant except to the degree that they constitute the vessel for the curriculum to be handed off.

At some level, this coordination might make sense. For example, take the case of Johnny, a third-grader who transfers from George Washington Elementary to Abraham Lincoln Elementary in a district. Curriculum coordination means that Johnny should be able do this without missing anything; his new teacher would know what he has done and where he is supposed to be in his studies in every subject, and his education might not suffer from the move.

As helpful as curriculum coordination sounds in the above example, the problem is that the district is concerned with the curriculum, not the student. Furthermore, the emphasis on curriculum requires that Johnny be at exactly the same place as every student in his class and at the exact same place as every third grader in the entire district.

We just do not think this is likely or reflective of reality. Anybody with experience in a third grade class knows that there is no way twenty or thirty kids will be at the same place. Even if they were, by some small miracle, all at the same place, they would not be moving at the same pace.

Curriculum coordination and articulation ultimately takes as its core assumption a practical impossibility. The reason that this approach continues to be used is that in a big school, there may appear to be no other option and it has the happy result of making the district appear to be using the best and newest approaches to managing education. Unfortunately, managing education takes resources away from actually providing it.

Prepared Programs—Reading, Math, and Others

Just as curriculums tell teachers and schools what to teach, districts and schools frequently adopt reading programs, usually offered by a major publisher. There are many such programs with which we are familiar, but legal counsel advises against naming names. In the abstract, the programs may be a good idea and fit a need, but as with any curriculum or grade-centered approach, following the program tends to become the goal, rather than educating students.

We have heard teachers say in essence, "I'm sorry that Jane is bored and reading below her level, but this is the program." Certainly, anything taken to the extreme becomes ridiculous, but truly, why let the curriculum or prepared program dictate to the teacher and the student? We think that a student's needs and a teacher's resources should guide the educational process, not a lesson concocted in New York to instruct every student in Texas.

One last thought on prepared programs, for this section at least. Excellent teachers are almost universally creative, adaptive, and proactive. Prepared programs and canned curriculums tend to stifle these abilities and turn the teacher into an assembly line worker, passing out the next assignment on cue.

POSITIVE BEHAVIOR SUPPORT (PBS) AND POSITIVE BEHAVIOR INTERVENTION SUPPORT (PBIS)

These two programs, PBS and PBIS, are emblematic of a larger group of behavior management strategies used in schools, especially at the grade school level. Programs such as these focus on tangible rewards for performance. For example, children might receive an eraser for every book they read, or the class may get an ice cream party when everyone completes enough read-at-home tally sheets. The roots of these programs reach back to B.F. Skinner and are based on "Behaviorism."

How can anyone be against rewarding desired behavior?—a thoughtful reader may ask, and our answer is that the programs are used as bandages and what is more they are poorly applied.

Behaviorism in its classic form focuses on incentives and disincentives that an individual finds "rewarding" or "punishing." Programs, such as PBS or PBIS treat all kids in a class or a school the same, as if an award eraser or pencil is not just desirable to all students, but equally desirable. Anyone with two children knows that oftentimes what is punishment for one child is blessed reward to another. Send one child to their room and it is agony, send the second child to their room and it is a relief.

As with so many of the bandages discussed in this chapter, most schools apply programs such as PBS far too universally to be effective and the results are haphazard at best. Far better, we think, to know the children and apply rewards and punishments in a way that has personal meaning. Even better, find ways to encourage intrinsic motivation within each student so that he or she learns for the sake of discovery, interest, and joy, rather than for an eraser or a pencil.

We suppose an aside of some sort is in order here. There is a strong under-current in American education today that stresses self esteem and not doing anything to damage it. One of the manifestations of this concern is a dogged insistence that all children be treated equally. Hence, behavior programs such as PBS or PBIS are doggedly consistent in terms of incentives for each child.

We will be the last to argue for discrimination and unjust treatment, but truly, schools must be able to respond to the needs of individual children. Just as a great carpenter uses more than one tool, an excellent school and teacher must be able to use the appropriate tool as well.

On this same topic of "self esteem," there is a burgeoning movement that argues that society has taken the idea of self-esteem development too far. Consequently, the argument goes, we now have a generation of indulged young people who would have been better served knowing that they are not all that special, or that everyone else is just as special.

Dr. Dan Kindlon at Harvard University is one of the leading proponents of the idea that young people are in danger of being over-indulged. Indeed, one of Dr. Kindlon's books "Too Much of a Good Thing," argues that well-intentioned parents are too generous with material possessions and allow too much freedom, creating unrealistically high expectations for performance.

The book The Over-Scheduled Child, by Dr. Alvin Rosenfeld and Nicole Wise also supports this notion. The two argue that "by scrutinizing every detail of how they (their children) look and act, by expecting them all to achieve at a notable level, we are setting them up for a fall—and ourselves for trouble down the road" (Rosenfeld and Wise, 2000, p. 147). Apropos of nothing perhaps, except that an excellent school should focus on intrinsic awards, rather than extrinsic; certainly children will be better served and, likely, so will society.

To return to the point that excellent schools focus on individuals, consider Johnny and Timothy, Johnny loves recess and gym, while Timothy is indifferent about recess, but loves free time in the library.

A competent teacher, to say nothing of an excellent one, knows each student's preferences and uses extra recess time to encourage and reward Johnny, but picks something different for Timothy. This strategy is obvious and yet the adoption of most canned behavior programs discourages this and instead emphasizes treating everyone equally. Once again, the tyranny of averages asserts itself even when it comes to rewards and incentives.

One last point about the PBS and PBIS rendering of behaviorism and its tenants: specifically, their reward schedule is all wrong. One of the many concerns of Behaviorism as an academic and therapeutic approach is the identification of a reward schedule. From B.F. Skinner to the present, much effort has gone into researching the most effective reward schedules and by all accounts, the "intermittent-random" reward schedule produces the best results.

Unfortunately, as most behavioral systems used by schools employ incentives that are regular and predetermined, and a student can decide whether or not to get them. For example, in one program if students reads a book, they get a "golden horseshoe" and when they have read twenty they get a pencil. Nothing in this approach is random, nothing is intermittent, and nothing is intrinsic.

Questioning Rewards and Incentives

At a more fundamental level, we believe that the application of a reward-based system for education is dubious. We think that ultimately reading, math, and learning must be their own reward. Purely extrinsic rewards will ultimately break down and learning will only take place when the student wants and values the external reward.

We think that if Caitlin reads books only to get an eraser, then it would seem that someone has failed. Moreover, if Caitlin already reads voraciously the eraser will not mean much because it is easy to get, while poor Jennifer who struggles to read may decide, "Who wants a stupid eraser anyway?"

"Who wants a stupid eraser anyway," is a fair enough question that eventually most students will answer with the simple, "Not me." We question how well served students are when they learn only to get a tangible award, and we also question how well society is served with that approach. We are not so naïve as to believe that there is no place for extrinsic rewards and that nobody should use them. Everybody uses and responds to extrinsic rewards, and there are plenty of jobs we would not do for $5 but would for $50,000.

We recognize that this can work and that there is a place for extrinsic rewards, but it cannot be the basis for an effective, intellectually consistent educational philosophy. The process of discovery, or learning, of understanding the world around them must be the focus of the educational process. High expectations, not a gimmicky prize or a gold star, will motivate students.

The impact of developmental stages is another important variable that must be calculated when considering rewards and incentives. The development stage of a student affects how a teacher reaches a student and again, not all students in a given grade will be at the same developmental stage.

Clearly, we realize that this is a slippery slope and that all schools wind up creating and giving incentives and prizes. However, an excellent school will carefully construct these programs so that the learning or activity is not done for the sake of the incentive, but for the sake of education and progress. For this reason, we recommend experiential rewards whenever possible that address intrinsic traits, acquired abilities, and honed skills, rather than tangible things or "stuff."

As an aside, to say nothing of being inconsistent and running counter to our own argument, let us pose a challenge. (Remember what Ralph Waldo Emerson said: "A foolish consistency is the hobgoblin of little minds." We would hate to be foolish or be accused of having too little a mind; instead, we are aiming at wise consistency, apropos of nothing we suppose.) Back to our challenge: we would bet at least a dollar that we could cut the high school dropout rate in half or more, and this is what we would do if we were appointed King.

We would institute a $1,500 payment to all high school students for each year in high school that they completed up to four years, with a bonus for a high school diploma. The difference with this challenge compared to more general behavioral programs is that we can state clearly what we want to encourage and propose a direct quid pro quo reward, which we have strong evidence to believe will be of value to those students who are at risk of dropping out of high school.

DEPARTMENT CHAIRS AND OTHER "LEADERS"

Significantly, the self-inflicted wounds caused by big schools not only impact or apply to programs aimed at students, but to teachers as well. One poultice applied to the wound of bigness is the creation of high school disciplinary departments and a department chair. Be it the science department, the English department, the social studies department or math department, each has a chairperson, who reports to an administrator, and likely a vice or assistant principal who in turn reports to the principal.

If a teacher has a problem or an issue, that person goes to the chair, who goes to the vice or assistant person, who goes to the principal. The lanes of communication, the chain of command, or the lines of authority if you prefer, are clear, and everyone knows to whom they can talk. If the teacher tries to talk directly to the vice principal then the chair gets offended and the vice principal probably will get upset too.

This system seems to work fine for the military and it has for centuries. Lieutenants report to commanders who report to captains who report to admirals. The admirals make decisions that they send to the captains for action who detail commanders who give orders to lieutenants who inevitably order around the enlisted personnel. Again, while it works for the military, perhaps it is not the best model for a school and the collaborative learning process.

The difference at a small school cannot be greater; there are no departmental chairs, no team leaders, no chains of command, just teachers and a principal. A principal must necessarily be more available, fewer things get lost in translation, and fewer messages and less information go astray. The biggest thing missing is a chance for promotion.

As we have asked before, which system would you, gentle reader, prefer to work in? By gosh, in a small school students can even access the principal directly. Clearly, creating departmental chairs is a dressing that big schools use to bandage the wounds caused by their very size. At a school with thousands of students, it is impossible for a principal to know all of the teachers, let alone all of the students; consequently, they create a structure to allow the administration to issue orders and collect information without personal relationships.

This strategy creates separation between teachers and the administration, supporting an "us-them" dichotomy that cannot be good. This strategy also adds to the paperwork, bureaucracy, and record-keeping burden with which a school must deal. More layers, more bureaucracy, and more records translate directly into an expense and by definition, this takes resources away from the classroom and the core mission of a school to educate the students. Why would anyone opt for this approach?

Staff Mentoring

A byproduct of the departmental system and big schools are the self-inflicted wounds on new teachers. One way to dress this wound is to create a staff-mentoring program for new teachers. Such programs are necessary, for without them, advocates argue, a new teacher may feel lost or abandoned in the strange new environment. This simply does not happen at a small school; a new teacher stands out and quickly becomes known by everybody. In a small school, the principal is accessible and the teacher is by definition part of a community, rather than a cog in an educational factory.

As with student mentoring discussed below, we find it difficult to believe that mentor relationships can be created by directive any more than we can tell you with whom you must become friends. Time, common experiences, mutual respect, and shared interests are what build relationships, not directives and assignments.

TEACHERS ON SPECIAL ASSIGNMENT

Some schools assign teachers to duties that remove them from the classrooms, designating them "Teachers on Special Assignment." Like everything in education, this practice has an acronym: "TOSA." Many schools embrace the TOSA as a reform that improves education because it theoretically takes the expertise of a teacher and applies it to education-related undertaking, thereby ensuring that the task benefits from the perspective of a teacher.

The list of TOSA duties is long, and what follows is hardly exhaustive, but should give a taste of what types of TOSA assignments exist in the educational world:

- Testing
- Choosing curriculums
- Coordinating curriculums

- Advising
- Academic coaching
- Mentoring new teachers
- Coordinate writing across the curriculum
- Coordinating other activities or approaches across the curriculum
- Creating or leading interdisciplinary teams
- Reading or other subject specialists

Usually we advocate for more teachers, but this practice requires us to qualify our admonition that teachers need to be in the classroom. Taking teachers out of the classroom is nothing less than taking resources and funding away from the classroom. Moreover, all of these special assignments are all individual band-aids that schools use to respond to the fundamental problems of size and grade level.

SPECIALISTS

Taking teachers out of the classroom and placing them on special assignment or making them specialists destroys relationships and undermines the effort to create an environment to support excellence. Hearken if you will, gentle reader, back to the six secrets discussed in Chapter Three. Secret number one exhorts schools to keep no more than twenty-four students paired with one excellent teacher, and Secret two argues that excellent teachers stay with their students. Creating specialist teachers and TOSAs violates these principles.

Specialists are used almost exclusively in high school, and there are good reasons for this specialization within disciplines, but they are also used in earlier grades with dubious results. Elementary schools may use specialists for physical education, music, reading, and library time among others. Perhaps the one area in which it makes sense is to use specialists to free time for teachers' planning periods.

Certainly, we do not quibble with a music teacher who serves the entire school and frees up planning time for teachers. Beyond this function, specialists fracture relationships and violate the core principles necessary to create an excellent school.

SMALL LEARNING COMMUNITIES

Admittedly, this may be our favorite reform and as an acronym, SLC at least has the virtue of being short and including all of the words in the title. The reason we have some relative like for this reform, is that it tends to reinforce one of the main themes of this work, namely that small schools are a good idea. Small learning centers are a bandage that schools apply to salve the wounds caused by bigness. With the small learning communities, large schools attempt to recreate a small school environment in pursuit of the intrinsic benefits of a small school.

The Schools to Watch Program identifies small learning communities as a "best practice" and advocate the use of such an approach. They report, "Small Learning Communities attempt to create a personalized environment to support each student's intellectual, physical, and ethical needs and development." We concur, indeed we advocate going further. Instead of faking a small school, why not just go ahead and create one? Would you rather pretend you work with people who know and care about you, or would you rather just go be a part of a small company where it is true across the board?

As attractive as small learning communities are as a reform and a method to address the inherent problems of a big school, they are ultimately doomed to failure. If the history of education suggests anything, it is that all trends, be they "small learning communities" or any other good idea, will eventually run their course and be replaced.

This is why it is imperative to address the fundamental structure of schools. Small learning communities need to be built into the nature of the school; in short, the school needs to be small. Otherwise, when administrators change, the budget gets tight, or teachers leave, the small learning communities will collapse. When that happens, they will be replaced with the same old big school, grade level approach that created them in the first place.

Another problem is that small learning communities can only serve a small portion of a big school and they cannot extend the benefits to everyone. This circumstance leads to the question—whose children should be left out? The cynical answer is that the poorer children and those who are behind and could use them the most will be the ones left out and left behind. Why not give every child the benefit of a small learning community? Why not construct and maintain small schools in the first place and obviate the need for expensive solutions and acronyms?

STUDENT MENTORING PROGRAMS

Mentoring programs come in and out of vogue and they are a deceptively easy fix and allow schools to appear to be actively engaged and on the cutting edge. Typically, mentoring programs bring in a person from the community to work with at-risk students on a one-on-one basis. Champions of mentoring programs usually point out that one of the prime selling points is that with a mentoring program, "someone will get to know that student really well and be able to build a relationship with him or her." This sounds to our ears like a bandage applied to bigness.

When a school has to bring in outsiders because none of the staff know a student well enough to build a relationship with him or her, it should be a clear signal to the school that it has a problem internally. As most mentoring programs are configured, they subdivide students and community members ethnically and by gender. This process may be logical, but it does not serve the effort to create a heterogeneous learning environment.

While mentoring programs do offer the chance for students in large schools to build a relationship, most of those relationships are not maintained beyond the school year, and the long-term data on their effectiveness is marginal. Moreover, a mentoring program invariably involves pulling students out of class, and the educational value of this approach is dubious. A mentor may be able to do many things, but it also introduces new variables that schools cannot control.

No matter how carefully a school reviews and checks a mentor, that person is rarely a teacher or trained educator. The mentor's accountability is limited at best and the approach creates new monitoring and oversight responsibilities, diverting resources from the classroom. The potential liabilities from an insurance and management standpoint are monumental, and mentoring programs create an unending need to recruit mentors and to respond to their concerns.

Yet another drawback is that mentoring programs are targeted only to specific students; the majority are left out and at least some programs choose students based on the perceived ability to stick with the program as opposed to those who need it the most. Further, the mentoring program singles out students for something special, highlighting differences and "otherness" that works against the environment that an excellent school must create.

Finally, our experience is that real mentors appear in an individual's life by circumstance, mutual respect, and common interests. Forcing a mentoring relationship seems to be problematic. We know that the Big Brothers and Big Sisters program works to good results in many places, but in this case, it is the sole focus of an entire organization and its training process. We find it difficult to believe that a meaningful friendship or mentoring relationship can reliably be created by fiat simply because a school matches an adult with an at-risk student.

Once again, we think it makes more sense to put resources into cultivating excellent teachers and building relationships between students and teachers. Keep teachers with students for as long as possible, and keep students together with their peers, and thereby create an environment that is mutually supportive of achievement and excellence.

BELLS

Creating an environment that cultivates excellence takes thought and consideration and it must be done carefully and with multiple perspectives. Throughout this book, we have argued for an individualized, student-centered approach and a fundamental attempt to be humane. Loud, intrusive bells that signal the end of one period and the start of another seem to work against the sort of environment that we believe fosters learning.

Certainly, teachers can tell time; we do not think that there is a need to regiment the day to such an extent that it is not possible to finish a lesson, a thought, or even a sentence at a preprogrammed time. In an excellent school, a teacher who consistently holds students too long will hear about it from his or her colleagues and the problem will be self corrected.

Even if the bells were not problematic in and of themselves, they are emblematic of a factory or institutional approach to education that is unhelpful. Who among you, dear readers, would opt to live or work in an environment where the start and end of every activity or time period were marked by a loud, intrusive bell? A few people would perhaps, but not many.

What the bell signals is that whatever is going on in a classroom is not as important as stopping at that instant and going to a pre-arranged "next." Bells become the ultimate authority; programmed and thoughtless, the bells reflect a way of thinking that ultimately deters the creation of an excellent school. Doing away with bells will not make an excellent school, but it will not hurt either, and will eliminate some noise pollution along the way.

SCHOOL-SPONSORED CLUBS

Clubs and extra-curricular activities have a long history in the country and are popular for good reasons. Clubs help kids feel connected to one another and to their schools. Clubs help build a sense of community and they are an ideal bandage to help control the bleeding caused the self-inflicted wound of alienation, abandonment, and isolation of a large school. They work as well as athletics to help inculcate a sense of belonging and connection, but not nearly as well as creating a similar environment throughout an excellent, small school.

This discussion is not advocacy of doing away with clubs. We certainly do not argue that schools should get rid of clubs, only that they are not necessary to create an excellent school. Furthermore, they help students identify or feel connections with a school, but that should be an ancillary benefit, not their only opportunity to do so.

OFF-CAMPUS EDUCATORS

Limited resources are a fact of life for all but the wealthiest schools, and one way that some states and districts have responded to this reality is to make use of community colleges and Internet courses. The popularity of online education notwithstanding, abdicating responsibility for education is not a well thought out or viable long-term solution.

In at least some states, school districts have to pay for community college classes, for example, and in so doing give up a great deal of control and oversight. Moreover, putting students in a community college setting removes them from what should be an excellent learning environment and puts them into a place with a much looser structure where they are unknown. We do not see this as a gain in much of anything.

TEACHER-ACCOUNTABILITY PROGRAMS
AND INITIATIVES

Just as many bandages appear in the form of "carrots" for the proverbial mule, there are others that attempt to employ the "stick." On balance, accountability is more about the stick than anything else. This bandage is a favorite of outsiders and especially legislators, precisely because they see the "bleeding" and recognize the need to fix something; unfortunately the solution is not particularly appropriate.

The attractiveness of holding teachers responsible for student achievement is clear, and we have been arguing to focus on teachers, so a reader might well ask how this could be problematic. The approach is problematic because it is typically a last resort.

The proponents of accountability efforts recognize bleeding is happening and think it is the teacher's fault. They arrive at this conclusion because nobody else knows the kids or understands the circumstances well enough to offer a more sophisticated solution, so this particular bandage is about blame. As a last resort, the bandage becomes a club that is used to threaten teachers to get those students educated "or else."

When it comes time to assess or hold a teacher accountable, there is no good method. Some advocate the crude measurement of looking at the percentage of students that passed a benchmark test. Left out of this equation is any understanding of student progress or even of individual students.

We are much more impressed with teacher #1 who takes low achieving students and brings them close to the benchmark, than teacher #2 who has high achieving students who simply maintain their place. However, with most merit schemes, it is teacher #2, who actually accomplished less but had more students pass the benchmark, who would be rewarded.

The problems for which accountability initiatives are proposed are always complex. However, accountability programs assume that by fixing one thing, one teacher, they can solve the entire problem. Consider that a single teacher may see six different groups of thirty kids in a day; achievement or test scores can hardly be the result of a single teacher. Even a single teacher who has a group of grade school kids has them for just 180 days. How much of the resulting test scores are attributable to that teacher, compared to the scores that the students had the previous year or years?

Aside: We have noticed that it has become fashionable to quote dead Russian authors when it comes to discussing the nature of problems. As far as we can tell, the preference for quoting a Russian is to show off, but only so far as a limited reading will allow. According to these capricious winds of fashion, we believe that it is time to try to make you believe that we actually read Anna Karenina and cite Tolstoy's famous assertion that goes something like: "Happy families are all alike, but unhappy families are all unhappy in their own way." That is an approximation, but should suffice.

By extension, the implication here is that problems in any given school are all unique and no one bandage or solution can address those "special circumstances." Alas, we do not really believe this so much as we think people tend to take the path of least resistance unless they are challenged and rewarded. Yes, there probably are many ways to make an excellent school, but what we have been advocating is the way that we know, and the way that we know works.

In the long run, accountability programs cannot be sophisticated enough to differentiate and quantify the precise contributions or failure of a teacher. This is especially true for efforts that simply focus on student performance on a benchmark test. Consider that a spectacular teacher may help very low-performing students improve remarkably, but not to the point where they pass a test, and a lousy teacher may be lucky enough to have high-achieving kids who do not gain anything from the teacher but pass the benchmarks anyway.

In a similar fashion, a profound problem with teacher accountability efforts is that they needlessly complicate the obvious. Anyone with any sense at all can go to a given school and, within a few days, figure out who is a good teacher and who is not. Students know which teachers are effective and which are not. Other teachers know as well; there is no hiding in front of a classroom, and the challenge is to create an environment that demands excellence and supports it effectively.

As a bandage to the problems with schools, merit pay and teacher accountability also suffers from the problem that it is not clear what problem it is supposed to solve. Is merit pay supposed to address low teacher salaries, is it supposed to improve student performance, is it supposed to attract more students to teaching while in college, or is it a punishment for poor schools? Like the boy with a hammer for whom everything is a nail, teacher accountability is a cudgel of dubious effectiveness, especially when aimed generally, rather than precisely.

Any reader who is still with us at this point should recognize by now that we have been deliberate in our phrasing and our admonitions to hire excellent teachers and support them. Excellent teachers typically support one another, and a good administrator cultivates an environment that encourages teachers sharing resources, helping one another, and providing informal mentoring.

A good administrator also celebrates success, helps motivate teachers, and makes sure they have the tools and resources they need to not just be excellent teachers, but to sustain that excellence and make continual progress, the same as their students.

In short, teacher accountability initiatives are nothing more than an imagined bandage for the self-inflicted wounds of bigness and mediocrity. Accountability would suggest that administrators and school boards had nothing to do with hiring the teachers and providing professional development opportunities and resources. This bandage typically regards teachers as existing in perfect isolation, able to educate or not.

If a school district is insistent on using this salve, then we recommend that administrators, school boards, and legislators likewise be accountable for creating such a system, for hiring teachers that are deemed poor performing, and for creating an environment in which such results were tolerated.

CONCLUSIONS

At last, the chapter comes to a close. We have certainly left out some bandages that schools in the United States use to salve the self-inflicted wounds of bigness and grade level. The permutations of curriculum oversight alone could have filled the chapter. Our point is not to overwhelm you, dear reader, but to help you identify the bandages in which your own schools are swathed.

In the short term, bandages, poultices, dressings, and salves are fine, no individual should wander around bleeding, and neither should an institution. At the same time, schools and districts must stop creating the wounds. To do this, to stop inflicting wounds on our schools, demands fundamental changes to the ways in which schools are conceived of, built, organized, and operated.

To be sure, the current configuration of schools and the education system is the result of good intentions and thought, but we believe that causes and effects are divorced too often and there is a profound disinclination to take a hard look at the underlying problems, and even more so to take the dramatic steps necessary to fix them. The bandages we discussed above demonstrate as much wrong thinking as good design and planning.

To be fair, we do not think that many of the bandages and even the self-inflicted wounds are malicious, but when the system is as imperfect as many schools patently are, we think we would all be better off starting over. It is time to stop adding bandages; instead let us cut the patent out of the layers of corrective systems and start over with deliberate and thoughtful policies and configurations, rather than continuing to patch patches.

NOTE

1. See CHADD website: http://www.help4adhd.org/en/education/rights/idea

Chapter 12

The Future and Thoughts on Trends Toward and Away from Excellence

We have included this chapter as a way to discuss some critical and current debate and discussion that simply did not fit elsewhere. Consequently, what follows is a discussion of federal legislation, state testing behavior, and other challenges that present schools with demands that tend to take the emphasis away from making and sustaining an excellent school.

NO CHILD LEFT BEHIND

The authors have reworked this section several times in an effort to be gentle, careful, and clear. At a minimum, the authors agree that leaving children behind is a bad thing and should be avoided. Indeed, the name of the federal legislation was well chosen and unfortunately, it sometimes appears that more thought went into the name than into its provisions.

Throughout this book, we the authors have argued that resources are always limited and that we as a nation must make hard choices between competing and sometimes equally noble objectives.

Education will always have to struggle about the best way to allocate scarce resources. Unfortunately legislation tends to ignore this fact, as do most of the public discussions. Legislators legislate, and the public demands excellence in language that tends to assume that resources are abundant, and this is never more obvious than when it comes to educating those in the tail ends of the distribution curve. Simply put, we the authors advocate for a clear public discussion and agreement about how to allocate resources.

Consider, for example, a child with cerebral palsy, who will require a full-time aide and other accommodations throughout his or her education. A child such as this may cost over $100,000 per year to educate, compared to the average cost of under $10,000 per pupil.[1] Thus, an average pupil may cost $130,000 to educate from Kindergarten to twelfth grade. A child with cerebral palsy, however, will likely remain in the school system until age twenty-one and cost approximately $1.6 million dollars to the school system.

The last thing that the authors wish to do is to argue for not educating the child with cerebral palsy, and we do not push for warehousing the differentially-abled, but we do believe that the nation needs to make informed decisions.

The ultimate cost-benefit ratio to society for education spending does not need to be calculated precisely to recognize that ultimately the child who cost $1.6 million to educate will likely contribute fewer tax dollars and economic activity than the average child. Again, we are not arguing for anything other than recognizing the implications of our collective education choices. Today, the choices tend to be made by legislators without an apparent understanding of the costs and trade-offs. To put it simply, this is a problem.

The underlying problem with much of the educational legislation and No Child Left Behind in particular is that legislators frequently mandate that money be spent on one purpose or another. Unfortunately, they do not identify a source of funds, nor do they tend to provide those funds. The assumption appears to be that the funds for each new mandate exist. We would be much less critical if each new mandate came with a funding stream, or at least instructions regarding what to cut in order to pay for the new mission.

Percentages

Consider a high school class with nineteen students, two of whom are severe needs special education students. Then ask yourself how likely it is that at least 90 percent of students will make "adequate yearly progress" as defined by the Department of Education? Each student constitutes approximately 5.25 percent of the class, and two are by the nature of their condition mathematically eliminated from reaching the standard. This is but one illustration of the problems of setting arbitrary percentages as goals.

Some may argue that two out of nineteen students being identified as SPED students is painting a picture that is not true. They are correct. It is higher than that! In Oregon, the state assumes that 11 percent of the population will be SPED identified. Furthermore, they assume that this will be the baseline for districts because much effort is expended on providing an avenue for districts to apply for funding above the 11 percent "cap." In fact, most, if not all, of the large districts in Oregon routinely report their SPED identification rates at closer to 15 percent.

One might think that the obvious problem of small classes and small sample sizes would warrant some sort of exemption or application of common sense, reason, or humanity. However, no one who expects such accommodation has faced the overwhelming momentum of a federal bureaucracy.

We believe that the impossibility of small sample sizes is one of the inherent problems with legislation such as "No Child Left Behind." By itself, the problem is not debilitating, but compounded with others, the problem becomes another crippling blow that ultimately destroys the good intent and noble purpose.

Measurements

The federal government and the No Child Left Behind legislation leaves much of the testing and measuring in state hands. Some states opted to set the bars very low, obviating the purpose of the law. These states seem to expect that the legislation will be overturned or eliminated before the magic date when 100 percent achievement is slated to be attained.

Other states, such as Oregon, opted to set the bar high, with standards devised by academics from state universities. In this case, the standards became closer to ideals than real targets for mastery by 100 percent of the population. Indeed, in the 2006–2007 school year, when test scores improved appreciably, the Oregon Department of Education took this as evidence that the tests were too easy.

Stated another way, the State of Oregon identified standards that were to be attained by 100 percent of the high school population and then decided too many people were meeting them. This is inherently self-contradictory, but it certainly did not deter the Oregon Department of Education. This is but one example of the difficulties of measuring achievement. Perhaps even more confusing is that while the states spend millions of dollars on testing standards and measures, they tend to ignore existing tests and fail to connect their tests.

In Oregon, students are tested at the third through eighth and tenth grades. Presumably, nothing important happens after the tenth grade; otherwise they would test for it. (This has changed. Now they test at third, fourth, fifth, sixth, seventh, eighth, and tenth grade. But, they do not test everything at every grade level . . . . and apparently, the case is still that nothing important happens after tenth grade.)

While it is possible to compare a third grade from one year to the next, it is difficult to compare the same student, class, or cohort over time. Surprisingly, the third grade test is only slightly connected to the fifth grade test and so forth. There is no way to tell if a group of students or a single student has improved from one test to the next, for each grade level test stands alone.

We believe, as you probably have figured out, that progress should matter. We believe it is more impressive if a school takes a kid from a score of 170 to 230 in twelve years than it is to take one from 228 to 240. We believe that the gains should be rewarded more than the final score, but that is not the way current legislation figures things and this is a big problem.

Another remarkable fact of the Oregon testing regimen is that passing rates fall as students get older. Apparently, the longer students are in school the worse they do, and their passing rates get worse. Another hypothesis is that teachers get worse, elementary teachers are universally great, high school teachers are lousy, and middle school teachers fall between the two. For the record, the authors believe that the truth can be found in the nonsensical testing handed down from on high.

Despite the convoluted mishmash of data, results, and inferences, the newspapers, newsletters, magazines, and local television news programs dutifully report the test scores as if they made sense or revealed anything. If they do tell us anything, it is probably just how much people like to have scores reported and to simplify complicated things like education into quantified segments.

Again, what is remarkable about the testing methods is that the nation's colleges and universities already have sets of tests that they have used for decades to help them make decisions about admissions. The ACT, SAT, and AP subject tests all provide much more useful data to colleges and universities than the tests devised to meet federal standards. Admittedly, these tests are not useful for identifying achievement by elementary students, but the fact remains that when faced with a need to test, the knee-jerk reaction seems to be to the engineering equivalent of re-inventing the wheel.

Moreover, the reinvention is not merely a one-time event, but an ongoing and expensive attempt to perfect what is by definition a measure, an approximation, a snapshot of attainment at a moment in time that cannot remain static. Call it what you will: "herding cats," "nailing Jell-O to the wall," or some equally evocative image, the upshot is that we, the authors, believe that much of the money spent on creating and revising tests would be better spent actually educating children.

TEACHER EDUCATION AND QUALIFICATIONS

Admittedly, this is a big topic and it probably deserves a book or two, and surely thousands have been written over the years describing how to teach or train a teacher. At the same time, it is instructive to note that there is no reliable method for hiring an excellent one, or determining with certainty who will thrive and who will barely survive or fall below the knives. (We know it is a bad rhyme.) The fact remains, a teaching credential is no guarantee of teaching ability, and it is not particularly a great predictor of effectiveness.

Some states, jurisdictions, and districts have made provisions to allow for teachers who do not have teaching credentials. These exceptions are typically reserved for specialists at the high school level. For example, an engineer may be able to teach math, a chemist may be allowed to teach chemistry. In general, these efforts make sense; why not try hiring competent professionals who know their topic to teach what they know? This is what colleges and universities do.

Almost no college or university professors have any formal education in being an instructor; they know their topic, and away they go. That being said, if you hire a competent chemist or engineer and they cannot teach, they need to be removed.

Certainly, there are advantages to classes in pedagogy. Understanding the ways people learn and the art of teaching should contribute to creating better teachers. On the other hand, there are so many more factors and traits that contribute to creating an excellent teacher that it may be time to consider embracing people with expertise and relevant experience who seek to teach mid-life or to switch careers.

NOTE

1. The average cost per student varies considerably across the nation and within states. The figure used here for illustrative purposes is relatively low, but reasonable, and the authors can point to several places in the United States where it fits. The cost for educating a child with cerebral palsy likewise varies considerably based on many factors including individual circumstances, but again, is a defensible figure based on known cases.

Chapter 13

How to Create an Excellent School if You Are a: Parent, Teacher, Student, Administrator, or School Board Member

After the last twelve chapters, we concede that we may be on the verge of overwhelming some readers with bad news. The list of the things that American schools should start or stop doing is discouragingly long, and we have tried to be precise and to demonstrate our points. Of course, we hope we have made our points convincingly, but one additional result may be that we have painted a disheartening picture. Now that we are drawing toward the end, we thought it important to buoy spirits and point to the ways that individuals can make a difference, and how things can be improved.

Truly, if things could not be improved, we would not have dragged you this far. However, things can be improved and improved dramatically, which is why we have worked to point out better ways to organize schools and strategies that a concerned school can adopt to produce better results.

Our purpose is to demonstrate what can work and why districts and schools should change their methods and approach. We would have preferred to find a magic potion or formula, since that would be much easier to implement, and we could probably sell it for a handsome price too. Alas, we can only point you to hard, albeit honest work, and strategies that are demonstrably better and more logical than those employed by most schools.

As we look back at the previous chapters and survey the ground that we have covered, several things became apparent to us. First, the list of what could be done and what specific people could do varies considerably by their role and their relationship to the schools. When it comes to adopting our recommendations, different people in different positions have advantages over others.

Administrators, including superintendents and principals undoubtedly yield the most influence and have the greatest freedom to take our advice.

However, they cannot, or should not act without support and consent. In our experience, leading by fiat works best in times of crisis and is never as effective as leading by consensus.

Some might reasonably argue that American schools are in crisis now. Even if American schools are not in crisis, we certainly think there is an urgent need to act now. However, we do think there is a crisis, one that is now so long-lived that it might be arguably called status quo. The upshot of these observations is that there is much that anyone with an interest in, or commitment to, education can do to move their schools and district toward excellence.

EDUCATE YOURSELF—OR IF YOU PREFER BIG WORDS: BE AUTODIDACTIC

First, anyone interested in creating an excellent school must be willing to learn and advocate. The initial step must be education for you, coupled with a commitment to keep learning. We appreciate past accomplishments and credentials, but we are much more impressed with ongoing learning, and it may well be that new research and practice will refine or replace some of the methods we advocate here.

Regardless, if as an advocate you are going to convince the rest of the interested community to change, you will have to provide (1) a good reason, (2) compelling evidence that there is a need for the change and that the proposed pathway will work and (3) a pathway. Consequently, a person must understand not only what should be done, but also what is currently happening within a school or district.

Nothing is so easy to dismiss as an ignorant reformer. Imagine a person trying to convince a school that it needs to change without knowing what is actually happening. Anyone wishing to create an excellent school must be informed and understand the environment, limitations, and restrictions within which a school operates.

There are some positions from which it will be easier to advocate; teachers, for example, will have a good understanding of what a school does. Students, too, should have a unique perspective and understanding. Regardless, before launching a protracted campaign to encourage excellence, a concerned citizen, teacher, or parent needs to understand the unique pressures and challenges their schools face.

We strongly recommend that people secure a copy of the school and district budget and understand the funding streams. Similarly, it is impossible to change what a school does without considering legislative mandates. Some schools also operate under court mandates, which may bear heavily on what is and is not possible. Someone pushing change without understanding these mandates will likely be dismissed as ignorant, and for good reason.

BE AN ADVOCATE

If we the authors can claim expertise in only one field, it must be in the field of being wrong. We freely admit to two lifetimes of fieldwork in figuring out what will not work and ways to not get things done. We have variously proven that engines without fuel will not run, that wet matches and wet wood will not make a fire, that reservations would have been a good idea, that whatever it was that we said was the wrong thing to say, and that not just "any" fool can assemble that thing.

We think that our credentials when it comes to being wrong are exemplary and, compared to the average person, we have as much or more experience in being wrong. In fact, our biggest fear is that we have been doing it again with you, gentle reader. With our error credentials established, we can safely say that if you want someone to listen to you and follow your advice, then telling them that they are messing up and that they should listen to you is not a good strategy.

In our experience, this approach just creates another problem, barrier, and obstacle. Notably, the effect seems to be the same for men and women, children and adults, the wise and foolish, as well as the people who already know they are screwing up and those who do not.

When advocating for an excellent school it is instructive to remember the old business school admonishment that "nobody will care what you know until they know that you care." Of course, there are exceptions, but if anyone really does want to help a school become excellent, he or she must do so in a collaborative, cooperative fashion. The permutations may be many, but ultimately, an advocate for change has to win the school and the teachers over; otherwise they will sabotage the effort, either passively or actively.

This is true for administrators as well as parents or community members. An outsider—that is, people who are not teachers or administrators—may face bigger challenges to becoming a partner, but ultimately it is a critical step for lasting improvements.

Simply put, we think that our mothers were correct. You ought to treat folks as you would like to be treated, and after all, it is easier to catch flies with honey than it is with vinegar. Of course, what you do with those flies once you catch them is your own business. What that has to do with education is also not clear, but our moms sure said it a lot. Understanding the challenges, issues, and needs of teachers and of the school in general will make it easier to recruit partners and ultimately help ensure success.

WHAT TO DO IF YOU ARE A PARENT OR COMMUNITY MEMBER

The first thing a parent should do is to care; the second thing is to be predisposed to give the teacher(s) and the school the benefit of the doubt. We would bet that no parent has ever improved things while belittling or antagonizing a teacher. Human nature is too strong. If you are a parent and want to see your school improve, it has to be done collaboratively and by finding ways to achieve common goals.

To be a parent who helps create an excellent school, a person must begin with the aforementioned understanding of the school and develop relationships within the school. Even if you think you know the solution, as advocated in this book for example, you must find a way to help teachers and staff buy into that solution and make it their solution.

Aside—This reminds us of the old chemistry joke about how if you are not part of the solution then you are part of the precipitate. If only we had a way to work it into the narrative.

Getting teachers or staff to embrace any solution will take work at listening, and it will take time. We would like to be able to provide a short cut or a prescription for immediate results. Unfortunately, we do not know of one and the work of creating an excellent school is too important to rely on short cuts and tricks.

Perhaps it is obvious, but for a parent, the place to start is likely with the grade level or school in which a child is enrolled. The enrollment creates an obvious "stake" in the school and provides entry or at least some leeway. We caution parents or any champion of change and excellence, that it will require perseverance.

Schools and teachers have seen reformers before and have often been able to wait them out. Champions become tired, distracted, and willing to move on, allowing schools to avoid commitments or investments. This is especially true when their child graduates or moves up a grade or to another school. If a parent is only interested in third grade while they have a child there, they are probably not going to be very effective in the end. Creating an excellent school is a long-term undertaking that demands continuous work.

As a parent attempts to help and encourage a school or district towards excellence, we believe it is important to heed the sentiments of John Dewey.

Loosely quoted, Mr. Dewey reminded parents that we as parents must want for all kids what we want for our own. Thus, parental advocates must be focused on the good of the whole, not just the good of their child. For example, while they may want a specific teacher for their child, there are undeniable benefits from heterogeneous classrooms, and that means schools may have to configure classes in ways that may or may not fit a specific parent's wishes.

Another important caution for parents who seek to foster excellent schools: do not expect glory or thanks. You may well be heaped in blame in the short term. Ultimately the glory will adhere to the school, teachers, administrators, and students—hopefully your children, but not likely to you. Right or wrong, if a parent really is concerned about the excellence of a school then excellence must be the objective. If a parent is looking for glory, validation, or affirmation, then they and the school or district would be better served if the parents focused on something else.

This rejoinder takes us to another point, which is that working to make an excellent school is hard work and requires a degree of selflessness, especially for parents. We have reworked these paragraphs several times, trying to avoid putting anyone off, while remaining honest. If we have not done this sufficiently, we really do apologize.

However, we think it is critical and strongly recommend that if you are a parent and are considering taking our recommendations to try and change your school, first you should carefully consider your own motivation.

There is nothing more debilitating that an important job badly done. A good idea poorly implemented is a mess; if a parent is going to push for solutions, it must be done for the good of the students, not for praise or attention for the parent pushing those goals. Consider the example of advertising campaigns. Companies carefully consider whom to hire as a spokesperson. The effort to encourage educational changes or reforms should be done just as carefully, with a friendly, non-accusatory, and committed spokesperson.

WHAT TO DO IF YOU ARE A TEACHER

Teachers face unique challenges when trying to encourage change and they are most likely better qualified to recount them than we are. However, to a surprising degree, the injunctions on how to proceed are similar to those of parents. Obviously, teachers are "insiders" and understand how their school works, but many are, have been, or will be parents of students in the school(s).

Like a parent, a teacher will have to build a partnership with a school to advocate for change. The most effective partnerships will be built with other teachers and the administrators. Further, like a parent, a teacher will face opposition from other teachers who have seen reform come and go, as well as from those who are resistant to change regardless of its vector. However, the willingness of a teacher to lead by example will carry greater weight than a parent cannot muster.

Teachers seeking to improve their schools or districts would do well to make sure they have an understanding of the school's budget, the legislative mandates, and the larger picture. Likewise, a good understanding of the current research is important, as is a healthy skepticism about programs in general.

While we certainly think that this document is a fine guide for teachers, a really good and effective strategy will include specific steps and proposed actions that fit the local school and condition. If a teacher or any advocate of change can enter the discussion with specifics, rather than vague generalities, they will have greatly improved their likelihood for success.

A final point is that we know it is possible for a grassroots movement to start with one teacher making a difference. One teacher can fundamentally alter practices and convince others to follow. As we were working on this book, Randy met a person teaching in a neighboring district who did exactly this; namely, he led by example. This teacher, working in a traditional grade level district, managed to convince a reluctant administration to allow him to teach a group of seventh graders their entire core curriculum.

This remarkable teacher accomplished what he did by using the lens of sustainability and the creation and operation of a greenhouse. All students in his class stay together, and their achievement has been significantly higher than that of other students. In this example, this teacher's program certainly got our attention, and he was recently named Oregon's Middle Level Teacher of the Year. Hopefully his approach will be embraced and replicated.

WHAT TO DO IF YOU ARE A STUDENT TEACHER OR NON-TENURED TEACHER

The people who are student teachers or non-tenured teachers are in a rather unique situation. First, they have no entrenched bad habits and they are not hostage to the notion that "this is the way we have always done it." Instead, the proverbial slate is clean and they have the ability to do anything and to adopt new approaches. Moreover, new teachers have the ability to question and ask why things are done a certain way, because they typically receive some leeway as new teachers with those "new ideas."

We are dubious of the ability of novices to rally teachers to wholesale change. On the other hand, new teachers can lead by example and question the norms. If done in the spirit of delivering the best possible education to students, a thoughtful new teacher will find that results will follow.

WHAT TO DO IF YOU ARE A SCHOOL BOARD MEMBER

The local school board is a wonderfully American institution that helps ensure that schools are responsive to local needs, conditions, and values. School boards are supposed to provide community oversight of the schools, and across the nation thousands of people volunteer to perform the duty. Given the de facto power and responsibility of a school board member, they have considerable power to shape a school district, providing that a majority of the members concur.

Given the case we continue to make even as the number of pages remaining is diminishing, namely that comprehensive, fundamental changes are in order, we urge school board members to take a collaborative approach. Of course, a board member should do everything in his or her power to avoid building large schools and to avoid building comprehensive high schools, but assuming that no capital projects are in the offing, he or she must work within the existing structure.

Ultimately, the biggest decision facing a school board is the hiring of the superintendent. The question for a school board should be: is the superintendent leading the district in the direction that the board wants to go? Further, does this person have the vision of the board and the ability to lead the district toward excellence or not?

The budget is certainly a powerful tool for the board members, but ultimately, meaningful change requires that staff buy into them and it cannot be done by fiat, at least not as effectively as it could be. The question of "chain of command" also begs at least mention. Board members should not be directing teachers or even principals; that is the job of the principal and superintendent respectively.

Different boards and districts operate differently, but in some places, administrators are likely to resent board members who do not work through channels. As an advocate for reform, a board member's biggest asset may be access—access to administrators, to policy decisions, and to communicate with other staff. The perception that a board member can offer both the "carrot" and the "stick" can help, but at the same time, some districts have entrenched adversarial relationships between teachers and the school board.

A thoughtful board member will find a way to educate other board members and hire like-minded administrative staff. We simply want to affirm that it is possible, desirable, and practical. A committed board member should be able to find like-minded partners. As with all of our recommendations, a board member should take time to understand the specifics of the school(s) and identify action steps to provide the sort of leadership that can produce meaningful results.

WHAT TO DO IF YOU ARE A STUDENT

The student's biggest asset in pushing for change is his or her biggest liability. A student advocating for change will likely always be able to get a hearing, but a serious hearing may be tougher. Students working to improve schools carry an inherent "cute" factor that, more than anything, needs to be acknowledged as part of the dynamic.

We believe that serious student involvement can be a real strength, but if a student or group of students is serious, then the first thing that he, she, or they must do is to demonstrate that seriousness. This requires understanding not only the situation in a given school or district, but a mastery of the larger issues and research. In particular, a young person must understand the budget and the legislative mandates under which a district operates. Bemused adults and professionals are sure to patronize until they come to understand that the young people really do understand the issues.

As important as it is for students to understand the larger issues, they must also enlist allies such as parents and teachers who are willing to stand up and be supportive in public. Ideally, students will be an integral part of any effort to push for change, simply because all of the effort and discussion is ultimately aimed at them.

WHAT TO DO IF YOU ARE AN ADMINISTRATOR

The first thing an administrator should do after reading this book is to give due consideration to Abraham Lincoln's rejoinder "with malice toward none and with charity toward all," when you think of us. Of all the groups profiled, with the possible exception of counselors, administrators may feel the most offended or attacked in the preceding pages. At the same time, administrators have considerable power to make changes and implement new programs. What we advocate however, is a radical departure for many, and this is unavoidable.

We recognize that in advocating for smaller schools we are advocating for jobs that tend to pay principals and superintendents less than do larger, comprehensive schools. Ultimately, this non-incentive to do what is best for students and must be addressed. Probably only school boards have the power to fix the problem, and they can only do so in a piecemeal fashion. The fact remains that administrators, superintendents, and principals are the professional staff to whom school boards turn when considering strategic questions, and they generally advocate for larger schools and "standard practices."

Depending on the type of school an administrator presides over, what that person should do varies considerably. Most of the places where schools and administrators are willing to try new methods and radical changes are in schools in severe distress. Specifically in places where things are already so bad that an administrator cannot really be held responsible if something new fails because everything else has.

What we advocate is not necessarily the opposite, but we do encourage administrators to embrace the changes and methods we have described here even if a school or district is not visibly failing or far below average. We encourage administrators to view average as unacceptable, to challenge themselves and the staff to be excellent, and to at least consider the pathways we have described in the previous chapters.

Administrators have the power to do more than apply bandages to self-inflicted wounds; they can take steps to stop the self-flagellation and make substantive, fundamental improvements that will push achievement higher and higher.

If you are an administrator, we encourage you to challenge traditional assumptions and lay aside the erroneous common knowledge. Look at what each school does with a clear and uncluttered eye and eliminate the activities that do not contribute to education. Reward teachers, transfer resources to the classroom, focus on individual students, and challenge the focus on grade-level and curriculum-focused activities. This is only a beginning list, but it should make for a very good start, maybe even an excellent one.

Chapter 14

Pathway to Excellence: Next Steps and Conclusions

The foregoing chapters have been rather unremitting in their criticism of modern American schools and it could be tempting to conclude that it is hopeless. Manifestly, we do not believe it is hopeless; indeed, we think there are many reasons for being hopeful, not the least of which is the fact that there are solutions to each problem.

Moreover, hard work and intelligence can make a difference, which is not always true when facing problems with bureaucratic components. Even more hopeful is our belief that the solutions can be implemented piecemeal or be phased in over time in a manner best suited to individual schools, districts, and their circumstances.

Considering what to do next can be as daunting as the problem. Moreover, this ground is well trod. The organization "Teacher's Mind Resources," noted in 2003 that "in the past 50 years, dissatisfaction with public education has risen exponentially. . . . Everyone from the President to school superintendents are falling all over themselves to respond to the criticisms by instituting one reform after another. As a result, education reform is now the norm rather than the exception. And yet, despite the constant parade of reforms, little of substance changes."[1]

The rejoinder must be that in moving toward an excellent school, an advocate will encounter a great deal of justifiable cynicism from individuals who have seen other efforts fail and even do more harm than good.

Since the above cited article appeared in 2003, the calls for change have continued to magnify, due in no small part to the new problems introduced by the legislation No Child Left Behind. As the Bush administration passed into the history books and the Obama administration replaced it, the calls for educational improvement, change, or reform have only gotten louder.

For example, the online magazine *"Slate"* reviewed the state of education in the United States in April of 2008, and called for specific solutions and changes. In this case, the recommendations included paying teachers more and restoring prestige to the teaching profession.[2] Generally we agree with Mr. Ryan, the article's author, especially when he notes "what we think we know may be wrong." However, as is typical of many commentators, just how one does these things is not explained.[3] We have identified specific strategies to move funds to the classroom, but the challenge of implementation remains.

As is probably to be expected, when national politics bring change, the nation sees that educational reform finds its way into the national discussion. For example, then presidential candidate John Edwards argued for a plan in late 2007 to pay teachers up to $15,000 more in high poverty areas to be financed with capital gains taxes. That is an idea that might make sense, but it does not address the underlying problems with the ways schools operate and teach. Neither do most political campaigns care to understand the complicated interrelated variables and needs of each school and district.

We certainly tend to support efforts to bring more resources to schools. At the same time we are also pragmatic, and believe that ultimately the solution has to involve changing the way funds are expended. This is necessary precisely because changing the way dollars are spent requires fundamental changes that simply throwing more money at the problem will not accomplish.

As part of the Project 2061, the American Association for the Advancement of Science has weighed in on educational reform. Among other things, they noted that reform takes time and that education in the United States is a $200 billion a year undertaking with more than 80,000 schools.[4]

The pressures to perform and conform are tremendous. Not surprisingly, anyone advocating the types of core changes that we do here will find that the existing system does not facilitate change, even for the better. The educational landscape is littered with good programs that were effective, but lacked institutional support or the endorsement of administration and they fell by the wayside. The upshot is that taking the next steps is not easy; no matter how simple they might be, the momentum arrayed against meaningful improvements is considerable.

Focusing on teachers is certainly a good way to begin building excellent schools, but if it were simple to recognize great teachers from bad ones in an interview process then presumably only good ones would get hired. Unfortunately, this is not the case and in the absence of better screening, other methods will have to suffice. Some school districts, such as in Toledo, Ohio, have adopted teacher-led performance reviews. Other places, such as in Public

School 49 (PS 49) located in Queens, New York, have gotten attention of late for the vigorous attempts by the administration to get rid of bad teachers.

Returning to the question of "next steps," we believe that there are many things that individuals, programs, schools, and districts can do to address the most significant problems and begin to build an excellent school. Even more importantly, successes will build on one another and make implementation easier as the process moves forward.

The previous chapter discussed what teachers, parents, administrators, and school boards can do and the list is impressive, especially since it is not exhaustive but rather is merely a starting point. Regardless of an individual's role, the next step for anybody or any school wishing to become excellent is to begin with a focus on understanding the needs of the community, the conditions of the schools, and what can be done.

There is no one way to proceed, no one place to start, and no one solution to implement first. Community conditions as well as the psychologies and individuals involved will bear every bit as much on identifying how best to proceed as will costs and benefits.

Schools that have seen efforts at reform will have teachers who may be more resistant to change, or conversely may be more ready for something that will work; either way, the dynamic will affect the strategy. Some districts, schools, or communities may find it is easier to implement reforms in the grade school, while others will focus on high school. No approach is inherently wrong, but each could be wrong for a specific place.

WHERE TO START

Step 1: Commitment

With a nod to the last two paragraphs and our belief that the next step must be appropriate to the community, we do think that there is a critical commitment that must constitute the first step. Specifically, those involved must be committed to creating an excellent school.

If a school or district is not concerned with academic excellence, then it is hard to imagine how such excellence could be achieved as broadly and universally as it could be. Therefore, the first step must include a deliberate commitment by the partners involved to build an excellent school. If the teachers, parents, administrators, and community are willing to entertain the idea that they can make a better school and then commit to being a part of that move, then subsequent steps will be easier. This step will make things easier to be sure, but not necessarily easy.

As discussed in the previous chapter, there are many things that individuals can do. While the most powerful individuals are administrators, for they have the most ability to implement a vision, they cannot do anything without commitment from other staff. An administrator might have even more power to screw things up; that is to say, they have more power to make a school bad than excellent, but they still need help.

Regardless of relative power to affect change, any meaningful change has to be rooted in the organization itself; nobody from the outside or in a peripheral position is likely to be able to drag a school to excellence without assistance from the institution.

Step 2: Assessment

Within the very broad spectrum of what is possible, the next step for a district or a school is to assess its own condition as well as its needs, opportunities, strengths, weaknesses, and barriers. In consulting and MBA circles this is called a SWOT analysis (Strengths, Weaknesses, Opportunities, and Threats). We do not like acronyms and like to appear original, thus the differing list of analytical points. Regardless of your choice of names, different schools will have different traditions, and history will help dictate what subsequent actions may be easier or more difficult.

Under the rubric of assessment must come a close look at the problematic assumptions about schools and how vigorously people in powerful positions hold them. For example, the idea that schools need to measure progress, rather than achievement of an arbitrary standard based on testing averages, will be difficult to propagate.

If the administration contains individuals unwilling to consider a continuous-progress model, then change would be better focused on other options. As much as we think the focus on grade level and curriculum is problematic, we do not advise tilting at windmills, especially when there are so many other places to which energy can be devoted.

CHOICES, CHANGE, AND ENVIRONMENTS

Steps 3, 4, and 5, which come next, are very much about making choices and creating an environment where excellence is possible. Significantly, a school or district has many choices, one of which is to stand pat, or continue with business as usual. If a school or district does this, it is quite probable that nothing will change and it may be that no one will even notice.

If the school or district is committed to excellence, then the next step is to choose a solution and implement it. We recognize that making a change is daunting and will invite scrutiny. The Japanese are credited with the reminder, "It is the nail that sticks out that gets hammered." An excellent school tends to stick out and it may invite as many hammers as an awful school

The next steps involve picking a solution and implementing it. This injunction may be simple, but it is not easy. Change, by definition, will threaten existing interests and will unsettle people as it introduces uncertainty and upsets the existing status quo. Assuming a school is not excellent already, we believe it is a good thing to unsettle things. As we have been at pains to point out, different communities and different locations will require different approaches.

However, we recommend that the next step be to make a commitment to the teacher. Specifically, the next step is to make a commitment to excellent teachers. A good place to begin is to reward good teachers, eliminate ineffective ones, and spend lavishly on professional development and teacher resources. Not only are teachers critical, but there is no stronger signal that the changes are in earnest and that excellence is the goal than that of investing resources in the teachers. Their attitude, their faith, and their commitment will ultimately be the force behind adopting and embracing meaningful change.

Step 3: Shift Resources to Classrooms and Teachers—Specifically Pay Teachers More

Clearly, the most important element in any school are the teachers. The teachers are the people who are directly responsible for educating students; without excellent teachers, no school is going to be excellent. Rearranging schedules, changing job titles, adding mentoring programs or adopting new curriculums are akin to rearranging the deck chairs on the Titanic, compared to focusing on the teachers. At the same time, the best teachers in the world can be undone by incompetent organization and misguided incentives.

How to shift resources is discussed at length in earlier chapters. A school can turn food preparation into an academic exercise, the school week could be cut to four days, administrative staff can be reduced, or schools can use a combination of methods to help them move funding to teachers, the classrooms, and professional development. Regardless of the specific of the method, teachers need to become the focus of the school, and class sizes need to be manageable, which means not more than 24 students.

One of the many practical reasons for shifting resources as soon as possible to the classroom is that it will demonstrate that the school is serious in its efforts. "Money talks," we are reminded; shifting resources to the classroom and to teachers is the best—and for some, the only—way to co-opt teachers into the change process.

We realize that this may seem mercenary, but we also know that any teacher with experience will have seen changes and reforms come and go and will be suspicious if not cynical of the next one. This response is understandable and logical; therefore, the strategy should account for this resistance and work to lessen, if not eliminate it.

Step 4: Elementary School—Move Grade and Curriculum Focus to a Continuous-Progress Model
Middle School—Eliminate Subject Area Teachers and Pair Teacher and Students
High School—Move Toward Smaller Schools and Abandon the Comprehensive Approach K–12—Employ the Continuous-Progress Model Throughout

The steps here vary by school, but they all focus on changing fundamental assumptions about how schools work and are organized.

For elementary schools, the next step is to move toward a continuous-progress model. Obviously, grade levels are not going to go away, but what can go away is the reliance on measuring a child against a grade-level norm. By adopting an individual approach that emphasizes progress for the individual, the school will improve and the child will be better served. In our experience, the results of this approach include happier children and teachers, fewer discipline problems, and greater achievement on standardized tests of all types.

Of all the fundamental changes proposed here, this may be the toughest, because elementary schools are dogmatically organized around grade level in a way that middle and high schools are not.

For middle schools, the next step must be to move away from school days where students move through six or more classrooms and teachers. Moving toward a single-teacher model will be a challenge, but a good faith effort will be rewarded with happier teachers and students as well as increased achievement. In our experience, no one who has worked with this type of system ever wants to go back to a traditional middle school environment.

The change for high schools at some level may be the easiest because there have been persistent critics of large schools and of the comprehensive approach for years. However, this is no less of a fundamental change than it is for the other schools. Furthermore, a shift from a comprehensive approach to one that focuses on a particular goal needs to operate in concert with a shift toward smaller schools. Retaining large schools in any form does students and the educational process a disservice, and this philosophical change is critical for the long-term achievement of students.

Step 5: Adopt a Single Focus for the School if Not the District

This step acknowledges the importance of Secret Number 5 from Chapter 3. A school must have a purpose, and this purpose must be identified, acknowledged, and internalized by the staff and even the students. We have made our argument for this approach and we continue to believe that it is the rare individual or organization that can do many things at an excellent level. Excellence is rare enough, without demanding excellence in multiple fields or activities.

Significantly, it is much easier to do this in a holistic fashion and is best done with a campus organized around K–12. By using a K–12 approach that keeps children in a single school unit, it is much easier to adopt a focus and to be successful in pursuing it. Moreover, by creating a single campus and integrated structure, achievement will improve as we have discussed at length in earlier chapters.

Step 6: Set High Standards and Help Staff and Students Internalize High Expectations

As tempting as it is for mediocre schools to center their attention on meeting state standards, this is the wrong approach. Minimal standards must be just that—minimal, something that students surpass while aiming for something much higher. At the same time, the expectations have to be internalized so that they are clearly aimed at and directed toward the single focus identified as Step 5.

Step 7: Adopt Practices and Policies that Stress Progress of Individual Students

Admittedly, we discussed this under Step 4, but it is so important that it deserves reiteration and adoption by every school and district, regardless of size and situation. The most obvious strategy to use to pursue this step is to focus on a continuous-progress model and de-emphasize curriculum. As we detailed earlier, we think this is a good way to proceed, but truly, schools must find a way that works for them to focus on individual students and not classes or grade levels.

As a rule, we tend to be dismissive of solutions that are based in a form or a redesigned form. In this case, however, redesigning the quarterly report cards, especially for elementary and even middle school students, is a good way to help make this transition.

Some schools already do this to some degree. For example, a Kindergarten report card that we saw recently reported the number of letters a student recognized, how far he or she could count, and other tasks. The subsequent report cards allows parents and teachers to chart a student's progress, and we think this is good, but there is no reason to stop with letter fluency, or the number of words a student can read a minute.

We discussed narrative report cards in earlier chapters, notably in Chapter Five, and urge school districts to use them for all grade levels, but especially in grades K–8. The social expectations for grades in high school may well be too much to avoid, but until then, we believe effort and progress are more important than meeting a standard imposed from on high.

If teachers had to report progress, rather than grades, the report cards would be much more useful to everyone. The reason that this approach makes sense is that it would help teachers and parents to focus on progress and effort, as well as individual needs, as opposed to grades and measures that compare students to one another. We have discussed the problems inherent in grades throughout earlier chapters enough to just note here that the road to excellence must be built on a base that stresses individuals and progress, rather than a snapshot in time of a grade.

Step 8: Evaluate Everything, Keep What and Who Works, and Eliminate the Rest

Perhaps this step should come earlier; regardless, it is the most mercenary of the prescriptions here. However, it is perhaps the most critical. An excellent school or district has to get rid of people and programs that do not contribute to the goal.

Significantly, this must include staff, including administrators, support personnel and teachers. If some staff persons cannot excel, cannot embrace the goals and the methods, and cannot meet the performance requirements, they need to seek employment elsewhere. Not every person is a good fit for every organizational culture or environment. Indeed, many very good teachers may thrive in one place and fail in another.

Manifestly, the job of a school must be to educate its students, and nobody faults a for-profit business for getting rid of employees who under-perform, or who do not fit with their colleagues and clients. Therefore, we cannot see why a school should be different. We do not advocate being cruel or inhumane, but the purpose must be to provide an excellent education.

An excellent school must have excellent staff who fit into the organizational environment. Some teachers, for example, may thrive with close supervision;

they will not do as well with a principal and colleagues who prefer more flexibility. Likewise, a teacher may be the best in the world at team teaching, but in a school that does not use that approach, this person may not fit.

In earlier chapters, we discussed making sure that the programs a school offers fit with the community, and here again we stress that it is essential that a district or a school assess whether or not its programs do indeed fit or complement other activities. We have no idea what programs will fit with your school, but we strongly recommend that each district and school figure that out and act accordingly.

Step 9: Continue to Shift Money to the Classrooms and to Teachers

This step is more than a device to fill up a chapter, it is our attempt to remind everyone that classrooms must be the focus of a school and they must have the majority of funding. Teachers, teacher development, and classroom materials must be funded, and everything else is necessarily less important. The attempt to move money toward the classroom must be ongoing, not a one-time undertaking.

We truly cannot emphasize this point sufficiently.

Step 10: Develop Staff

Closely related to the last step is the need to devote resources to developing staff, and it could have been rolled into step eight but for one critical point. The point we wish to make is that staff development demands an understanding of the goals and preferences of each staff member. An excellent school will have an excellent administrator who knows the staff. The administrator must work to make it possible for teachers to pursue their own educational goals and must move them within a school or district to allow them to pursue their passions.

Consider the example of a school that has a good high school science teacher who has a passion for integrating science into all studies. Imagine too that your school district has just reconfigured the middle school to meet our recommendations. Moving that teacher to the middle school could create an excellent middle school teacher and make a much happier, indeed grateful employee who is even more motivated to succeed. The result is good for everyone, but it is only possible when the administrator knows the staff and works to develop them.

Step 11: Reassess and Celebrate

An excellent school faces one final, recurring challenge—namely to stay excellent. Ultimately, this is likely the biggest challenge any excellent school will face, and for that reason it must never stop assessing results, considering feedback, and fine tuning the school and the approach. What works for one group of students may not work five years later with a different group. If a school is already focusing on individuals rather than grade level or curriculum, this is easier to do.

In many ways, reassessing should be a way to habituate staff and the community to change. Change, while it may be inevitable, is invariably unpopular and can be unsettling. If a school is always willing to make improvements and adjustments, then the process of change becomes familiar, constant, and normal. So long as the changes are collaborative and based in logic that is communicated, new developments will be welcome.

Finally, we realize that we are asking a lot. That excellence is harder to achieve than mediocrity is obvious, but what to do about that is not. Average is usually good enough, and creating an excellent school will be hard, and maintaining it will be even harder; therefore, we believe it is imperative for staff to be reminded of their achievements and excellence and to celebrate. This matter of celebration creates a wonderful opportunity for the school's administration to make a critical difference.

CONCLUSIONS

Much of what we read in the course of our duties and lives, as well as in preparing this book, reminds us how daunting the prospect of creating an excellent school can appear. The sheer size of the American educational system is nothing short of amazing. More than 3 million people are employed by the industry, and there are more than 80,000 schools with capital assets totaling over $1 trillion, educating 50 million elementary and secondary students. From villages in Alaska to inner cities in St. Louis, to affluent suburbs, to the very heart of Washington D.C., devising a system to achieve excellence would be difficult if there were centralized control and a dictatorship.

Given the dispersed nature of control by local districts and boards of education, the best that we hope for from the federal government is greater flexibility and a leadership role in dismantling some of the old ideas that are just plain wrong. In particular, there is a role for the federal government in encouraging small schools, lowering the student-teacher ratio, and focusing on individual progress rather than on curriculum, grade level, and arbitrary performance targets based on the tyranny of averages.

There is also a role for the federal bureaucracy to play in encouraging schools to focus on education, rather than becoming a way to address every social ill from obesity to volunteerism to trade school to social service provider. We would love to see the US Department of Education take the lead in arguing that schools need fewer unfunded mandates.

Fortunately, most schools, districts, parents, and teachers do not have to worry about 80,000 schools, only one or two. Most teachers, parents, administrators, and community members are able to work on the human scale of a school, with a few dozen teachers and a few hundred students. We have given up faith, if we ever held it, in top-down improvements. There is no reason for any community to settle for less than an excellent school.

At the same time, it is incumbent on each community to demand an excellent school and to help create it. As trite and clichéd as it may be, the future of the nation is at least partially decided in the schools, and each mediocre school compounds the difficulties and problems, while each excellent school gives its students, community, and nation a decided advantage.

We know categorically that it is possible to remake a school and a district to deliver an excellent education. Moreover, we have seen how success builds on itself and how teachers, students, and parents come to invest themselves in the process. The result is more people pushing on the "flywheel of excellence" improving things further and being proud of the work they do.

There is no reason that the schools in each district cannot do the same thing. The federal government will never be able to mandate excellence as it cannot create excellence, but can stand in the way and make things much more difficult. Similarly, individuals in specific schools may be able to block change and make things more difficult, but if there is an underlying commitment to excellence, it can be achieved and sustained.

We hope after all this that you, gentle reader, will see a practical and relevant role for yourself in creating an excellent school. We also hope that each reader will believe that not only is it necessary to make fundamental changes to the assumptions underlying education, but more importantly, that it is possible to make the changes.

The improvements we have detailed here will not perfect anything. However, they will give each individual student a better chance at a superior education and allow the purpose of education to square more closely with the methods employed. What the student does with those tools is another matter, just as what happens next in the educational process at the post-secondary level is also another matter.

Lastly, we thank you for reading this far and considering our points. We would love to know if anything comes of it. If you make changes, use the ideas, or modify them, we would love to know about it. We would hate for this chapter to really be the end of things. Instead, we hope that this is a beginning, a good one we hope, but we would settle for the beginning of the beginning.

The talk of beginnings brings us back around to our opening, and we want to reiterate what we claimed at the beginning but with a twist. We stated that "much of what you know or were taught about education is wrong," but we also believe that it does not have to get in the way. Indeed, we hope you will agree that much of what you used to take for granted about education is not only wrong but also counter-productive.

Finally, we hope that we have convinced you that the status quo needs to be replaced with the strategies and approaches we have outlined here. We certainly do not think our strategies cannot be improved upon, but we know they work and are unwavering in our belief that the proper emphasis of the American educational system must be on the students in a classroom with a teacher focused on the core academic subjects.

RT and BI

NOTES

1. "Reforming or Transforming Education: More than Just Words," *Focus on Teacher's Newsletter*, January 2003.

2. Jim Ryan, "Education: Fixing Education Policy," *Slate*, posted Tuesday April 1, 2008.

3. Ibid.

4. American Association for the Advancement of Science, "Reforming Education," available at: http://www.project2061.org/publications/rsl/online/SFAA/CHAP14.HTM

Appendix: Multi-Age Resources and FAQs

Why would a school go multi age?

There are two main reasons that schools use multi-age education. First, it is pedagogically sound; in short, it is better than single grade level education. Second, it is economically the most efficient way to operate a school.

Corbett provides an interesting case study in what can happen to achievement when a district adopts a multi-age approach. Since Corbett has gone to multi-age education, both the high school and middle school have gained national recognition as being among the best schools in the country. The success of the high school and middle school can be traced directly back to the move to multi-age classrooms.

Corbett's most thoroughly multi-age program is their math program. When you allow students to work in a multi-age environment and combine that configuration with a continuous progress approach, great things happen. Math students are expected to make progress at their own rate without regard to their age; this is what we call continuous progress. Corbett uses this approach in all disciplines, not just math. This forces a school to regroup students according to achievement level rather than grade level.

When this multi-aged approach is used, it is not uncommon to find 3rd–6th grade students working in the same math room, or 7th–12th-grade students working together in pre-calculus. The end result of this approach has led Corbett High School students to take and pass Advanced Placement Calculus exams at a rate more than 1000 times what would be expected of a school their size.

Who Says that Multi-Age Classrooms are Better?

Looking at Corbett's steady improvement over the last 10 years provides evidence that this method of instruction is better than the old single grade level configuration. Comparing Corbett's K–12 achievement to all other schools in the state, the vast majority of which are still using the assembly line, single grade level model of Henry Ford's era, provides evidence that this way is better. So, we say it is better. But does anyone else?

A review of more than 2,000,000 peer reviewed articles on education, when filtered for articles pertaining to multi-age education, produces a unified voice from the education community that this model is better than the single grade level model, particularly with regard to social, emotional, and developmental needs of students. In fact, there appears to be no serious dissenting voices in the peer reviewed literature with regard to multi-age classrooms.

What does the literature say about traditional grade level classrooms?

According to Hallion (1994), John Dewey, one of the foremost authorities on education, considered graded classrooms too confining and machine like.

Pardini (2005) says that graded education is the antithesis of developmentally appropriate practice and that, despite its popularity, there is no research showing that it helps students.

Placing students in classrooms according to their age with a given time to cover curricular expectations is detrimental to their academic, social, and psychological growth (Goodland & Anderson, 1987).

Children's learning is affected negatively when they are forced to follow grade level constraints (Copeland, 1998).

Although traditional classrooms continue to be the most common way of organizing elementary students, there is no evidence to show that all children of the same 12-month age range are able to learn the same things, the same way, at the same time (Katz, 1995).

Drawbacks of traditional classrooms include the following. First, children of the same age vary in readiness to learn. Second, children have different learning styles, so a single grade level classroom is unlikely to be effective for all children. Third, traditional classrooms compare children with each other. Children who are not within the norm are considered failures. This leads to feelings of discouragement and low self esteem (Gaustad, 1992).

What does the literature say about achievement in multi-age classrooms?

Research studies reporting significant outcomes for students in non graded classroom have demonstrated improved performance in language, including vocabulary and literacy, and in mathematics (Kinsey, 2002).

A continuous progress approach produces superior academic performance, and children do better academically (Calkins, 1992).

Teachers report that through a continuous progress approach they experience fewer classroom behavior problems. Classrooms that use a continuous progress approach experience more time on task, become self regulators, and help enforce classroom rules (Hanes, 2008).

First graders in multi-age classrooms function at significantly higher average cognitive development then first graders in traditional classrooms (Cromey, 1999).

Continuous progress multi-age schools make students responsible for their own learning and produce increased learning (Mack, 2004).

New Zealand, the country with the highest literacy rate in the world, uses multi-age grouping as a common educational practice (Kasten & Clark, 1993).

In 1981, Milburn compared the reading achievement scores of 6–11 year old children in multi age and single grade level classrooms. Children in multi-age classrooms scored significantly higher on standardized tests, especially the young children.

In non-graded classrooms, students of different abilities, interests, and backgrounds can interact, and student in all ranges of ability can benefit from non-gradedness, (Merrit, 2008).

The state of Kentucky mandated non-graded programs. A review of Kentucky's top 20 percent of all students showed that they outperformed the top 20 percent of all other states (Viadero, 1996).

Applying a continuous progress approach utilizing grouping children of various age and ability levels maximizes teaching and learning (Nye, 1993).

Students in multi-age classrooms have more positive attitudes about school, develop and exhibit more advanced social skills, benefit in the areas of cognitive development, and show improved performance in reasoning skills (Merrit, 2008; Green, 1997; Kruglik, 1993; Stegelin, 1997; Thelin, 1981).

Children in multi-age classrooms attained a higher cognitive developmental level at a faster pace compared to children in traditional classroom, and they scored significantly higher on a standardized reading achievement test (Fosco, et. al., 2004).

According to Maeda (1994), there is mounting evidence that multi-age classrooms have the following benefits:

• Optimal learning occurs in a nurturing environment.
• They foster self esteem and improved decision making.
• Individual differences are accommodated.
• Learning is more holistic.
• Students construct their own knowledge rather than having it transmitted to them.

A major meta analysis of 57 multi-age studies that examined standardized academic achievement test scores of multi-age and traditional grade level found that in 91 percent of the studies, the multi-age students scored as well or better than their grade level peers (Paven, 1992).

Learning in non-graded classrooms is more developmentally sound (Kruglik, 1993).

Multi-age classrooms maximize student learning (Aina, 2001).

Mixed-age programs permit flexible learning arrangements for developmentally appropriate instruction of all students. The approach creates an active learning environment that encourages individual development and fosters growth of staff and students (Hanes, 2008).What does the literature say about social/emotional development in multi-age classrooms?

One of the most important benefits of multi-age groupings is the opportunity to learn nurturing behaviors (Tangen-Foster, 1998)

Mixed-age groups were shown to be better at taking turns than single-age groups, and to exhibit greater social responsibility and sensitivity to others (Chase & Dolan, 1994).

Social competence develops for younger children as they observe and emulate the behavior of older classmates, who in turn grow in their role as nurturers and teachers (Katz, 1995).

In multi-age groups, fewer children are isolated or rejected by peers. Children are more willing to watch out for one another, to include less popular children in play, and to ask one another for assistance with problems (Mclellan & Kinsey, 1996).

Multi-age classrooms improve life for middle school students particularly in the social, emotional, and developmental arenas (Petrie, Lindauer, Dotson, & Tountasakis, 1996).

Students in multi-age classrooms have more positive attitudes about school, develop and exhibit more advanced social skills, benefit in the areas of cognitive development, and show improve performance in reasoning skills (Merrit, 2008; Green, 1997; Kruglik, 1993; Stegelin, 1997; Thelin, 1981).

Teachers report that when using a continuous progress approach they experience fewer classroom behavior problems. Classrooms that use a continuous progress approach experience more time on task, become self regulators, and help enforce classroom rules (Hanes, 2008).

When students are placed in same-age groups and asked to complete a task there is more bullying behavior than in multi-age group (Chase & Dolan, 1994).

According to Maeda (1994), there is mounting evidence that multi-age classrooms have the following benefits:

- Optimal learning occurs in a nurturing environment.
- They foster self esteem and improved decision making.
- Individual differences are accommodated.

- Learning is more holistic.
- Students construct their own knowledge rather than having it transmitted to them.
- Multi-age classrooms allow teachers and students to develop long-term learning partnerships (McLaughlin, Irvin, & Doda, 1999).

Mixed-age programs permit flexible learning arrangements for developmentally appropriate instruction of all students. The approach creates an active learning environment that encourages individual development and fosters growth of staff and students (Hanes, 2008).

What does the literature say about special populations and multi-age classrooms?

Multi-age grouping is good for special needs children since it creates a classroom where individual differences are more likely to be accepted and, more importantly, are expected; roles are found to suit the strengths of all children (Clark, 1996, Tangen-Foster 1998).

In non-graded classrooms, students of different abilities, interests, and backgrounds can interact, and student in all ranges of ability can benefit from non-gradedness (Merrit, 2008)

In a review of a K-2 school, Fu et al. (1999) found that for single-age classrooms the first week of school is the hardest week for teachers, while the teachers in the K–2 classrooms had a far different experience. The teachers knew most of the parents and students, and instead of one teacher having to train 24 new students each year, the teacher had 16 classroom helpers to welcome the 8 new Kindergarten students each year.

Fu et. al. further found that Kindergarten students and their older peers enjoyed a much smoother start to the school year than other children in single grade classrooms. Furthermore, parents expressed satisfaction with the arrangement and also had a much smoother start to the school year.

When students are placed in same-age groups and asked to complete a task, there is more bullying behavior than in multi-age group (Chase & Dolan, 1994).

According to Maeda (1994), there is mounting evidence that multi-age classrooms have the following benefits:

- Optimal learning occurs in a nurturing environment.
- They foster self esteem and improved decision making.
- Individual differences are accommodated.
- Learning is more holistic.
- Students construct their own knowledge rather than having it transmitted to them.

What does the literature say about parents and multi-age classrooms? Communication lines between parents and teachers are open and maintained better in multi-age classrooms (Aina, 2001).

As noted earlier in a review of a K-2 school, Fu et al. (1999) found that for single-age classrooms the first week of school is the hardest week for teachers, while the teachers in the K-2 classrooms had a far different experience. The teachers knew most of the parents and students, which made the start of the school year more fluid. Furthermore, parents expressed satisfaction with the arrangement and also had a much smoother start to the school year.

By working with students individually in multi-age classrooms, teachers are better able to provide useful information to parents about how to assist their child (Kruglik, 1993; Pardini 2005).

Schools often face difficulties with parents, or community members at large, who view themselves as experts on education simply because they themselves went through the primary grades, or that they "know what is best for their child," or because "it was good enough for me so why is it not good enough for my kid." Educating parents by showing them the literature as well as the success of schools that use multi-age education can help to minimize these distractions (Petrie, Lindauer, and McKinney, 1998)

Parents sometimes feel apprehension about new multi-age programs. They want to know what the benefits for their child will be, and whether they will learn more or less. Multi-age grouping is actually more natural and educationally more beneficial than many realize (Aina, 2001)

Often multi-age configurations never get off the ground because administrators are unwilling to take on and convince the inevitable "Doubting Thomases" in every community.

Taking on one more political task of reassuring anxious parents and community members is often one task too many for school leaders who have extensive responsibilities of advocating for school bonds, formulating yearly budgets, providing building maintenance, fighting drugs, etc. Yet, multi-age schools promise to deliver Americans the schools they demand and need. The challenge for administrators is to convince the public that yesterday's graded barriers need to be replaced with tomorrow's non-graded opportunities (Yarborough, B. & Johnson, R., 2000).

MULTI-AGE RESOURCES

Aina, O. (2001), Maximizing learning in early childhood multi-age classrooms: Child, teacher, and parent perceptions. *Early Childhood Education Journal,* Vol. 28, No. 4, 2001.

Calkins, T. (1992) Off the track: Children thrive in ungraded primary school. *School Administrator.* 49 (5) 8–133.

Chas, P. & Dolan, J. (1994). *Full Circle: A new look at multi-age education.* Portsmouth, NH: Heineman Publishers.

Clark, A. (1996). Special needs children and mixed-age grouping. *The Magnet Newsletter.* 5(1). Internet document retrieved from http://ericeece.org.pubs.mag. magfal96.html#b.

Copeland, K. (1998) Reflections. *Primary Voices K–6.* 6 (2) p 44–46.

Cromey, A. (1999). *Impact of Multi-age Programming on Social Competency in Five to Seven Year-old Children.* Unpublished doctoral dissertation, Illinois Institute of Technology, Institute of Psychology.

Fosco, A., Schlesser, R., & Andal, J.(2004). Multi-age programming effects on the cognitive developmental level and reading achievement in early elementary school children. *Reading Psychology,* 25:1–17, 2004.

Fu, D., Hartle, L., Lamme, L., Copenhaver, J., Adams, D., Harmon, C., and Reneke, S. (1999). A comfortable start for Everyone: The first week of school in three multi-age (K-2) classrooms. *Early Childhood Education Journal,* Vol 27, No. 2, 1999.

Gaustad, J. (1992) Non-graded education: Mixed-age, integrated, and developmentally appropriate education for primary children. *Oregon School Study Council,* 35(7) 1–38.

Goodland, J. I. & Anderson, R. H. (1987). *The Non-graded elementary school.* New York: Teachers College Press.

Green, B. G. (1997) Reading instruction in the non-graded classroom. *Reading Psychology,* 18(1), 69–76.

Hallion, A. M. (1994). *Strategies for developing multi-age classrooms.* Washington DC: Education Resources Research Center (document number ED 373 899), p 25.

Hanes, J. (2008). Continous Progress Approach. *Research Starters.* Ebsco Research Starters 1–7.

Kasten, W. C., Clarke, B. K. (1993) *The Multi-age Classroom: A Family of Learners,* Katonah, NY: Richard C. Owen.

Katz, L. G. (1995, May). The Benefits of mixed-age grouping. *ERIC Digest.*

Kinsey, S. G. (2002). Multi-age grouping and academic achievement. Washington, DC: Education Resource Center (document number ED 466 328).

Kruglik, M (1993). Results from non-graded classroom program: Good, bad, and unclear. *Curriculum Review,* 33(4),16.

Mack, J. (2004) Continuous progress schools see the "whole child." *Education,* Vol. 129, No. 2, p. 324–27.

Maeda, B. (1994) *The Multi-age Classroom: An Inside Look at One Community of Learners.* Los Angeles, CA: Creative Teaching Press.

McClellan, D. & Kinsey, S. (1996). Mixed-age grouping helps children develop social skill and a sense of belonging. *The Magnet Newsletter* 5(1).

McLaughlin, H., Irvin J. L., & Doda, N. M. (1999). Crossing the grade level gap: Research on multi-age grouping. *Middle School Journal,* 30(3), 55–58.

Merrit, R., (2008). Non-Graded Instruction. *Research Starters.* Ebsco Research Starters 1–9.

Milburn, D. (1981). A study of multi-age or family-grouped classrooms. *Phi Delt Kappan,* 62(7), 513–514.

Nye, B. (1993) Questions and Answers about multi-age grouping. *Educational Research Service (ERS) Spectrum.* 38–45.

Pardini, P. (2005) The slowdown of the multi-age classroom. *School Administrator.* 62(3) 22–30.

Paven, B. (1992). The benefits of non-graded schools. *Educational Leadership,* 50(2), 22–25.

Petrie, G.; Lindauer, P.; Dotson, K.; & Tountasakis, M. (1996) The non-graded middle school: Can it   improve life for early adolescents? *Education,* Vol. 121. No. 4, p 781–786.

Steglin, D. A. (1998). Creating contexts for middle-age learning. *Childhood Education, 74(4), 234–236.*

Tangen-Foster, J & Tangen-Foster, L (1998) The caring capacity: A case for multi-age experiential learning, Electronic Green Journal, 1998.

Viadero, D. (1996). Mixed Blessings. *Education Week,* 15:33, 31–33. Editorial project in education, Inc. Washington, DC.

Yarborough, B. & Johnson, R. (2000). Non-graded schools: Why their promise has not been realized and should be reconsidered. *Contemporary Education,* 2000, Vol. 71 Issue 3, p. 42.

About the Author

Dr. Randy K. Trani is a past Oregon Middle School and Oregon High School Principal of the Year and is currently principal of the Corbett School where he has worked for six years. Trani spent fourteen years as a teacher in Alaska and Oregon and has taught every grade from K–12.

Dr. Robert K. Irvine is the vice president of PARC Resources, a consulting firm focused on development specializing in working with tribes, nonprofits, and rural governments. He is resource faculty member at Eastern Oregon University and adjunct faculty member at Blue Mountain Community College, where he teaches primarily American History.